50 Questions on the Natural Law

CHARLES E. RICE

50
Questions
on the
Natural Law

What It Is and
Why We Need It

IGNATIUS PRESS   SAN FRANCISCO

Cover design by Roxanne Mei Lum

To my wife, Mary,
and our children
and grandchildren.

Contents

III. NATURAL LAW AND THE HIGHEST HUMAN LAW

IV. THE REASONED FOUNDATION OF THE NATURAL LAW

V. THE REASONED FOUNDATION: MAN AS KNOWN THROUGH REASON TO BE SPIRITUAL AND IMMORTAL

VI. THE REASONED FOUNDATION: GOD AS KNOWN THROUGH REASON

VII. REVELATION AS THE NECESSARY COMPLETION OF NATURAL LAW: WHAT GOD HAS TOLD US ABOUT HIMSELF AND ABOUT MAN

VIII. THE CENTRALITY OF CHRIST

IX. THE ROLE OF THE CATHOLIC CHURCH AS AUTHORITATIVE INTERPRETER OF THE NATURAL LAW

X. THE MAGISTERIUM: INDISPENSABLE INTERPRETER FOR THE COMMON GOOD

XI. SOME APPLICATIONS OF THE NATURAL LAW BY THE MAGISTERIUM

Acknowledgments

I gratefully acknowledge the generous assistance of Mrs. Lois Plawecki in expertly preparing and managing the manuscript from start to finish; of Carl Schmitt, an alumnus of Thomas Aquinas College and of Notre Dame Law School, in the research and evaluation of the manuscript; of John Murdock of Notre Dame Law School, in providing essential research and comments on the project; of Mrs. Carmela Kinslow, Dwight King, and the Notre Dame Law Library research staff in their prompt acquisition of often arcane materials; of Professors Douglas W. Kmiec and Edward J. Murphy of Notre Dame Law School in their helpful comments and guidance; of Fr. Robert Connor of the Prelature of Opus Dei in providing many indispensable insights and clarifications; and especially of my wife, Mary, in reviewing and evaluating the concepts and drafts.

Abbreviations

In this book abbreviations are used for frequently cited sources. In all quotations, unless otherwise indicated, emphasis is in the original.

C.A.   Pope John Paul II. Encyclical *Centesimus Annus* (1991).

C.C.C.   *Catechism of the Catholic Church* (1992).

E.V.   Pope John Paul II. Encyclical *Evangelium Vitae* (1995).

F.C.   Pope John Paul II. Apostolic Exhortation *Familiaris Consortio* (1981).

F.R.   Pope John Paul II. Encyclical *Fides et Ratio* (1998).

L.F.   Pope John Paul II. *Letter to Families* (1994).

P.C.H.P.   Pope John Paul II. *Letter to the Bishops of the Catholic Church on the Pastoral Care of Homosexual Persons* (1986).

S.T.   *Summa Theologica*. Saint Thomas Aquinas (Benziger Bros. ed., 1947).

V.S.   Pope John Paul II. Encyclical *Veritatis Splendor* (1993).

Introduction

"The ideas of natural justice are regulated by no fixed standard: the ablest and the purest men have differed upon the subject."[1] If this 1798 conclusion of Supreme Court Justice James Iredell is correct, then the natural law has no future as a workable criterion for law and morality. Over the past three centuries and more, the philosophy of the Enlightenment has isolated natural law from its author and his revelation and has denied the capacity of reason to know the essences of things. One result is a "natural law" devoid of ascertainable, objective content and therefore useless as a moral standard for private conduct and public law. The purpose of this book is to examine a natural law jurisprudence that does provide an alternative—a "fixed standard"—because it integrates the natural law into the plan of the Creator as seen in revelation as well as through reason.

This book approaches the subject on two levels. First, it offers to state, as plainly as possible, the natural law jurisprudence of Saint Thomas Aquinas and its bases in reason and revelation. On the second level, especially in Questions 35 through 49, it examines relevant teachings of the Magisterium, or teaching authority, of the Catholic Church. Saint Thomas accepted the Magisterium as the indispensable interpreter of morals as well as of faith. The Magisterium is the authoritative interpreter of the meaning of the natural law on specific issues. However, the Magisterium does not undertake merely to explain the natu-

---

[1] *Calder* v. *Bull*, 3 Dall. 386, 399, 1 L. Ed. 648 (1798) (opinion of Iredell); see Question 17 below.

ral law. Rather, it incorporates natural law as an aspect of the Truth, who is a person, Jesus Christ.[2]

A key element here is the emerging concept of person as relation. For the past three centuries and more, the jurisprudence of the Enlightenment has fostered a sterile individualism. The result is a pagan culture; autonomous individuals are locked in a perennial conflict of interests, with the outcome determined by the powerful unencumbered by any standard higher than their own will. The Magisterium, by contrast, integrates the natural law teaching of Saint Thomas into a vision in which relation to others is intrinsically an aspect of personhood and in which the moral norm—for society as well as for persons —is not a set of abstract principles but the person of Christ, who shows man what it means to be man. Without the Magisterium, the teaching of Saint Thomas would be subject to endless, inconclusive debate and would make little more sense than the "ideas of natural justice" criticized by Justice Iredell. The Magisterium accepts and approves the work of Saint Thomas and completes it on a higher plane. The result is a vision of the human person, with Christ himself as the moral norm, that provides the definitive corrective to the failed individualism of the Enlightenment.

For more than thirty years I have taught a course at Notre Dame Law School on the jurisprudence of Saint Thomas Aquinas. The topics in this book reflect persistent inquiries and concerns of students in that course. This book examines the current issues, such as abortion, euthanasia, or the family, only to the extent necessary to explain the teachings of Aquinas and the Magisterium. The style of the book, necessarily, oscillates between the formal exposition required for technical accuracy and a more colloquial discussion that applies principles

---

[2] See Jn 14:5–7.

to current issues. The question-and-answer format and the detailed index allow for precision and ease of reference. The answers include extensive direct quotations from Saint Thomas and the Magisterium because we understand them best if we allow them to speak for themselves.

This second edition incorporates quotations and references from Pope John Paul's *Veritatis Splendor*, *Letter to Families*, *Evangelium Vitae*, *Crossing the Threshold of Hope*, and *Fides et Ratio*, all of which were issued after publication of the original edition of this book.

I

THE IMPORTANCE
OF NATURAL LAW

1. Does anybody really care about natural law?

Ask Clarence Thomas. Before his nomination, Supreme Court Justice Thomas had voiced his approval of natural law jurisprudence. His opponents made the natural law the dominant issue in his confirmation process until attention shifted to the sexual harassment charges brought against him by Professor Anita Hill.

> One of the more curious displays of cultural illiteracy has been the consternation and bafflement created by Judge Clarence Thomas's expressions of esteem for "natural law." For some of the critics of the nominee to the Supreme Court, it was as though the man had let slip a reference to torture by thumbscrews. Others squinted as though Judge Thomas had disclosed an obscure and probably sinister belief in alchemy.
>
> These are strange reactions to a philosophical theory stretching back to Socrates, Plato and Aristotle, propounded by the Stoics, developed anew by medieval churchmen like Aquinas, elaborated in secular terms by Protestant jurists like Grotius and Pufendorf, reshaped to justify "natural rights" by Locke, Montesquieu, Jefferson and Adams, and invoked in the cause of racial equality by Abraham Lincoln, the Rev. Martin Luther King Jr. and, yes, even the man Judge Thomas has been nominated to replace, Thurgood Marshall.[1]

Thomas' enthusiasm for natural law evoked criticism that he was "the first Supreme Court nominee in 50 years to maintain that natural law should be readily consulted in constitu-

---

[1] Peter Steinfels, "Natural Law Collides with the Laws of Politics in the Squabble over a Supreme Court Nomination", *New York Times*, Aug. 17, 1991, p. A8.

tional interpretation".[2] Before his nomination, Thomas had endorsed "the higher law political philosophy of the Founding Fathers".[3] That philosophy, he said, "is far from being a license for unlimited government and a roving judiciary. Rather, natural rights and higher law arguments are the best defense of liberty and of limited government. Moreover, without recourse to higher law, we abandon our best defense of judicial review—a judiciary active in defending the Constitution, but judicious in its restraint and moderation. Rather than being a justification of the worst type of judicial activism, higher law is the only alternative to the willfulness of both run-amok majorities and run-amok judges."[4]

In his Senate hearings, before the Hill charges surfaced, Thomas underwent what Senator Howell Heflin (Democrat from Alabama) called a "confirmation conversion".[5] "I don't see a role", Thomas told the Senate Judiciary Committee, "for the use of natural law in constitutional adjudication. My interest in exploring natural law and natural rights was purely in the context of political theory."[6] "At no time", Thomas said, "did I feel nor do I feel now that natural law is anything more than the background to our Constitution. It is not a method

---

[2] Laurence H. Tribe, "Natural Law and the Nominee", *New York Times*, July 15, 1991, p. A15; see also Douglas W. Kmiec, "Natural Law, Unnatural Concern", *Chicago Tribune*, July 30, 1991, sec. 1, p. 13.

[3] Clarence Thomas, "The Higher Law Background of the Privileges or Immunities Clause of the Fourteenth Amendment", 12 *Harv. J. of Law & Public Policy* 63 (1989); see also Clarence Thomas, "Toward a Plain Reading of the Constitution—The Declaration of Independence in Constitutional Interpretation", 30 *Howard L. J.* 691 (1987).

[4] Clarence Thomas, "The Higher Law Background of the Privileges or Immunities Clause of the Fourteenth Amendment", 63–64.

[5] *New York Times*, Sept. 12, 1991, p. A1.

[6] *New York Times*, Sept. 11, 1991, p. A12.

of interpreting or a method of adjudicating in the constitutional law area."[7] "Instead of explaining your views," Senator Howard Metzenbaum (Democrat from Ohio) understandably told Thomas, "you actually ran from them and disavowed them."[8]

Why did Thomas' opponents care so much about his oblique endorsements of natural law? At the center of their concern was the fear that Thomas would use natural law theory to overturn legalized abortion.[9] Members of the Senate Judiciary Committee questioned him extensively on that point.[10] And Senate Majority Leader George Mitchell (Democrat from Maine) devoted the major part of his closing speech, moments before the Senate confirmation vote, to abortion. "Judge Thomas", he said, "will be confirmed and will soon be sitting on the Supreme Court. There he will vote to restrict the right of choice by women."[11]

So does anybody care about natural law? Lots of people do, on both sides of the aisle. Natural law is more than just a theory. Whether you accept it can determine whether you will accept or reject the legalized killing of innocent human beings. On abortion and other issues, jurisprudence kills people. Anyone who cares about life and death issues has to care about natural law, one way or the other.

---

[7] *New York Times*, Sept. 12, 1991, p. A10.

[8] Ibid.

[9] See Edward C. Smith, "For God and for Country", 10 *Lincoln Review* 15 (1992).

[10] See *New York Times*, Sept. 11, 1991, p. A1; Sept. 12, 1991, p. A1; Sept. 13, 1991, p. A1; Sept. 14, 1991, p. 6.

[11] *New York Times*, Oct. 16, 1991, p. A12.

2. *Can natural law thinking really make a difference?*

As a reminder to popular majorities and ruling politicians that their power is limited, natural law theory is always controversial and often unwelcome. The late Professor Anton-Hermann Chroust, of Notre Dame Law School, used to tell his students: "The academics repeatedly declare the natural law to be dead, but every twenty-five or so years it comes in again by the back door when some crisis shows the failure of utilitarian positivism." Two striking revivals of natural law in this century occurred in reaction to the evils of Nazi Germany and of racial segregation in the United States.

During the Nazi period in Germany, "all attempts at passive and active resistance to the regime were necessarily grounded on natural law ideas or on divine law, for legal positivism as such could offer no foundation."[12] After the war, the courts of the Federal Republic of Germany repudiated legal positivism. They recognized "the necessity of universal higher standards of objectively valid suprapositive principles for the lawmaker" and relied on the natural law in punishing actions that were legal under the Nazi regime.[13] "The positive legislative act", declared one court, "is intrinsically limited. It loses all obligatory power if it violates the generally recognized principles of international law or the natural law, or if the contradiction between positive law and justice reaches such an intolerable degree that the law . . . must give way to justice."[14] In reject-

---

[12] Henrich Rommen, "Natural Law in Decisions of the Federal Supreme Court and of the Constitutional Courts in Germany", 4 *Natural Law Forum*, 1, 11, n. 26 (1959).

[13] Ibid., 5.

[14] Ibid., 11.

ing the defense of accused physicians that their killing of prisoners in medical experiments had been authorized by the laws of the Third Reich, another court concluded that "law must be defined as an ordinance or precept devised in the service of justice. Whenever the conflict between an enacted law and true justice reaches unendurable proportions, the enacted law must yield to justice, and be considered a 'lawless law.' The accused may not justify his conduct by appealing to an existing law if this law offended against certain self-evident principles of the natural law."[15]

Part of the Nuremberg anti-Semitic legislation of 1935 declared that German citizens of Jewish origin who were then outside the country or thereafter left it would lose their German citizenship and their property would be confiscated by the state. After the war, the German courts recognized the claims of Jews to the restoration of their property:

> These laws of confiscation, though clothed in the formal rules . . . of a law, . . . [are] an extremely grave violation of the suprapositive principle of equality before the law as well as of the suprapositive guarantee of property. The equality principle is the foundation of any legal order and must remain inviolable. . . . [These provisions] were and are by reason of their unjust content and their violation of the basic demands of any legal order null and void; this law could not, even at and during the time of the Nazi regime, *produce any legitimate legal effect.*[16]

---

[15] 2 *Süddeutsche Juristen Zeitschrift* 521 (1947); see Ernst von Hippel, "The Role of the Natural Law in the Legal Decisions of the German Federal Republic", 4 *Natural Law Forum* 106, 111 (1959).

[16] Judgment of Feb. 28, 1955, 16 Entscheidungen des Bundesgerichtschofs in Zivilsachen 350 (emphasis by court); see Rommen, "Natural Law in Decisions of the Federal Supreme Court and of the Constitutional Courts in Germany", 14–15.

What might the history of the twentieth century have been if the German legal profession had reacted to the early Nuremberg laws with denunciation and refusal to cooperate? Instead they were "good lawyers" and "good Germans". "Positivism", wrote Heinrich Rommen, "with its thesis that 'law is law' has made German jurists and lawyers defenseless against laws of arbitrary or criminal content. Positivism simply holds that a law is valid because it is successfully enforced. 'Any legislative act is unconditionally binding upon the judge.' "[17]

In his letter from the Birmingham jail, Martin Luther King, Jr., echoed Saint Thomas Aquinas: "A just law is a man-made code that squares with the moral law or the law of God. . . . An unjust law is a code that is out of harmony with the moral law. To put it in the terms of Saint Thomas Aquinas: 'An unjust law is a human law that is not rooted in eternal law and natural law.' "[18] When Rosa Parks refused to give up her seat on the bus in Montgomery, Alabama, on December 1, 1955, a proper reading of the natural law supported her stand.[19] The legal positivist would have told Parks that no law could be rightly disobeyed as unjust.

The same issue was involved a century before when rescuers of fugitive slaves acted in reliance on the higher law. They maintained the Underground Railroad in violation of the Fugitive Slave Act of 1793 and the fugitive-slave provisions of the Compromise of 1850. Incidentally, no federal judge ever refused to enforce the fugitive-slave law on the ground that it

---

[17] Rommen, "Natural Law in Decisions of the Federal Supreme Court and of the Constitutional Courts in Germany", 1.

[18] Martin Luther King, Jr., "Letter from Birmingham Jail", *Why We Can't Wait* (1963), 76, 82.

[19] See Juan Williams, *Eyes on the Prize: America's Civil Rights Years, 1954–55* (1967), 61–73.

was unjust. Charles H. Langston, son of a Revolutionary War soldier and himself described as "part Negro", was convicted in a U.S. District Court in Ohio in 1859 for violating federal law in his rescue of John Price, a fugitive slave. In his speech before sentencing, Langston (as reported in the trial record) relied on the higher law:

> I will do all I can, for any man thus seized and held, though the inevitable penalty . . . hang over me! We all have a common humanity and you all would do that; your manhood would require it; and no matter what the laws might be, you would honor yourself for doing it, while your friends and your children to all generations would honor you for doing it, and every good and honest man would say you have done *right*! (Great and prolonged applause, in spite of the efforts of the Court and Marshal.)[20]

So can natural law thinking really make a difference? It did for the victims of racial segregation in the United States as it had for the fugitive slaves a century before. Had it been acted upon, it could have saved the lives of victims of the Nazi regime. And natural law made a difference to Ingo Heinrich and Andreas Kühnpast, two former East German border guards who were convicted of manslaughter by a German court in 1992 for having killed a fleeing refugee. The court rejected the defense that the guards had been ordered to "shoot to kill" refugees. "Not everything that is legal is right", declared Judge Theodor Seidel. "At the end of the 20th century, no one has the right to turn off his conscience when it comes to killing people on the orders of the authorities."[21]

---

[20] Paul Finkelman, ed., *Slavery, Race and the American Legal System*, 1700–1872 (1988), vol. IV, 11, 17–18.

[21] *New York Times*, Jan. 26, 1992, p. E6; Jan. 21, 1992, p. A1. On appeal, Andreas Kühnpast's conviction was quashed because the German Supreme

3. But what is natural law?

Natural law will seem mysterious if we forget that everything has a law built into its nature. The nature of a rock is such that it will sink if you throw it into a pond. An automobile will function if you feed it gasoline. If you put sand in the tank instead, you may be sincere in your belief that the car will run, but you will end up a pedestrian. The natural law is the story of how things work. If you eat a barbed-wire sandwich, it will not be good for you. If you want your body to function well, you ought not to treat it as if it were a trash compactor. Natural law is easy to understand when we are talking about physical nature. But it applies as well to the moral sphere.

Morality is governed by a law built into the nature of man and knowable by reason. Man can know, through the use of his reason, what is in accord with his nature and therefore good. Every law, however, has to have a lawgiver. Let us say up front that the natural law makes no ultimate sense without God as its author. "As a matter of fact," said Hans Kelsen, probably the foremost legal positivist of the twentieth century, "there is no natural-law doctrine of any importance which has not an essentially religious character."[22] The natural law is a set of manufacturer's directions written into our nature so that we can discover through reason how we ought to act. It " 'is

---

Court found that he had not shot to kill. *Agence France-Presse*, Mar. 25, 1993. On a new trial, Ingo Heinrich had his punishment reduced to a two-year suspended sentence. *Agence France-Press*, Mar. 14, 1994. See Micah Goodman, "After the Wall: The Legal Ramifications of the East German Border Guard Trials in Unified Germany", 29 *Cornell Int'l. Law J.* 727 (1996).

[22] Hans Kelsen, "The Natural-Law Doctrine before the Tribunal of Science", 2 *Western Political Quarterly* 481, 482 (1949).

nothing other than the light of understanding infused in us by God, whereby we understand what must be done and what must be avoided' ".[23] The Ten Commandments, and other prescriptions of the divine law, specify some applications of that natural law.

We ought to welcome those manufacturer's directions, whether written in our nature or on tablets of stone. If you were driving your new car on a lonely road at night and suddenly had a flat, you would be grateful for the manufacturer's directions in the owner's manual, which would tell you where to locate the jack and how to change the tire. It would be a strange motorist who would resent the existence of that manual and refuse to look at it. General Motors, the manufacturer of your Chevy, provides those directions because it wants your car to work well, and it wants to avoid tort and warranty liability. But it also wants you to be happy with your car so you will tell others about it and come back to buy another General Motors car.

Only an unusual car owner would believe that "General Motors loves me." But our "Manufacturer" wants more than to sell us a new car. As we shall see in later Questions in this book, he loves us and wants us to be happy during our life on earth. More important, he wants us to choose to love him so that we can share in his love in the eternal happiness of heaven. The natural law provides a guide through which we can safely and rightly choose to love God by acting in accord with our nature and by helping others to do the same. We can know the requirements of the natural law through reason unaided by explicit revelation. But, because of the weakness and disorder caused in our nature by original sin, we are likely to make

---

[23] *V.S.*, no. 12, quoting Aquinas, *In Duo Praecepta Caritatis et in Cecem Legis Praecepta*.

mistakes; so God has provided revelation to enable us to know with certainty how we ought to act. "The Commandments, that first charter of human rights, are a specific promulgation, to the wavering human conscience, of the natural moral law itself. Nor has our generation in the least outgrown the need for that authoritative, specific promulgation."[24] In a sense, the natural law and revelation complement each other. However, "there is not a natural morality and a supernatural morality but only one salvific morality . . . of which natural law morality is existentially a part. . . . [It] leads men to their ultimate end, God, by sanctifying them through obedience to its moral precepts, and to those of the Gospel ethics."[25]

One caveat is needed at the outset. The natural law provides an objective standard of right and wrong. But it is essential to distinguish the objective wrongness of an act from the subjective culpability, if any, of the person who does it. Jeffrey Dahmer committed objectively wrong acts when he lured fifteen men to his Milwaukee apartment and murdered them. The sole question in his trial, however, was whether he was sane and therefore culpable. The jury decided that he was sane.[26] John Hinckley, however, shot President Ronald Reagan and three others on March 30, 1981, and was found not guilty by reason of insanity; he was committed to a mental hospital.[27] To

---

[24] John M. Finnis, "The Foundations of Human Rights", *Position Paper* 217, Jan. 1992, 28, 37 (*Position Papers* are published by Four Courts Press, Kill Lane, Blackrock, Co. Dublin, Ireland); see the *Catechism of the Catholic Church* (hereafter cited as *C.C.C.*) (1992), no. 1955; on the Commandments generally, see *C.C.C.*, nos. 2052–2557.

[25] Joseph F. Costanzo, S.J., *The Historical Credibility of Hans Küng* (1979), 359.

[26] *Chicago Tribune*, Feb. 16, 1992, p. 1.

[27] *New York Times*, Aug. 10, 1982, p. 1; see Lincoln Caplan, "Not So Nutty: The Post-Dahmer Insanity Defense", *New Republic*, Mar. 30, 1992, p. 18.

be morally culpable for committing a wrong, one must know it is wrong and yet choose to do it. The abortionist, for example, performs actions that objectively violate the natural law and the divine law. But his subjective culpability may be diminished or perhaps even eliminated (or increased) by circumstances. In general, that culpability is not ours to judge. The presence or absence of subjective culpability, however, cannot change the objective rightness or wrongness of the act: the act either is or is not in keeping with the Manufacturer's directions written in our nature. "The distinction between yes and no, true and false, good and evil cannot be given up unless men want to give up being human."[28]

What is natural law? It is, of course, a guide to individual conduct. But it also serves as a standard for the laws enacted by the state. As we shall see in our discussion of Aquinas, if an enacted law is contrary to the natural law, it is not even a law. It is void, an act of violence rather than law. The natural law is therefore a standard for the state as well as for its citizens.

4. Isn't natural law just another Catholic dogma?

No. The natural law has been around a long time. It is neither a Catholic dogma nor even a Christian invention. Sophocles' *Antigone* recognizes the reality that human laws are subject to a higher law. Antigone was condemned to be buried alive for violating the order of Creon, king of Thebes, that Polynices, her dead brother, was not to be buried.

---

[28] Walter Kasper, *Transcending All Understanding: The Meaning of Christian Faith Today* (Boniface Ramsey, O.P., transl., 1989), 41; see Question 34 below.

CREON: [To Antigone] Now tell me, briefly and con-
            cisely: were you aware of the proclamation pro-
            hibiting those acts?

ANTIGONE: I was. I couldn't avoid it when it was made pub-
            lic.

CREON: You still dared break this law?

ANTIGONE: Yes, because I did not believe that Zeus was
            the one who had proclaimed it; neither did Jus-
            tice, or the gods of the dead whom Justice lives
            among. The laws they have made for men are
            well marked out. I didn't suppose your decree
            had strength enough, or you, who are human,
            to violate the lawful traditions the gods have
            not written merely, but made infallible. These
            laws are not for now or for yesterday, they are
            alive forever; and no one knows when they were
            shown to us first. I did not intend to pay, before
            the gods, for breaking these laws because of my
            fear of one man and his principles. I was thor-
            oughly aware I would die before you proclaimed
            it; of course I would die, even if you hadn't. Since
            I will die, and early, I call this profit. Anyone who
            lives the troubled life I do must benefit from
            death.

            No, I do not suffer from the fact of death.
            But if I had let my own brother stay unburied
            I would have suffered all the pain I do not feel
            now. And if you decide what I did was foolish,
            you may be fool enough to convict me too.[29]

Aristotle (384–322 B.C.) observed that "one part of what is
politically just is natural, and the other part legal. What is nat-

---

[29] Sophocles, *Antigone* (Richard Emil Braun, transl., 1973), 38–39.

ural has the same validity everywhere alike, independent of its seeming so or not. What is legal is what originally makes no difference [whether it is done] one way or another, but makes a difference whenever people have laid down the rule, e.g., . . . that a goat rather than two sheep should be sacrificed."[30] Aristotle believed that "there is in nature a common principle of the just and unjust that all people in some way divine [discern], even if they have no association or commerce with each other."[31]

Marcus Tullius Cicero (106–43 B.C.) described "Law" as "the highest reason, implanted in Nature, which commands what ought to be done and forbids the opposite".[32] He said that "right is based, not upon men's opinions, but upon Nature."[33] And "Socrates was right when he cursed, as he often did, the man who first separated utility from Justice; for this separation, he complained, is the source of all mischief."[34] Cicero continued: "But the most foolish notion of all is the belief that everything is just which is found in the customs or laws of nations. . . . But if the principles of Justice were founded on the decrees of peoples, the edicts of princes, or the decisions of judges, then Justice would sanction robbery and adultery and forgery of wills, in case these acts were approved by the votes or decrees of the populace."[35] According to Cicero:

---

[30] Aristotle, *Nicomachean Ethics*, book V (Terence Irwin, transl., 1985), 133; see Saint Thomas Aquinas, *Summa Theologica* (Benziger Bros., ed., 1947; hereafter cited as *S.T.*), which similarly divides "right" into "natural right" and "positive right".

[31] Aristotle, *On Rhetoric*, book I, chap. 13 (George A. Kennedy, transl., 1991), 102.

[32] M. Cicero, *Laws*, in *Great Legal Philosophers* (C. Morris, ed., 1959), 44.

[33] Ibid., 45.

[34] Ibid., 46.

[35] Ibid., 48.

What is right and true is also eternal, and does not begin or end with written statutes. . . . From this point of view it can be readily understood that those who formulated wicked and unjust statutes for nations, thereby breaking their promises and agreements, put into effect anything but "laws." It may thus be clear that in the very definition of the term "law" there inheres the idea and principle of choosing what is just and true. . . . Therefore Law is the distinction between things just and unjust, made in agreement with that primal and most ancient of all things, Nature; and in conformity to nature's standard are framed those human laws which inflict punishment upon the wicked but defend and protect the good.[36]

Natural law ideas found later expression in the common law. Sir Edward Coke, in his dictum concluding that an Act of Parliament could not justify the London College of Physicians in punishing Dr. Bonham for practicing medicine in London without a license from the college said:

And it appears in our books, that in many cases, the common law will controul Acts of Parliament, and sometimes adjudge them to be utterly void: for when an Act of Parliament is against common right and reason, or repugnant, or impossible to be performed, the common law will controul it, and adjudge such Act to be void.[37]

That same year, in his report in *Calvin's Case*, Coke described the "law of nature" as "that which God at the time of creation of the nature of man infused into his heart, for his preservation and direction and this is *lex aeterna*, the moral law, called also the law of nature. And by this law, written with the finger of God in the heart of man, were the people of God a long time

---

[36] Ibid., 51.
[37] *Dr. Bonham's Case*, 8 Coke's Rep. 107(a); 7 Eng. Rep. 638, 652 (1610).

governed before the law was written by Moses, who was the first reporter or writer of law in the world."[38]

Sir William Blackstone, perhaps the greatest commentator on the common law, said:

> As man depends absolutely upon his Maker for everything, it is necessary that he should, in all points conform to his Maker's will. This will of his Maker is called the law of nature. . . . This law of nature being coeval with mankind, and dictated by God himself, is, of course, superior in obligation to any other. It is binding over all the globe, in all countries, and at all times: no human laws are of any validity, if contrary to this; and such of them as are valid derive all of their force and all of their authority mediately or immediately from this original.[39]

Incidentally, despite his affirmation of the law of nature, Blackstone endorsed the English political reality, a product of the Revolution of 1688, that nobody had authority to overturn an Act of Parliament.[40] "After 1688", wrote Roscoe Pound, "there was no fundamental law superior to Parliament."[41]

Alexander Hamilton "maintained a lifelong belief in a divinely ordained eternal law. . . . 'No tribunal, no codes, no systems can repeal or impair this law of God, for by his eternal

---

[38] *Calvin's Case*, 8 Coke's Rep. 113b, 118(a); 77 Eng. Rep. 377, 392 (1610).

[39] William Blackstone, "Introduction", *Commentaries on the Laws of England*, sec. 2 (William Draper Lewis, ed., 1897), vol. I, 29–31.

[40] "Yet it is certain that if Parliament were to pass a law clearly inconsistent with those principles, no court in England would venture to pronounce it void. And if it could not be repealed . . . , it would have to be submitted to as the law of the land, unless the people chose to resort to a revolution. Revolution means nothing more nor less than a peaceable or forcible change by a people of their constitution." Ibid., vol. I, 49, note 34.

[41] Roscoe Pound, "The Development of Constitutional Guarantees of Liberty", 20 *Notre Dame Lawyer* 347, 367 (1945).

laws it is inherent in the nature of things.' "[42] In 1772, George Mason argued before the General Court of Virginia against a slavery statute:

> All acts of legislature apparently contrary to natural right and justice are, in our laws, and must be in the nature of things, considered as void. The laws of nature are the laws of God; Whose authority can be superseded by no power on earth. A legislature must not obstruct our obedience to him from whose punishments they cannot protect us. All human constitutions which contradict his laws, we are in conscience bound to disobey. Such have been the adjudications of our courts of Justice.[43]

Today, if he argued in such terms, Mason might be laughed out of court. At least he would hardly be confirmed by the Senate for appointment to the federal bench. Neither would Blackstone nor Coke.

The affirmation of natural law by Martin Luther King[44] further indicates that natural law is neither the invention nor the exclusive property of Catholics.[45] Professor John T. McNeill of Union Theological Seminary, discussing the views of Martin Luther, Philip Melanchthon, Holdreich Zwingli, and John Calvin, concluded:

> There is no real discontinuity between the teaching of the Reformers and that of their predecessors with respect to nat-

---

[42] Alfons Beitzinger, "The Philosophy of Law of Four American Founding Fathers", 21 *Am. J. of Jur.* 1, 5 (1976); quoting H. C. Syrett, ed., *The Papers of Alexander Hamilton* (1961), vol. I, 87, 47; and Julius Goebel, *The Law Practice of Alexander Hamilton* (1964), vol. I, 821, 838.

[43] *Robin* v. *Hardaway*, 2 Va. (2 Jefferson) 109, 114 (1772).

[44] See Question 2 above.

[45] See also Carl. E. Braaten, "Protestants and Natural Law", *First Things*, Jan. 1992, p. 20.

ural law. Not one of the leaders of the Reformation assails the principle. Instead, with the possible exception of Zwingli, they all on occasion express a quite ungrudging respect for the moral law naturally implanted in the human heart and seek to inculcate this attitude in their readers. Natural law is not one of the issues on which they bring the Scholastics under criticism. With safeguards of their primary doctrines but without conscious resistance on their part, natural law enters into the framework of their thought and is an assumption of their political and social teaching. . . . For the Reformers, as for the Fathers, canonists, and the Scholastics, natural law stood affirmed on the pages of Scripture.[46]

Although natural law is not the property of Catholics, Saint Thomas Aquinas (1225–1274), a Catholic, does provide the most systematic explanation of the natural law in the context of reason as well as revelation. But his work is not a merely sectarian enterprise. "Aquinas' perspective on human law became a major component of Christian tradition."[47] In the part of his *Summa Theologica* known as his *Treatise on Law*, Aquinas frequently used scriptural quotations to support his positions. On self-evident truths, "Aquinas' view is drawn directly from the apostle Paul."[48] However, although he did emphasize the role of reason, the revelational component is essential to Saint Thomas' treatment of law. Aquinas' *Treatise on Law*[49] is only part of his formal treatment of law, which includes also his discussion of the moral, ceremonial, and judicial precepts of the

---

[46] John T. McNeill, "Natural Law in the Teaching of the Reformers", 27 *J. of Religion* 168 (1946).

[47] Lynn Buzzard and Paula Campbell, *Holy Disobedience* (1984), 125.

[48] Gary Amos, *Defending the Declaration: How the Bible and Christianity Influenced the Writing of the Declaration of Independence* (1989), 75.

[49] *S.T.*, I, II, Q. 90–97.

Old Testament.[50] Saint Thomas puts the natural law within the context of the eternal law and divine law as part of God's design. Through reason—and with the aid of revelation—we can attain certainty as to the meaning of the natural law.[51]

In later Questions we will discuss the role of the Magisterium in completing the meaning of the natural law within the context of Christ. But the natural law is not "just another Catholic dogma". As Antigone testified to Creon, its principles are rooted in nature and knowable to reason: "These laws are not for now or for yesterday, they are alive forever; and no one knows when they were shown to us first."[52]

5. How does natural law differ from the dominant jurisprudence today?

Francis Canavan, S.J., aptly described the present stage of American culture as "the fag end of the Enlightenment".[53] American jurisprudence today is a product of the Enlightenment philosophy, which gained influence in the eighteenth century.[54] Although the Protestant Reformation formally, and tragically, severed the bonds of Christian unity, Thomas Hobbes (1588–1679) and other Enlightenment figures went further. The Enlightenment rejected not only the Catholic Church but all revealed religions, and it sought to replace

---

[50] See *S.T.*, I, II, Q. 98–108.

[51] See discussion in Charles E. Rice, "Some Reasons for a Restoration of Natural Law Jurisprudence", 24 *Wake Forest L. Rev.* 539, 557 et seq. (1989).

[52] Sophocles, *Antigone* (Richard Emil Braun, transl., 1973), 38–39.

[53] Francis Canavan, S.J., "Commentary", *Catholic Eye*, Dec. 10, 1987, p. 2.

[54] See discussion in William Smith, "The First Amendment and Progress", *Humanitas*, Summer 1987, pp. 1, 5.

them with a new and worldly religion of reason. "The fundamental dogma of the Enlightenment is that man must overcome the prejudices inherited from tradition; he must have the boldness to free himself from every authority in order to think on his own, using nothing but his own reason."[55] This "[i]ndividualism presupposes a use of freedom in which the subject does what he wants, in which he himself is the one to 'establish the truth' of whatever he finds pleasing or useful. . . . Individualism thus remains egocentric and selfish."[56]

The Enlightenment further involved a denial of the power of reason to know objective truth.

> Truth is no longer an objective datum. . . . It gradually becomes something . . . which each one grasps from his own point of view, without ever knowing to what extent his viewpoint corresponds to the object in itself. . . . The idea of the good in itself is put outside of man's grasp. The only reference point for each person is what he can conceive on his own as good. Consequently, freedom is no longer seen positively as a striving for the good which reason uncovers with help from the community and tradition, but is rather defined as an emancipation from all conditions which prevent each one from following his own reason.[57]

As John Paul II put it, "some philosophers have abandoned the search for truth in itself and made their sole aim the attainment of a subjective certainty or a pragmatic sense of utility.

---

[55] Cardinal Joseph Ratzinger, *Address* to Consistory of College of Cardinals, Apr. 4, 1991, "The Problem of Threats to Human Life", *L'Osservatore Romano* (English ed.), Apr. 8, 1991, p. 2; 36 *The Pope Speaks* 332–33 (1991); see also Question 46 below.

[56] *L.F.*, no. 14; see also, *E.V.*, nos. 20, 21.

[57] Ratzinger, "The Problem of Threats to Human Life", 36 *The Pope Speaks*, 333–34 (1991); see also *V.S.* nos. 32, 33, 46.

This in turn has obscured the true dignity of reason."[58] "As a result of the crisis of rationalism, what has appeared finally is nihilism. As a philosophy of nothingness, it has a certain attraction for people of our time. Its adherents claim that the search is an end in itself, without any hope or possibility of ever attaining the goal of truth. In the nihilist interpretation, life is no more than an occasion for sensations and experiences in which the ephemeral has pride of place. Nihilism is at the root of the widespread mentality which claims that a definitive commitment should no longer be made, because everything is fleeting and provisional."[59]

Whereas Aristotle, Aquinas, and others affirmed that man is social by nature, Enlightenment thinkers postulated a mythical "state of nature" populated by autonomous individuals who were not social but "sociable".[60] Those individuals formed the state according to the social contract. The purpose, according to Hobbes, was to achieve security; according to John Locke (1632–1704), it was for the protection of rights; for Jean Jacques Rousseau (1712–1778), it was to implement the "general will". The origin of the state was therefore not in nature and the divine plan but in the social contract, with rights coming not from God but from man and ultimately from the state. "The Declaration of the Rights of Man at the end of the eighteenth century", wrote Hannah Arendt, "was a turning point in history. It meant nothing more nor less than that from then on Man, and not God's command or the customs of history, should be the source of Law."[61]

---

[58] *F.R.*, no. 47.

[59] *F.R.*, no. 46.

[60] See Heinrich Rommen, *The Natural Law* (1948), 75–109.

[61] Hannah Arendt, *The Origins of Totalitarianism* (1966), 290.

The theories of the social contract . . . were elaborated at the end of the 17th century (cf. Hobbes): that which would bring harmony among men was a law recognized by reason and commanding respect by an enlightened prince who incarnates the general will. Here, too, when the common reference to values and ultimately to God is lost, society will then appear merely as an ensemble of individuals placed side by side, and the contract which ties them together will necessarily be perceived as an accord among those who have the power to impose their will on others. . . . By a dialectic within modernity, one passes from the affirmation of the rights of freedom, detached from any objective reference to a common truth, to the destruction of the very foundations of this freedom. The "enlightened despot" of the social contract theorists became the tyrannical state, in fact totalitarian, which disposes of the life of its weakest members, from an unborn baby to an elderly person, in the name of a public usefulness which is really only the interest of a few.[62]

The jurisprudence of the Enlightenment is an individualist, utilitarian positivism. It leaves no room for mediating institutions, such as the family and social groups, between the individual and the state. It tends to deteriorate into either an extreme, individualist capitalism or a totalitarian collectivism. The natural law tradition, by contrast, includes the principle of subsidiarity, which emphasizes the role of intermediate family and voluntary groups, such as labor unions, which stand between the individual and the state.

In the natural law tradition, law involves the will of the lawgiver who ordains and promulgates it, but the essence of law is reason. In Enlightenment jurisprudence, law is essentially an

---

[62] Ratzinger, "The Problem of Threats to Human Life", 36 *The Pope Speaks*, 334–35 (1991).

exercise of will.[63] In the traditional natural law, for example, all human beings are entitled to be regarded as persons. In positivist jurisprudence, this natural and necessary correspondence between humanity and personhood is rejected. Human beings who are black, as in the Dred Scott Case,[64] or unborn, as in *Roe v. Wade*,[65] can be deprived of rights, at the will of the lawmakers who define them as nonpersons. In *Cruzan v. Director, Missouri Dept. of Health*, dissenting Justice John Paul Stevens even argued that "for patients like Nancy Cruzan, who have no consciousness and no chance of recovery, there is a serious question as to whether the mere persistence of their bodies is 'life' as that word is commonly understood, or as it is used in both the Constitution and the Declaration of Independence."[66]

Professor Harold Berman wrote:

> Only in the past two generations, in my lifetime, has the public philosophy of America shifted radically from a religious to a secular theory of law, from a moral to a political or instrumental theory, and from a historical to a pragmatic theory. . . . Rarely does one hear it said that law is a reflection of an objective justice or of the ultimate meaning or purpose of life. Usually it is thought to reflect at best the community sense of what is expedient; and more commonly it is thought to express the more or less arbitrary will of the lawmaker. . . . The triumph of the positivist theory of law—that law is the will of the lawmaker—and the decline of rival theories—the moral theory that law is reason and

---

[63] See the discussion of Nietzsche's critique of Enlightenment philosophy in Alasdair MacIntyre, *After Virtue* (1984), 109–20; Friedrich Nietzsche, *The Gay Science* (1974), sec. 335, 263–66.

[64] *Scott v. Sandford*, 60 U.S. (19 How.) 393, 15 L. Ed. 691, 709, 720 (1857).

[65] 410 U.S. 113 (1973).

[66] 110 S. Ct. 2841, 2886 (1990).

conscience, and the historical theory that law is an ongoing tradition in which *both* politics and morality play important parts—have contributed to the bewilderment of legal education. Skepticism and relativism are widespread.[67]

Any serious espousal of natural law poses a potentially mortal threat to the prevailing jurisprudence. A coherent natural law approach affirms objective norms, rooted in nature, that are higher even than the Constitution or the Supreme Court. It points to God as the lawgiver, and it threatens to bring up for public discussion the claim of the Catholic Church that the Pope, as Vicar of Christ, is the authoritative interpreter of the natural law. It is interesting to speculate as to whether the vehemence of the opposition to Clarence Thomas' nomination perhaps was due in part to his Catholic upbringing and to the fact that he was a graduate of the College of the Holy Cross. Even considering the anemic contemporary state of Jesuit education, that background could have added a threatening dimension to Thomas' mild espousals of natural law theory.

---

[67] Harold Berman, "The Crisis of Legal Education in America", 26 *Boston Coll. L. Rev.* 347, 348 (1985).

II

AQUINAS ON NATURAL LAW
AND OTHER KINDS OF LAW

6. Let's talk about Aquinas. Why is he so important? How does he define natural law and where does he put it in the big picture?

Saint Thomas' most significant philosophical achievement was "his successful integration of Christian theology and Greek, or perhaps better, Aristotelian philosophy".[1] In this he was indebted to Saint Augustine (354–430), who integrated legal philosophy and theology and who insisted that "theological-Christian considerations not only permeate the whole of law and legal theory, but in fact constitute the only sound foundation of true law and true jurisprudence."[2] "Saint Thomas", said John Paul II, "is an authentic model for all who seek the truth. In his thinking, the demands of reason and the power of faith found the most elevated synthesis ever attained by human thought, for he could defend the radical newness introduced by Revelation without ever demeaning the venture proper to reason."[3] Saint Thomas, following Saint Augustine, understood and affirmed the order in the universe. The world is not a product of chance. Rather it was created by a loving God whose existence and attributes we can demonstrate and who has ordered his creation in accord with his design.

Saint Thomas defines "law" in general as "an ordinance of reason for the common good, made by him who has care of

---

[1] Anton-Hermann Chroust, "The Philosophy of Law of St. Thomas Aquinas: His Fundamental Ideas and Some of His Historical Precursors", 19 *Am. J. of Jur.*, 1, 23 (1974).

[2] Anton-Hermann Chroust, "The Fundamental Ideas in St. Augustine's Philosophy of Law", 18 *Am. J. of Jur.*, 57 (1973).

[3] *F.R.*, no. 78.

the community, and promulgated".[4] He then enumerates four kinds of law: the eternal law, the natural law, the human law, and the divine law.

The Eternal Law

In a human manner of speaking, it might be said that God, the Creator, has a "plan" for the world. God, of course, is eternal, and eternity is timeless. He does not make plans for the future and then proceed to carry them out. Rather a "universal rational orderliness" is "characteristic of the whole universe".[5] The "whole community of the universe is governed by Divine Reason. Wherefore the very Idea of the government of things in God the Ruler of the universe, has the nature of a law."[6] This law, "the Divine Reason's conception of things", is called by Saint Thomas the eternal law.[7] "The [Second Vatican] Council refers to the classic teaching on God's *eternal law*. Saint Augustine defines this as 'the reason or the will of God, who commands us to respect the natural order and forbids us to disturb it.' "[8]

The Natural Law

Man is a rational creature.

Since all things subject to Divine Providence are ruled and measured by the eternal law . . . it is evident that all things

---

[4] *S.T.*, I, II, Q. 90, art. 4.

[5] Chroust, "The Philosophy of Law of St. Thomas Aquinas", 24.

[6] *S.T.*, I, II, Q. 91, art. 1.

[7] Ibid.

[8] *V.S.*, no. 43, quoting *Contra Faustum*.

partake somewhat of the eternal law, in so far as, namely, from its being imprinted on them, they derive their respective inclinations to their proper acts and ends. Now among all others, the rational creature is subject to Divine providence in the most excellent way, in so far as it partakes of a share of providence, by being provident both for itself and for others. Wherefore it has a share of the Eternal Reason, whereby it has a natural inclination to its proper act and end: and this participation of the eternal law in the rational creature is called the natural law.[9] [The] light of natural reason, whereby we discern what is good and what is evil, which is the function of the natural law, is nothing else than an imprint on us of the Divine Light. It is therefore evident that the natural law is nothing else than the rational creature's participation of the Eternal Law.[10]

The natural law is therefore a rule of reason, promulgated by God in man's nature, whereby man can discern how he should act. "The natural law is promulgated by the very fact that God instilled it into man's mind so as to be known by him naturally."[11] Just as the maker of an automobile builds into it a certain nature (it drives, it does not fly) and gives directions for its use so that it will achieve its end—that is, to be dependable transportation—so God has built a certain, knowable nature into man to follow if he is to achieve his final end, which is eternal happiness with God in heaven.

The first, self-evident precept of the natural law is that "good is to be done and pursued, and evil is to be avoided. All other precepts of the natural law are based on this: so that whatever the practical reason naturally apprehends as man's good (or evil) belongs to the precepts of the natural law as something

---

[9] *S.T.*, I, II, Q. 91, art. 2.
[10] Ibid.
[11] Ibid., art. 4; see also *V.S.*, nos. 44, 46.

to be done or avoided."[12] Because the good is to be sought and evil is to be avoided, and because the good is that which is in accord with the nature of whatever it is we are talking about, the next question is: What is the nature of man? The essential nature of man is unalterable because it is a reflection of the unchanging divine essence.[13] Saint Thomas says that "all those things to which man has a natural inclination are naturally apprehended by reason as being good, and consequently as objects of pursuit, and their contraries as evil, and objects of avoidance."[14] The basic inclinations of man are five:

1. To seek the good, including his highest good, which is eternal happiness with God.[15]

2. To preserve himself in existence.

3. To preserve the species—that is, to unite sexually.

4. To live in community with other men.

5. To use his intellect and will—that is, to know the truth and to make his own decisions.[16]

These inclinations are put into human nature by God to help man achieve his final end of eternal happiness. From these in-

---

[12] *S.T.*, I, II, Q. 94, art. 2.

[13] See discussion in Heinrich Rommen, *The Natural Law* (1948), 50.

[14] *S.T.*, I, II, Q. 94, art. 2.

[15] Saint Thomas states that "moral virtues . . . are about matters that are ordered to God as their end. And religion approaches nearer to God than the other moral virtues, in so far as its actions are directly and immediately ordered to the honor of God. Hence, religion excels among the moral virtues." *S.T.*, II, II, Q. 81, art 6; see also *S.T.*, II, II, Q. 85, art. 1.

[16] See Thomas E. Davitt, S.J., "St. Thomas Aquinas and the Natural Law", *Origins of the Natural Law Tradition* (1954), 26, 30–31; Rommen, *The Natural Law*, 49; *S.T.*, I, II, Q. 94, art. 2.

clinations we apply the natural law by deduction: Good should be done; this action is good; this action therefore should be done. However, because of "concupiscence or some other passion, . . . evil perversions . . . or . . . vicious customs and corrupt habits", people may come to the wrong conclusions in their understanding or application of the secondary principles of the natural law.[17] For example, among some people, as Saint Thomas points out, homosexual activity is not considered sinful although it is specifically stigmatized by him as the "unnatural crime".[18] The fact that people are in error in their perception of the natural law may reduce or eliminate their subjective culpability. But whether or not such people are culpable, some acts are always objectively wrong.[19]

The Human Law

"It is from the precepts of the natural law, as from general and indemonstrable principles, that the human reason needs to proceed to the more particular determination of certain matters. These particular determinations, devised by human reason, are called human laws, provided the other essential conditions of law be observed."[20] Those essential conditions of law are encompassed in Saint Thomas' definition of law, which, as we have seen, is "an ordinance of reason for the common good, made by him who has care of the community, and promulgated".[21] "Since . . . the eternal law is the plan of government in the Chief Governor, all the plans of government in

---

[17] *S.T.*, I, II, Q. 94, art. 6; see Question 7 below.

[18] *S.T.*, I, II, Q. 94, art. 3.

[19] *C.C.C.*, nos. 1755–56; see nos. 1950–86 on the moral law.

[20] *S.T.*, I, II, Q. 91, art. 3.

[21] *S.T.*, I, II, Q. 90, art. 4.

the inferior governors must be derived from the eternal law. But these plans of inferior governors are all other laws besides the eternal law. Therefore all laws, in so far as they partake of right reason, are derived from the eternal law."[22]

The Divine Law

Saint Thomas affirmed the necessity of revelation, which includes the Old Testament and the New Testament.[23] Saint Thomas calls this revelation the divine law. The natural law can be known by reason without the aid of explicit supernatural revelation. However, he states:

> Besides the natural and the human law it was necessary for the directing of human conduct to have a Divine law. And this for four reasons.
>
> *First*, . . . since man is ordained to an end of eternal happiness which is inproportionate to man's natural faculty . . . therefore it was necessary that, besides the natural and the human law, man should be directed to his end by a law given by God.
>
> *Secondly*, because, on account of the uncertainty of human judgment, especially on contingent and particular matters, different people form different judgments on human acts; whence also different and contrary laws result. In order, therefore, that man may know without any doubt what he ought to do and what he ought to avoid, it was necessary for man to be directed in his proper acts by a law given by God, for it is certain that such a law cannot err.
>
> *Thirdly*, because man can make laws in those matters of which he is competent to judge. But man is not competent

---

[22] *S.T.*, I, II, Q. 93, art. 3.
[23] See *C.C.C.*, nos. 1961–86.

to judge of interior movements, that are hidden, but only of exterior acts which appear: and yet for the perfection of virtue it is necessary for man to conduct himself aright in both kinds of acts. Consequently human law could not sufficiently curb and direct interior acts; and it was necessary for this purpose that a Divine law should supervene.

Fourthly, because . . . human law cannot punish or forbid all evil deeds: since while aiming at doing away with all evils, it would do away with many good things, and would hinder the advance of the common good, which is necessary for human intercourse. In order therefore, that no evil might remain unforbidden and unpunished, it was necessary for the Divine law to supervene, whereby all sins are forbidden.[24]

The divine law complements the natural law as well as the human law. Elsewhere, Saint Thomas affirms the necessity of revelation even with respect to things we can know through reason:

It is necessary for man to accept by faith not only things which are above reason, but also those which can be known by reason: and this for three motives. *First*, in order that man may arrive more quickly at the knowledge of Divine truth. . . . *Second*, . . . in order that the knowledge of God may be more general. For many are unable to make progress in the study of science, either through dullness of mind, or through having a number of occupations and temporal needs, or even through laziness in learning, all of whom would be altogether deprived of the knowledge of God, unless Divine things were brought to their knowledge under the guise of faith. The *third* reason is for the sake of certitude. For human reason is very deficient in things concerning God. A sign of this is that philosophers in their researches, by natural investigation, into human affairs, have fallen into many errors,

---

[24] *S.T.*, I, II, Q. 91, art. 4 (emphasis added).

and have disagreed among themselves. And consequently, in order that men might have knowledge of God, free of doubt and uncertainty, it was necessary for divine matters to be delivered to them by way of faith, being told to them, as it were, by God Himself Who cannot lie.[25]

In summary, Saint Thomas places the human law within the context of the natural law and places them both within the overall design of God, the "Chief Governor".[26] By contrast, the secular jurisprudence of the Enlightenment attempts to organize society as if God and his revelation did not exist. If it talks about natural law, that law is a secular version divorced from the divine law. It may be helpful to visualize the contrast in this respect between the jurisprudence of Aquinas and that of the Enlightenment:

Eternal law
Divine law

Natural law
Human law

Aquinas integrates the natural and human laws with the eternal and the divine law. Enlightenment jurisprudence, by contrast, operates entirely below the line, even when it affirms a natural law, without reliance on God or his revelation. Secular and humanistic, it leaves man entirely on his own. In fact, however, "the true philosopher, if he wishes to reach the ultimate questions, cannot free himself from the question of God, the question about the foundation and end of being itself."[27]

---

[25] *S.T.*, II, II, Q. 2, art. 4.

[26] *S.T.*, I, II, Q. 93, art. 3.

[27] Cardinal Joseph Ratzinger, "Faith, Philosophy and Theology", 11 *Communio* 351, 357 (1984).

7. *Is the natural law the same for everybody? Does everybody know what it requires? Can it be changed?*

Saint Thomas distinguishes the general principles of the natural law from its particular applications.

> As regards the general principles whether of speculative reason or of practical reason, truth or rectitude is the same for all, and is equally known by all.[28] As to the proper conclusions of the speculative reason, the truth is the same for all, but it is not equally known to all: thus it is true for all that the three angles of a triangle are together equal to two right angles, although it is not known to all. But as to the proper conclusions of the practical reason, neither is the truth or rectitude the same for all, nor, where it is the same, it is equally known by all. Thus it is right and true for all to act according to reason: and from this principle it follows as a proper conclusion, that goods entrusted to another should be restored to their owner. Now this is true for the majority of cases: but it may happen in a particular case that it would be injurious, and therefore unreasonable, to restore goods held in trust; for instance if they are claimed for the purpose of fighting against one's country.[29]

This is applied common sense. If you borrow a target pistol from another, you are bound in justice to return it according to the terms of your agreement with him. However, if you discover, when the owner comes to reclaim it, that he intends to use it to murder someone, the ordinary obligation to return

---

[28] With respect to the natural law, rectitude here means the objective rightness or wrongness of an act.

[29] *S.T.*, I, II, Q. 94, art. 4.

a borrowed item no longer applies. You are obliged in justice not to return it as long as you have reason to believe that the lender wants it back so that he can use it to harm or kill another person.

Aquinas concludes:

> Consequently, we must say that the natural law, as to general principles, is the same for all, both as to rectitude and as to knowledge. But as to certain matters of detail, which are conclusions, as it were, of those general principles, it is the same for all in the majority of cases, both as to rectitude and as to knowledge; and yet in some few cases it may fail, both as to rectitude, by reason of certain obstacles, . . . and as to knowledge, since in some the reason is perverted by passion, or evil habit, or an evil disposition of nature; thus formerly, theft, although it is expressly contrary to the natural law, was not considered wrong among the Germans, as Julius Caesar relates (*De Bello Gall.* vi).[30]

Peter Kreeft neatly summarized this teaching of Aquinas:

> Thus the natural moral law tells what is naturally and usually right (e.g., "pay debts"), just as natural physical law tells us how nature usually behaves (e.g., "birds fly"); but there are exceptions to both when we come to detail. "Do not give a murderer his gun back" is an exception to "Justice means paying what is owed," and dodos are an exception to "birds fly." The natural moral law is also naturally *known*, as is much of natural physical law; yet there are exceptions to both: e.g., in the case of natural moral law, St. Thomas' example of those Germans in Caesar's day who justified theft (or, in our own day, genocide); and in the case of natural physical law, some South Pacific natives believed women got pregnant by sitting under a sacred tree.[31]

---

[30] Ibid.

[31] Peter Kreeft, ed., *A Summa of the Summa* (1990), 519–20, note 272.

Saint Thomas makes a related point:

[As to] certain most general precepts that are known to all,
. . . the natural law, in the abstract, can nowise be blotted
out from men's hearts. [However, the natural law] is blotted
out in the case of a particular action, in so far as reason is
hindered from applying the general principle to a particular
point of practice, on account of concupiscence or some other
passion. . . . But as to the other, i.e., the secondary precepts,
the natural law can be blotted out from the human heart,
either by evil persuasions, just as in speculative matters errors occur in respect of necessary conclusions; or by vicious
customs and corrupt habits, as among some men, theft, and
even unnatural vices, as the Apostle states (*Rom.* i), were not
esteemed sinful.[32]

Here, too, Saint Thomas speaks common sense. A person can
so dull his conscience with repeated sin that he will no longer
acknowledge that what he is doing is wrong. As Saint Thomas
said, "Through sin, the reason is obscured, especially in practical matters, the will hardened to evil, good actions become
more difficult, and concupiscence more impetuous."[33] As John
Paul II put it, "the systematic violation of the moral law, especially in the serious matter of respect for human life and its
dignity, produces a kind of progressive darkening of the capacity to discern God's living and saving presence."[34]

The natural law cannot be changed in its essentials.[35] Saint
Thomas affirmed that the natural law "does not vary according to time, but remains unchangeable."[36] He distinguished,

---

[32] *S.T.*, I, II, Q. 94, art. 6.

[33] *S.T.*, I, II, Q. 85, art. 3; see also Saint Thomas Aquinas, *Summa contra Gentiles* (Vernon J. Bourke, transl., 1975), book III, chap. 108, p. 105.

[34] *E.V.*, no. 21.

[35] See *V.S.*, no. 53.

[36] *S.T.*, I, II, Q. 94, art. 5, quoting the Decretals (Dist. V).

however, addition to the natural law from subtraction from it. "Nothing hinders the natural law from being changed" by way of addition.[37] However, "by way of subtraction, so that what previously was according to the natural law, ceases to be so . . . the natural law is altogether unchangeable in its first principles: But in its secondary principles, which . . . are certain detailed proximate conclusions drawn from the first principles, the natural law is not changed so that what it prescribes be not right in most cases. But it may be changed in some particular cases of rare occurrence, through some special causes hindering the observance of such precepts."[38] Saint Thomas cites here his earlier reference to the inapplicability of the general rule requiring return of a borrowed item when it is known that it will be used to commit a crime. As Monsignor Paul J. Glenn summarized the adaptability of the natural law:

> The natural law is changeless in the sense that its precepts cannot be upset or destroyed. It can change by extension, by new applications, as experience brings new situations and circumstances. Such a change is not in the natural law itself; it is extrinsic to the natural law; it is merely a new use of the natural law. For instance, the question may arise as to the use of atom bombs in warfare; we may inquire whether the use of such weapons is in conflict with the natural law. Such a question is new; it could not arise in the days when atom bombs were entirely unknown. The question seeks to apply the unchanging natural law in a changing world.[39]

The natural law, in sum, provides an objective, knowable standard that is as old as human nature but ever adaptable to new and changing situations.

---

[37] Ibid.
[38] Ibid.
[39] Paul J. Glenn, *A Tour of the Summa* (1978), 169.

8. How does the law enacted by the state — the human law — relate to the natural law?

According to Saint Thomas, the human law is the fourth type of law, in addition to the eternal law, natural law, and divine law. Human law, an integral part of God's plan, is designed to promote the common good and help man attain his highest end of happiness with God.[40] Saint Thomas' realistic view of human nature can be seen in his explanation as to why we need the human law:

> Man has a natural aptitude for virtue; but the perfection of virtue must be acquired by man by means of some kind of training. . . . Now it is difficult to see how man could suffice for himself in the matter of this training: since the perfection of virtue consists chiefly in withdrawing man from undue pleasures, to which above all man is inclined, and especially the young, who are more capable of being trained. Consequently a man needs to receive this training from another, whereby to arrive at the perfection of virtue. And as to those young people who are inclined to acts of virtue, by their good natural disposition, or by custom, or rather by the gift of God, paternal training suffices, which is by admonitions. But since some are found to be depraved, and prone to vice, and not easily amenable to words, it was necessary for such to be restrained from evil by force and fear, in order that, at least, they might desist from evil-doing, and leave others in peace, and that they themselves, by being habituated in this way, might be brought to do willingly what hitherto they did from fear, and thus become virtuous. Now this kind of training, which compels through fear of punishment, is the

---

[40] On the political community and civil authority in the context of the Fourth Commandment, see *C.C.C.*, nos. 2234–57.

discipline of laws. Therefore, in order that man might have peace and virtue, it was necessary for laws to be framed: for, . . . "as man is the most noble of animals, if he be perfect in virtue, so is he the lowest of all, if he be severed from law and righteousness;" because man can use his reason to devise means of satisfying his lusts and evil passions, which other animals are unable to do.[41]

The human law is derived from the natural law. It may be derived by conclusion, as the law "that one must not kill may be derived as a conclusion from the basic principle that one should do harm to no man."[42] Or it may be derived by determination, as, for example, "the law of nature has it that the evildoer shall be punished", but the human law decrees whether the punishment should be "in this or that way" by fine, imprisonment, or other penalty.[43]

The natural law has two functions with respect to human law; they might be called the "constructive" and the "protective". In its "constructive" function, natural law provides a guide for the formulation of laws to promote the common good. Natural law principles of morality and social justice ought to inform the public discussion of issues such as the family, the economy, and the prevention of racial discrimination. For example, in light of the harmful effects of permissive divorce, especially on the children involved, legislators ought to consider restrictions on divorce as a means of restoring the status of the family as a divinely ordained natural society entitled to the protection of the human law. This constructive function includes the limitation that the human law should not attempt to prohibit

---

[41] *S.T.*, I, II, Q. 95, art. 1, quoting Aristotle, *Politics*, i, 2.
[42] Ibid., art. 2.
[43] Ibid.

every vice or enforce every virtue.[44] But the natural law can plan an important role as a guide to the way things ought to work according to the Manufacturer's directions. It would be a mistake, however, to claim that natural law "pretends to be some sort of magic formula that furnishes handy answers for whatever practical legal questions may arise".[45] In its constructive role, the natural law offers not a cookbook of legal and social recipes but a reasonable guide to principles and general objectives. The Magisterium of the Church provides further specification of those principles and objectives; thus, for example, the general norms of economic justice include support for the specific objective of the "family wage".[46]

The second, or "protective", function of natural law provides a shield against laws that violate the natural law. This role involves criticism of the human law. Although it is critical in that sense, its primary effect is to protect the rights of the people. Without the natural law, the people have no basis other than the pragmatic and utilitarian on which to respond to unjust laws. The ability, provided only by natural law, to challenge the very validity of an unjust law is an important safeguard against the enactment and enforcement of such laws. In this function, the natural law provides a basis for drawing the line and criticizing an act of the state as unjust and void. This protective function is also constructive in that the recognition of a protective line beyond which the state may not go can encourage the enactment of laws that are truly just.[47]

---

[44] See Questions 13 and 14 below.

[45] Davitt, "St. Thomas Aquinas and the Natural Law", 45.

[46] Pope John Paul II, *Laborem Exercens* (1981), no. 19; see Pope John Paul II, *Centesimus Annus* (1991) (hereafter cited as *C.A.*), no. 8.

[47] See discussion in Charles E. Rice, "Some Reasons for a Restoration of Natural Law Jurisprudence", 24 *Wake Forest L. Rev.* 539, 566–67 (1989).

In summary, Saint Thomas makes it clear that the human law is not some arbitrary imposition, but, as a rule of reason for the common good, it is itself, along with the natural and divine laws, part of God's design.

9. *What is the "common good" that the human law is supposed to promote? Shouldn't the focus be on individuals and their rights?*

Aristotle, Aquinas, and the natural law tradition affirm that man is social by nature. The jurisprudence of the Enlightenment regards society as composed of autonomous individuals who are related to others not by nature but only insofar as they consent to be related. In that view, the purpose of law becomes the protection of individual rights, as those rights are determined by the political process and, ultimately, according to the greatest good of the greatest number or other utilitarian criteria. For Aquinas, however, law is not merely whatever legislative product results from the contentions of rival individuals and interests. Rather, there is a common good that is more than merely the total of individual goods.[48] Saint Thomas quotes the statement of Saint Isidore of Seville (c. 570–636) that "laws are enacted for no private profit, but for the common benefit of the citizens."[49] Aquinas continues:

> [The] first principle in practical matters, which are the object of the practical reason, is the last end: and the last end of human life is bliss or happiness. . . . Consequently the law must needs regard principally the relationship to happiness.

---

[48] On the common good generally, see *C.C.C.*, nos. 1905–27.
[49] *S.T.*, I, II, Q. 90, art. 2.

Moreover, since every part is ordained to the whole, as imperfect to perfect; and since one man is a part of the perfect community, the law must needs regard properly the relationship to universal happiness. Wherefore the Philosopher [Aristotle] . . . says . . . that we call those legal matters "just, which are adapted to produce and preserve happiness . . . for the body politic:" since the state is a perfect community.[50]

The human law cannot rightly be directed toward the merely private welfare of one or some of the members of the community. Nor can the law be directed toward the benefit of the present generation to the undue detriment of generations to come or vice versa. Saint Thomas quotes the dictum of the Byzantine emperor and lawgiver Justinian (483–565) that "laws should be made to suit the majority of instances; and they are not framed according to what may possibly happen in an individual case".[51] Saint Thomas continues, "Now the common good comprises many things. Wherefore laws should take account of many things, as to persons, as to matters, and as to times. Because the community of the state is composed of many persons; and its good is procured by many actions; nor is it established to endure for only a short time, but to last for all time by the citizens succeeding one another."[52]

Incidentally, the common good is Saint Thomas' basis for his justification of capital punishment:

Moreover, the common good is better than the particular good of one person. So, the particular good should be removed in order to preserve the common good. But the life of certain pestiferous men is an impediment to the common good which is the concord of human society. Therefore,

---

[50] Ibid.

[51] *S.T.*, I, II, Q. 96, art. 1.

[52] Ibid.

certain men must be removed by death from the society of men. . . . Therefore, the ruler of a state executes pestiferous men justly and sinlessly in order that the peace of the state may not be disrupted. . . . [However], the execution of the wicked is forbidden wherever it cannot be done without danger to the good. Of course, this often happens when the wicked are not clearly distinguished from the good by their sins, or when the danger of the evil involving many good men in this ruin is feared.[53]

If a man be dangerous and infectious to the community, on account of some sin, it is praiseworthy and advantageous that he be killed in order to safeguard the common good, since "a little leaven corrupteth the whole lump" (1 *Cor.* v. 6).[54]

Evangelium Vitae, Pope John Paul's 1995 encyclical, affirms the Church's traditional teaching that the state has authority to impose the death penalty in some situations.[55] But it mandates that a much heavier burden of proof than previously required must be met before one can rightly support the use of that penalty:

[T]here is a growing tendency, both in the Church and in civil society, to demand that [the death penalty] be applied in a very limited way or even that it be abolished completely. The problem must be viewed in the context of a system of penal justice ever more in line with human dignity and thus, in the end, with God's plan for man and society. The

---

[53] Aquinas, *Summa contra Gentiles* (Vernon J. Bourke, transl., 1975), book III, chap. 146, pp. 220–22.

[54] *S.T.*, II, II, Q. 64, art. 2; see also *S.T.*, II, II, Q. 66, art. 6.

[55] See discussion in "The Bishops on the Death Penalty" (editorial), *America*, Dec. 20, 1980, p. 400; Rev. Richard P. Hire, "Society Kills: Can It Ever Be Justified?" *Our Sunday Visitor*, Oct. 23, 1977, p. 8; see also *C.C.C.*, nos. 2266–67.

primary purpose of the punishment which society inflicts is "to redress the disorder caused by the offence." Public authority must redress the violation of personal and social rights by imposing on the offender an adequate punishment for the crime, as a condition for the offender to regain the exercise of his or her freedom. In this way authority also fulfills the purpose of defending public order and ensuring people's safety, while at the same time offering the offender an incentive and help to change his or her behaviour and be rehabilitated.[56]

The final text of the Catechism of the Catholic Church severely limits the permissible use of the death penalty.

Assuming that the guilty party's identity and responsibility have been fully determined, the traditional teaching of the church does not exclude recourse to the death penalty, if this is the only possible way of effectively defending human lives *against the unjust aggressor*.

If, however, nonlethal means are sufficient to defend and protect people's safety *from the aggressor*, authority will limit itself to such means, as these are more in keeping with the concrete conditions of the common good and more in conformity with the dignity of the human person.

Today, in fact, as a consequence of the possibilities which the state has for effectively preventing crime, *by rendering one who has committed an offense incapable of doing harm*—without definitively taking away from him the possibility of redeeming himself—the cases in which the execution of the offender is an absolute necessity are very rare, if not practically nonexistent.[57]

---

[56] *E.V.*, no. 56, quoting *C.C.C.* no. 2267.

[57] No. 2267; 27 *Origins* 57, 261 (Sept. 25, 1997) (emphasis added).

A Catholic can now rightly support the use of the death penalty only in cases when it is "the only possible way of effectively defending human lives against the unjust aggressor." The death penalty cannot be justified as a means to promote a generalized protection of society by deterring potential offenders. The test is the protection of society *from this convicted criminal.* "Among the signs of hope," John Paul stated in *Evangelium Vitae*, "there is evidence of a growing public opposition to the death penalty, even when such a penalty is seen as a kind of legitimate defense on the part of society. Modern society in fact has the means of effectively *suppressing crime by rendering criminals harmless without definitively denying them the chance to reform.*"[58]

Under the new criterion one could apparently still argue for the death penalty in very limited situations, such as that of a prisoner already serving a life sentence who murders a guard or another inmate. What sense would it make to give him another life sentence? Or would it be consistent with his dignity to wall him up permanently in a cell, with food and wastes passed through an aperture, and with no direct contact ever with any other human being? The death penalty could be argued to be absolutely necessary in such a case, although even there it is debatable. Other cases could be argued, such as a condition of unrest in which the authorities would lack the means to keep a murderer securely imprisoned.

Before *Evangelium Vitae*, this writer and others supported the use of the death penalty, among other reasons, because it seemed to be necessary to restore the balance of justice with respect to some crimes and because it uniquely promoted respect for innocent life by inflicting a punishment for murder which was qualitatively different from the punishment for other

---

[58] *E.V.*, no. 27 (emphasis added).

crimes. But the Vicar of Christ has raised the discussion to a new level, making the old arguments obsolete. After discussing the death penalty, *Evangelium Vitae* states, "If such great care must be taken to respect every life, even that of criminals and unjust aggressors, the commandment, 'You shall not kill' has absolute value when it refers to the *innocent person*."[59] If we owe such respect to life of the guilty, so much the more, and absolutely so, with respect to the innocent. But this works the other way, too. If we would maintain the absolute inviolability of innocent life, we must begin by safeguarding even the life of the guilty from termination except according to the very restrictive law of God.

John Paul's practical condemnation of the use of the death penalty derives its significance from the overall context of *Evangelium Vitae*, which is "meant to be . . . a pressing appeal addressed to each and every person, in the name of God: *respect, protect, love and serve life, every human life!*".[60] The Pope urges a "culture of life" as the only answer to the "culture of death". He sees the restriction, if not the abolition, of both war and capital punishment as important elements in the building of that "culture of life".[61]

Although Saint Thomas analogizes capital punishment to the situation where "the physician quite properly and beneficially cuts off a diseased organ if the corruption of the body is threatened because of it",[62] his emphasis here, as in other respects, on the limited power of human law shows that the

---

[59] *E.V.*, no. 57.

[60] Ibid., no. 5.

[61] Ibid., no. 27. See Charles E. Rice, "Showdown in Texas: The Pope vs. the Culture of Death", *Catholic Dossier* (Sept.-Oct. 1998), p. 16.

[62] Aquinas, *Summa contra Gentiles* (Vernon J. Bourke, transl., 1975), book III, chap. 146, p. 221.

authority of the state over the person cannot be simply and wholly analogized to the authority one has over the members of one's own body. One commentator noted:

> Between the organism of the human body . . . and that of the State there is one fundamental difference. . . . The organs and parts of the human body belong essentially to a greater whole. They have no special end or purpose of their own, distinct from those of the body to which they belong; and therefore no rights independent of the rights of the human person that owns them. . . . Hence, no limits can be set to the demands which the human being may make, should need require, upon any part or faculty of his bodily organism. Even a limb may be amputated or an arm worked till it becomes permanently useless. It is quite otherwise in the State, whose ultimate purpose is not the good, or seeming good, of the body politic, but that of the individual members that compose it. These latter being persons, and having each a destiny of his own and a purpose in life far transcending his position in the social organism, can never be made into mere instruments for promoting the interests of any other person or thing in the created universe.[63]

Saint Thomas justifies capital punishment on the ground that "the common good is better than the particular good of one person."[64] In that context, the "particular good" of the life of a "pestiferous" criminal may be required to yield to the common good.[65] However, this justification cannot be trans-

---

[63] R. E. Cahill, S.J., *The Framework of a Christian State* (1932), 279–80, quoted in F. P. LeBuffe, S.J., and James V. Hayes, *The American Philosophy of Law* (1953), 406–7.

[64] Aquinas, *Summa contra Gentiles* (Vernon J. Bourke, transl., 1975), book III, chap. 146, p. 220.

[65] Ibid.

lated into an unlimited subjection of the good of the individual person to the common good. The human law is "an ordinance of reason for the common good".[66] But the function and authority of the human law and the state are limited. The state itself is part of God's plan, which is oriented toward the salvation of human persons. It is fair to say, therefore, that the "ultimate purpose [of the state] is not the good, or seeming good, of the body politic, but that of the individual members that compose it."[67] Thus, for example, "the Family is more sacred than the State" because "men are begotten not for the earth and for time, but for Heaven and eternity."[68] As Pope John Paul II stated in *Centisimus Annus*, "The social nature of man is not completely fulfilled by the state, but is realized in various intermediary groups, beginning with the family and including economic, social, political, and cultural groups which stem from human nature itself and have their own autonomy, always with a view to the common good."[69]

The common good cannot be equated with collectivism.

[Rather, it is] the sum total of all the presuppositions and arrangements of a general, public kind which a common body needs so that the individuals as members of a body can fulfill their earthly task and can themselves realize their earthly happiness by means of their own activity. According to this view the common good is a social state which in the first place guarantees to each person that place in the community which belongs to him and in which he can freely develop his God-given talents, so that he can attain his own bodily, spiritual and moral perfection and so that, through his

---

[66] *S.T.*, I, II, Q. 90, art. 4.

[67] Cahill, *The Framework of a Christian State*, 279–80.

[68] Pope Pius XI, *Casti Connubii* (1931), Part II.

[69] *C.A.*, no. 13.

service to the community, he himself can become richer in external and internal goods.[70]

As we shall discuss in Questions 36 and 37, the objective of the common good assumes increasing importance from the description by the Church of human personhood as intrinsically involving relation to others. The human person is not an isolated individual. Persons cannot even exist except in relation to others. The person is central to the common good as summarized by the *Catechism of the Catholic Church:*

1905. In keeping with the social nature of man, the good of each individual is necessarily related to the common good, which in turn can be defined only in reference to the human person: "Do not live entirely isolated, having retreated into yourselves, as if you were already justified, but gather instead to seek the common good together" (*Ep. Barnabae*, 4:10).

1906. By common good is to be understood "the sum total of social conditions which allow people, either as groups or as individuals, to reach their fulfillment more fully and more easily" (*Gaudium et Spes*, no. 26). The common good concerns the life of all. It calls for prudence from each, and even more from those who exercise the office of authority. It consists of *three essential elements:*

1907. First, the common good presupposes *respect for the person* as such. In the name of the common good, public authorities are bound to respect the fundamental and inalienable rights of the human person. Society should permit each of its members to fulfill his vocation. In particular, the common good resides in the conditions for the exercise of the natural freedoms indispensable for the development of the human vocation, such as "the right to act according to a sound norm of conscience and to safeguard . . . privacy,

---

[70] Walter Brugger, ed., *Philosophical Dictionary* (Kenneth Baker, S.J., transl., 1972), 62–63.

and rightful freedom also in matters of religion" (*Gaudium et Spes*, no. 26).

1908. Second, the common good requires the *social well-being* and *development* of the group itself. Development is the epitome of all social duties. Certainly, it is the proper function of authority to arbitrate, in the name of the common good, between various particular interests; but it should make accessible to each what is needed to lead a truly human life: food, clothing, health, work, education and culture, suitable information, the right to establish a family, and so on.

1909. Finally, the common good requires *peace*, that is, the stability and security of a just order. It presupposes that authority should ensure by morally acceptable means the *security* of society and its members. It is the basis of the right to legitimate personal and collective defence. . . .

1929. Social justice can be obtained only in respecting the transcendent dignity of man. The person represents the ultimate end of society, which is ordered to him. . . .[71]

Pope John Paul II, in a statement that could be applied to the United States, noted:

[There is] a crisis within democracies themselves, which seem at times to have lost the ability to make decisions aimed at the common good. Certain demands which arise within society are sometimes not examined in accordance with criteria of justice and morality, but rather on the basis of the electoral or financial power of the groups promoting them. With time, such distortions of political conduct create distrust and apathy, with a subsequent decline in the political participation and civic spirit of the general population, which feels abused and disillusioned. As a result, there is a growing inability to situate particular interests within the framework

---

[71] *C.C.C.*, nos. 1905–9, 1929.

of a coherent vision of the common good. The latter is not simply the sum total of particular interests; rather it involves an assessment and integration of those interests on the basis of a balanced hierarchy of values; ultimately it demands a correct understanding of the dignity and the rights of the person. The church respects the legitimate autonomy of the democratic order and is not entitled to express preferences for this or that institutional or constitutional solution. Her contribution to the political order is precisely her vision of the dignity of the person revealed in all its fullness in the mystery of the incarnate Word.[72]

As we have seen, the common good "can be defined only in reference to the human person. . . . [It] presupposes *respect for the person* as such. In the name of the common good, the public authorities are bound to respect the fundamental and inalienable rights of the human person."[73] The individualist jurisprudence of the Enlightenment has lost sight not only of the idea of the common good but also of the unique dignity of the human person, the protection of which is an aspect of the common good. Perhaps the most striking example of the gulf between the Enlightenment and the authentic natural law is in the treatment of animals and their "rights", which we will next discuss.

10. What about animals? Don't they have rights?

When an infant, Baby Fae, was born in 1984 with an incomplete heart and was near death twelve days after her birth,

---

[72] *C.A.*, no. 47.

[73] *C.C.C.*, nos. 1905, 1907; see also *E.V.*, no. 71.

physicians at California's Loma Linda Medical Center gave her a new heart—that of a baboon. Baby Fae died twenty days after the operation because her body rejected the transplanted heart.[74] Animal-rights activists opposed the effort to save Baby Fae. "That baboon was someone's baby, too", said Ingrid Newkirk, director of People for the Ethical Treatment of Animals (PETA).[75] "The baboon has rights", said philosophy professor Tom Regan of North Carolina State University. "The baboon doesn't exist for us; the baboon exists for the baboon."[76] PETA, the Animal Liberation Front, and other animal-rights groups oppose, in varying degrees and intensity, the use of animals for research, food, clothing, and sport.[77]

Jeremy Bentham (1748–1833) wrote: "The day *may* come where the rest of the animal creation may acquire those rights which never could have been withholden from them but by the hand of tyranny. . . . [A] full-grown horse or dog is beyond comparison a more rational, as well as a more conversable animal, than an infant of a day, or a week, or even a month, old. But suppose the case were otherwise, what would it avail? The question is not, Can they *reason*? nor, Can they *talk*? but, *Can they suffer?*"[78] Newkirk echoed Bentham: "How can we say that we will take care of only our own kind when what we call 'our own' didn't always include blacks or women? Today,

---

[74] *New York Times*, Nov. 16, 1984, p. A1.

[75] *Newsday Magazine*, Feb. 21, 1988, pp. 8, 26.

[76] *U.S. News & World Report*, Nov. 12, 1984, p. 58.

[77] See Andrew W. Rowan, "Why Scientists Should Seek Alternatives to Animal Use", 89 *Technology Review* 22 (May 1986); *Washington Post*, Nov. 13, 1983, p. B1; see the discussion of an opposing group, Putting People First, in the *Washington Post*, Mar. 27, 1992, p. B1.

[78] Jeremy Bentham, *Introduction to the Principles of Morals and Legislation* (1907 ed.), chap XVII, 310, n. 1.

our own takes in all people, but why shouldn't our own be all of us who are capable of suffering and pain?"[79]

An Australian philosopher, Peter Singer, inspired the modern animal-rights movement with his 1975 book, *Animal Liberation*. Singer criticizes "speciesism", which is prejudice against persons who are not members of the species *homo sapiens*, just as racism is prejudice against persons of a different race. For Singer a person is "a rational and self-conscious being".[80] He regards "newborn infants and some mental defectives" as non-persons.[81] But chimpanzees can make the personhood team.[82] So can "apes, whales and dolphins, . . . monkeys, dogs and cats, pigs, seals and bears".[83] "So it seems", concludes Singer, "that killing, say, a chimpanzee is worse than the killing of a gravely defective human who is not a person."[84] Singer even thinks that chickens might be persons,[85] raising the prospect that the greatest mass murderer in history was not Ghengis Khan, Stalin, or Hitler, but Colonel Sanders. "Six million people died in concentration camps," said Newkirk, "but 6 billion broiler chickens will die this year in slaughterhouses."[86]

The assertion of animal rights involves a rejection of the reality that man essentially differs from the lower animals in that he has a spiritual and immortal soul. It reflects also a loss of faith in the order of creation by which God gave man "dominion" over the lower creatures.[87] Singer maintains that "we

---

[79] *Washington Post*, Nov. 13, 1983, p. B1.

[80] Peter Singer, *Practical Ethics* (1979), 76.

[81] Ibid., 84.

[82] Ibid., 95.

[83] Ibid., 103.

[84] Ibid., 97.

[85] Ibid., 105.

[86] *Washington Post*, June 2, 1986, p. B1.

[87] Gen 1:26.

can no longer base our ethics on the idea that human beings are a special form of creation, made in the image of God, singled out from all other animals, and alone possessing an immortal soul."[88] Singer treats "ethics as entirely independent of religion".[89] The polio vaccine required fatal experiments on more than 100,000 rhesus monkeys.[90] Those experiments, of course, were premised on the dominion of man over animal. This dominion is not a function merely of power but of nature and the divine plan. Man, however, has a duty to God to make a right use of animals without being cruel or inflicting needless pain. This is a serious duty. Wanton cruelty to animals entails a brutalization of our own nature. And animals "cannot be maltreated without infringement of the rights of their creator, and . . . without dislocating God's order in nature."[91]

However, in the nature of things and in the light of God's design, animals themselves have no rights. One person cannot own another. But we can own animals, which are things and not persons. As Saint Thomas noted, "The rational plan of divine providence demands that the other creatures be ruled by rational creatures."[92]

Since man does participate somewhat in intellectual light, brute animals are subject to him by the order of divine providence, for they participate in no way in understanding. Hence it is said: "Let us make man to our own image and likeness," namely, according as he has understanding,

---

[88] Peter Singer, "Sanctity or Quality of Life", 72 *Pediatrics* 128, 129 (1983).

[89] Singer, *Practical Ethics*, 3.

[90] Bruce Rheinstein, "Animal Liberation *or* Animals Are People Too?" *Legal Backgrounder* (Heritage Foundation), June 23, 1989, pp. 1, 2.

[91] Don Ambrose Agius, O.S.B., *Cruelty to Animals: The Church's Teaching* (1959), 9.

[92] Aquinas, *Summa contra Gentiles* (Vernon J. Bourke, transl., 1975), book III, chap. 78, p. 261.

"and let him have dominion over the fishes of the sea, and the fowls of the air, and the beasts of the earth" (*Gen.* 1:26).[93]

In concluding that it is lawful for man to kill animals, Saint Thomas said, "The order of things is such that the imperfect are for the perfect. . . . Wherefore it is not unlawful if man use plants for the good of animals, and animals for the good of man. . . . Wherefore it is lawful both to take life from plants for the use of animals, and from animals for the use of men."[94] Animal-rights activists ignore the fact that "man is the only creature on earth whom God has 'wished for himself.'"[95]

However, those who reject any restraint on the use of animals can do so only by rejecting their own accountability to God for their use of creation. Interestingly, as one commentator on Saint Thomas' "environmental philosophy" noted, "In the thought of St. Thomas, virtue restrains overuse and forbids excessive interference with the environment, but does not require the notion of rights of nonhuman creatures or of claims owned by them. . . . In brief, the Thomistic environmental philosophy is balanced. It is satisfying to one saddened by consumerism and the consequent harm to plants, animals, land, water, and air. Yet it shows how such an environmentalist

---

[93] Ibid., chap. 81, p. 272.

[94] *S.T.*, II, II, Q. 64, art. 1.

[95] Congregation for the Doctrine of the Faith, *Instruction on Bioethics* (1987), Introduction, para. 5. This quotation is from the Second Vatican Council, *Pastoral Constitution on the Church in the Modern World* (*Gaudium et Spes*), no. 24. The text says "*seipsam*", which can be translated as "itself" or "himself". 58 *Acta Apostolicae Sedis* 1045 (Dec. 7, 1966). Either way, it refers to man: Man is the only creature on earth whom God has created for man's own sake rather than for the sake of other creatures. The Flannery edition of Vatican II, which is used in this book for quotations from the Council, translates this phrase as "man is the only creature on earth that God has wanted for its own sake." *Vatican Council II* (Austin Flannery, O.P., ed., 1975), 925.

may also be a proclaimed humanist and a theist. As such, it serves as a framework for balanced thinking about environmental policy. It integrates important values."[96]

> Man was created in the image and likeness of God: animals were not. Man is rational, animal is irrational. . . . Man therefore is a person; animals are non-persons. Man is a person because he is an end in himself, and not a mere means to the perfection of beings of a higher order. Animals are not persons or moral beings because devoid of reason and free will (and so of responsibility) and because they were created for the service of man, and as a means (if properly used) towards his perfection. . . . Now a right or "jus" is the moral faculty or power of doing, having, exacting, or omitting something. This is a moral, not a physical, power derived from eternal law, which is the fount of all laws and rights. Therefore animals, as non-moral beings, have no "jus" or right in themselves, no personal rights, as against man, and the question of "injustice" (which means acting against "jus") does not arise. . . . This is exactly where we have to be very careful. . . . While [God] refrained from raising animals to the moral order so as to put them on a level with man, He yet provided for them a greater safeguard than mere sentimental attachment; for He made care and consideration for animals an integral part of the moral order of the universe. Right thinking man acknowledges the animal world as a commission form God, given for his use; for which he will have to render an account to the Creator.[97]

---

[96] Patrick Halligan, "The Environmental Policy of Saint Thomas Aquinas", 19 *Environmental Law* 767, 806 (1989); see *E.V.*, no. 10.

[97] Dom Ambrose Agius, O.S.B., *Cruelty to Animals: The Church's Teaching* (1959), 4–5.

11. Did Aquinas have an opinion as to which form of government is best? Was he a conservative or a liberal?

The United States Constitution, as originally adopted, created a mixed form of government. The President represented the monarchical principle, the Senate (originally elected by state legislatures before the Seventeenth Amendment in 1913 provided for popular election) represented the aristocratic principle, and the popularly elected House of Representatives embodied the democratic principle.[98] Saint Thomas probably would have approved of this arrangement. He enumerated "the various forms of government", as listed by Aristotle:

> One is *monarchy*, *i.e.*, when the state is governed by one. . . . Another form is *aristocracy*, *i.e.*, government by the best men or men of highest rank. . . . Another form is *oligarchy*, *i.e.*, government by a few rich and powerful men. . . . Another form . . . is that of the people, which is called *democracy*, and there we have Decrees of the commonality (Plebiscita). There is also tyrannical government, which is altogether corrupt, which, therefore, has no corresponding law. Finally, there is a form of government made up of all these [monarchy, aristocracy, oligarchy, democracy], and which is the best: and in this respect we have law sanctioned by the Lords and Commons, as stated by Isidore.[99]

---

[98] See the discussion of the influence of English and French philosophies on the United States Constitution, in Harold J. Berman, "The Impact of the Enlightenment on American Constitutional Law", 4 *Yale J. of Law and the Humanities*, 311, 328 (1992).

[99] *S.T.*, I, II, Q. 95, art. 4 (emphasis added).

Elsewhere, Saint Thomas favored monarchy because "the rule of one man is more useful than the rule of many" for achieving "the unity of peace".[100] However, although Aquinas asserted that the rulership of one man is best when it is just, he also said that when it is unjust, it is the worst. "Just as the government of a king is the best, the government of a tyrant is the worst."[101] Saint Thomas advocated limitations on the power of the king in what we might describe today as a constitutional monarchy: "Once the king is established, the government of the kingdom must be so arranged that opportunity to tyrannize be removed. At the same time his power should be so tempered that he cannot easily fall into tyranny."[102]

It would be presumptuous and inaccurate to classify Saint Thomas as a conservative or liberal as those terms are used today. His analysis touched on political matters, but it transcended political categories. In a nonpolitical sense, however, he was conservative in that he was cautious about the role of the enacted law. For example, he believed that custom could have the force of law:

> All law proceeds from the reason and will of the lawgiver; the Divine and natural laws from the reasonable will of God; the human law from the will of man, regulated by reason. Now just as human reason and will, in practical matters, may be made manifest by speech, so may they be made known by deeds. . . . Wherefore by actions also, especially if they be repeated, so as to make a custom, law can be changed and expounded; and also something can be established which obtains force of law, . . . for when a thing is done again and again, it seems to proceed from a deliberate judgment of

---

[100] Saint Thomas Aquinas, *De Regimine Principum* (*On the Governance of Rulers*) (Gerald B. Phelan, transl., 1938), book I, chap. 2, 41.

[101] Ibid., chap. 3, 43.

[102] Ibid., chap. 6, 54.

reason. Accordingly, custom has the force of a law, abolishes law, and is the interpreter of law.[103]

However, while custom can obtain the force of human law, "the natural and Divine laws proceed from the Divine will, as stated above. Wherefore they cannot be changed by a custom proceeding from the will of man, but only by Divine authority. Hence it is that no custom can prevail over the Divine or natural laws."[104]

Saint Thomas was cautious about changing the human law.

[Human law] is rightly changed, in so far as such change is conducive to the common weal. But, to a certain extent, the mere change of law is of itself prejudicial to the common good: because custom avails much for the observance of laws, seeing that what is done contrary to general custom, even in slight matters, is looked upon as grave. Consequently, when a law is changed, the binding power of the law is diminished, in so far as custom is abolished. Wherefore human law should never be changed, unless, in some way or other, the common weal be compensated according to the extent of the harm done in this respect. Such compensation may arise either from some very great and very evident benefit conferred by the new enactment; or from the extreme urgency of the case, due to the fact that either the existing law is already unjust, or its observance extremely harmful.[105]

Saint Thomas' prudential approaches to the forms of government, the legal effect of custom, and the wisdom of changes in the law illustrate the difficulty of analyzing him except on his own terms. He resists classification according to modern

---

[103] *S.T.*, I, II, Q. 97, art. 3.
[104] Ibid.
[105] Ibid., art. 2.

political or ideological categories, as does the Church, whose teaching authority he accepted.

12. *Am I bound in conscience to obey the human law? What if that law is unjust?*

Aquinas places human law in the framework of the plan of God, who wants man to achieve eternal happiness by choosing to love and obey him. Human law and the state exist to promote the common good and thus to help man achieve his end of eternal happiness with God. The state is not a necessary evil, nor is it a mere contrivance of the majority or of a mythical social compact. Rather, it is good because it is an integral part of God's plan, with the objective of promoting the common good. But the state is not an end in itself; it is rather an instrument to help man achieve his end. Although Saint Thomas did not experience the modern state, his discussion of the human law provides principles to govern the state in any age. Aquinas directly contradicts the secularist and the positivist by grounding his theory of law on the reality of God. Only in this way can human law be limited. Otherwise, if God is not recognized, the state becomes god.[106]

> [If human laws are just,] they have the power of binding in conscience, from the eternal law whence they are derived, according to *Prov.* viii, 15: "By Me kings reign, and law-givers decree just things." Now laws are said to be just, both from the *end*, when . . . they are ordained to the common good,—and from their *author*, that is to say, when the law

---

[106] See Charles E. Rice, "Some Reasons for a Restoration of Natural Law Jurisprudence", 565.

that is made does not exceed the power of the lawgiver,—
and from their *form*, when . . . burdens are laid on the subjects, according to an equality of proportion and with a view
to the common good. For, since one man is a part of the
community, each man in all that he is and has, belongs to
the community; just as a part, in all that it is, belongs to the
whole; wherefore nature inflicts a loss on the part, in order
to save the whole: so that on this account, such laws as these,
which impose proportionate burdens, are just and binding
in conscience, and are legal laws.[107]

Elsewhere, Saint Thomas stated that "the order of justice requires that subjects obey their superiors, else the stability of
human affairs would cease."[108]

Aquinas can coherently affirm the obligation in conscience
of human law because he differs from the positivists and sec-
ularists in his view of the nature of law. The positivist and the
secularist reduce law to an act of will by the lawgiver. There
is, of course, an element of will in the law (every law is a
command), but, as Saint Thomas affirms, something more is
needed. In order that "what is commanded may have the nature of law, it needs to be in accord with some rule of reason".[109] This requirement proceeds from the fact that "the
whole community of the universe is governed by Divine Reason."[110] The divine will cannot act separately from the divine
reason because "God cannot be at variance with himself."[111]

The human law is itself part of God's plan. As such, it obliges
in conscience because the legislator ultimately derives his authority from God for the purpose of promoting the common

---

[107] *S.T.*, I, II, Q. 96, art. 4 (emphasis added).

[108] *S.T.*, II, II, Q. 104, art. 6.

[109] *S.T.*, I, II, Q. 90, art. 1.

[110] *S.T.*, I, II, Q. 91, art. 1.

[111] Rommen, *The Natural Law*, 51.

good. But if that legislator abuses his authority by enacting unjust laws, such laws are "acts of violence rather than laws".[112]
Aquinas' analysis is a prescription for limited government, providing a rational basis on which to affirm that there are limits
to what the state can rightly do. His insistence that the power
of the human law is limited implies a "right" of the person
not to be subjected to an unjust law. However, as noted in
other Questions, Aquinas' jurisprudence differs radically from
the rights-oriented, individualist and positivist jurisprudence
of the Enlightenment.[113]

"Man is bound to obey secular princes", according to Saint
Thomas, "in so far as this is required by the order of justice.
Wherefore if the prince's authority is not just but usurped, or
if he commands what is unjust, his subjects are not bound to
obey him, except perhaps accidentally in order to avoid scandal or danger."[114] If a human law "deflects from the law of
nature", it is unjust and "is no longer a law but a perversion
of law".[115] Saint Thomas explains that a law may be unjust in
two ways:

> *First, by being contrary to human good* . . . either in respect
> of the *end*, as when an authority imposes on his subjects
> burdensome laws, conducive, not to the common good, but
> rather to his own cupidity or vainglory;—or in respect of
> the *author*, as when a man makes a law that goes beyond
> the power committed to him;—or in respect of the *form*,
> as when burdens are imposed unequally on the community,
> although with a view to the common good. The like are acts
> of violence rather than laws; because as Augustine says, . . .

---

[112] *S.T.*, I, II, Q. 96, art. 4.

[113] See Questions 5, above, and 46, below; see also *S.T.*, II, II, Q. 57, art.
1, where Aquinas uses "right" as synonymous with "just".

[114] *S.T.*, II, II, Q. 104, art. 6.

[115] *S.T.*, I, II, Q. 95, art. 2.

"a law that is not just, seems to be no law at all." Wherefore such laws do not bind in conscience, except perhaps in order to avoid scandal or disturbance, for which cause a man should even yield his right, according to *Matth.* v. 40, 41.

Secondly, laws may be unjust through being opposed to the Divine good; such are the laws of tyrants inducing to idolatry, or to anything else contrary to the Divine law; and laws of this kind must nowise be observed, because, as stated in *Acts* v. 29, "we ought to obey God rather than men."[116]

An example of a law "contrary to human good" would be the income tax, which is riddled with arbitrary and even oppressive features in its substance and procedures. Yet the injustice of the income tax does not provide a justification for refusing to pay it because an unacceptable disruption of the common good would result from the affirmation of such a right. Moreover, at least in principle, means are available within the law to change the system. An example of a law "opposed to the Divine good" would be a law requiring a physician to perform an abortion. If there were such a law, the physician would be morally obliged to refuse even on pain of death.

An unjust law, such as a law permitting abortion, can raise the distinction between formal and material cooperation in evil.[117] "One *formally* cooperates in another's wrongful act when one participates in the immoral act in such a way that it becomes one's own."[118] As Pope John Paul said in *Evangelium Vitae*, "Christians, like all people of good will, are called upon under grave obligation of conscience not to cooperate formally

---

[116] *S.T.,* I, II, Q. 96, art. 4 (emphasis added).

[117] See, in general, Henry Davis, S.J., *Moral and Pastoral Theology* (1945), vol. 1, 341–43.

[118] Bishop John J. Myers, *"The Obligations of Catholics and the Rights of Unborn Children,"* 20 *Origins,* June 14, 1990, 65; see discussion in Charles E. Rice, *No Exception: A Pro-Life Imperative* (1991), 79–84.

in practices which, even if permitted by civil legislation, are contrary to God's law. Indeed, from the moral standpoint, it is never licit to cooperate formally in evil. Such cooperation occurs when an action, either by its very nature or by the form it takes in a concrete situation, can be defined as a direct participation in an act against innocent human life or a sharing in the immoral intention of the person committing it."[119] "One materially cooperates in another's wrongdoing", in Bishop Myers' words, "when one's acts help to make that wrongdoing possible, although one does not *intend* that wrongdoing. Material cooperation in abortion takes place . . . *where one's actions — although motivated by another purpose — nevertheless help to make an abortion possible.* All formal cooperation in abortion is gravely immoral. So is most material cooperation in abortion. However, there may be limited circumstances under which certain forms of material cooperation are permissible. For example, a hospital worker responsible for cleaning and maintaining an operating room where abortions are sometimes performed may carry out his or her tasks without being implicated in the immoral act. The worker may oppose abortion and *intend* only to facilitate the morally upright, indeed laudable surgical procedures performed there. He or she merely accepts as an unintended albeit foreseen consequence that the well-maintained facility will enable physicians to perform abortions."[120] Or a legislator "could licitly support", in some limited circumstances, "a more restrictive law, aimed at limiting the number of authorized abortions, in place of a more permissive law".[121] A separate question is whether such cooperation, even if morally jus-

---

[119] *E.V.*, no. 74.

[120] Bishop John J. Myers, above.

[121] *E.V.*, no. 73.

tified, is prudent.[122] Incidentally, *Evangelium Vitae* emphasized that the civil law should protect the right of "conscientious objection" to legalized abortion and euthanasia.

> To refuse to take part in committing an injustice is not only a moral duty; it is also a basic human right. . . . [T]he opportunity to refuse to take part in the phases of consultation, preparation and execution of these acts against life should be guaranteed to physicians, health-care personnel, and directors of hospitals, clinics and convalescent facilities.[123]

On a related point, Saint Thomas notes that a law does not have to be followed when noncompliance is required by the common good:

> It happens often that the observance of some point of law conduces to the common weal in the majority of instances, and yet, in some cases, is very hurtful. Since then the lawgiver cannot have in view every single case, he shapes the law according to what happens most frequently, by directing his attention to the common good. Wherefore if a case arises wherein the observance of that law would be hurtful to the general welfare, it should not be observed. For instance, suppose that in a besieged city it be an established law that the gates of the city are to be kept closed; this is good for public welfare as a general rule: but if it were to happen that the enemy are in pursuit of certain citizens, who are defenders of the city, it would be a great loss to the city, if the gates were not opened to them: and so in that case the gates ought to be opened, contrary to the letter of the law, in order to maintain the common weal, which the lawgiver had in view.[124]

---

[122] See discussion in Charles E. Rice, *No Exception: A Pro-Life Imperative*, (1991), 73–90.

[123] *E.V.*, no. 74; see also *E.V.* no. 89.

[124] *S.T.*, I, II, Q. 96, art. 6.

This principle of necessity or justification is recognized in the common law and by federal and state statutes or decisions.[125]

If you were walking down a street and saw, through a picture window, a man attacking a child with a knife in the living room of his house, you would have a privilege to commit what would otherwise be trespass in order to enter that house to save the child's life. You could even use reasonable force if necessary to prevent the murder of the child. This principle ought to apply to rescues at abortuaries, which involve trespass in an effort to save the lives of unborn children. The courts, however, regard the unborn child as a nonperson and generally deny the necessity defense in abortion rescues.[126]

With respect to necessity in general, it ought not to be regarded as a free pass for vigilante justice. Saint Thomas warns that "if the observance of the law according to the letter does not involve any sudden risk needing instant remedy, it is not competent for everyone to expound what is useful and what is not useful to the state: those alone can do this who are in authority, and who, on account of such like cases, have the power to dispense from the laws. If, however, the peril be so sudden as not to allow the delay involved by referring the matter to authority, the mere necessity brings with it a dispensation since necessity knows no law."[127]

Rightful action under necessity does not even involve a violation of law. Rather, the law itself implicitly authorizes such

[125] See *The William Gray*, 29 F. Cas. 1300 (Cir. Ct. N.Y. 1810) (no. 17,694); *U.S. v. Ashton*, 24 F. Cas 873 (2d Cir. 1834) (no. 14,470); American Law Institute, *Model Penal Code* (proposed official draft) (1962), sec. 3.02; *People* v. *Richards*, 269 Cal. App. 2d 768, 777–78, 75 Cal. Rptr. 597, 604 (1969); *U.S.* v. *Simpson*, 460 F.2d 515, 517 (9th Cir. 1972).

[126] See discussion in Charles E. Rice, "Issues Raised by the Abortion Rescue Movement", 23 *Suffolk Univ. L. Rev.* 15 (1989).

[127] *S.T.*, I, II, Q. 96, art. 6.

action. "No man"—and certainly no legislator—"is so wise as to be able to take account of every single case. . . . And even if a lawgiver were able to take all the cases into consideration, he ought not to mention them all, in order to avoid confusion: but should frame the law according to that which is of most common occurrence."[128]

13. Wait a minute. If people who follow Aquinas are so sure they are right as to the meaning of natural law, won't they compel everyone to follow their rules? Won't they use the law to make *people be "good"?*

Allan Bloom, in his introduction to *The Closing of the American Mind*, observed that, for American university students, "the relativity of truth is not a theoretical insight but a moral postulate, the condition of a free society."[129]

> Relativism is necessary to openness; and this is the virtue, the only virtue, which all primary education for more than fifty years has dedicated itself to inculcating. Openness—and the relativism that makes it the only plausible stance in the face of various claims to truth and various ways of life and kinds of human beings—is the great insight of our times. The true believer is the real danger. The study of history and of culture teaches that all the world was mad in the past; men always thought they were right, and that led to wars, persecutions, slavery, xenophobia, racism, and chauvinism. The point is not to correct the mistakes and really be right; rather it is not to think you are right at all. The students,

---

[128] Ibid.

[129] Allan Bloom, *The Closing of the American Mind* (1987), 25.

of course, cannot defend their opinion. It is something with which they have been indoctrinated. The best they can do is point out all the opinions and cultures there are and have been. What right, they ask, do I or anyone else have to say one is better than the others?[130]

Hans Kelsen, who has been well described as "the jurist of our century",[131] provided a jurisprudential foundation for this orthodoxy of openness. Kelsen espoused "philosophical relativism", which "advocates the empirical doctrine that reality exists only within human knowledge, and that, as the object of knowledge, reality is relative to the knowing subject. The absolute, the thing in itself, is beyond human experience; it is inaccessible to human knowledge and therefore unknowable."[132] He rejected "philosophical absolutism", the "metaphysical view that there is an absolute reality, i.e., a reality that exists independently of human knowledge".[133]

Kelsen believed that philosophical absolutism leads to political absolutism, while philosophical relativism leads to political relativism—that is, democracy. "For, just as autocracy is political absolutism and political absolutism is paralleled by philosophical absolutism, democracy is political relativism which has its counterpart in philosophical relativism."[134]

If one believes in the existence of the absolute, and consequently in absolute values, in the absolute good, . . . is it not meaningless to let a majority vote decide what is politically good? . . . Tolerance, minority rights, freedom of speech, and

---

[130] Ibid., 25–26.

[131] Hans Kelsen, *Essays in Legal and Moral Philosophy* (Ota Weinberger, ed., 1973), ix.

[132] Hans Kelsen, "Absolutism and Relativism in Philosophy and Politics", 42 *Am. Pol. Sci. Rev.* 906 (1948).

[133] Ibid.

[134] Ibid., 911.

freedom of thought, so characteristic of democracy, have no place within a political system based on the belief in absolute values. This belief irresistibly leads—and has always led—to a situation in which the one who assumes to possess the secret of the absolute good claims to have the right to impose his opinion as well as his will upon the others who are in error. And to be in error is, according to this view, to be wrong, and hence punishable. If, however, it is recognized that only relative values are accessible to human knowledge and human will, then it is justifiable to enforce a social order against reluctant individuals only if this order is in harmony with the greatest possible number of equal individuals, that is to say, with the will of the majority. It may be that the opinion of the minority, and not the opinion of the majority, is correct. Solely because of this possibility, which only philosophical relativism can admit—that what is right today may be wrong tomorrow—the minority must have a chance to express freely their opinion and must have full opportunity of becoming the majority. Only if it is not possible to decide in an absolute way what is right and what is wrong is it advisable to discuss the issue and, after discussion, to submit to a compromise.

This is the true meaning of the political system which we call democracy, and which we may oppose to political absolutism only because it is political relativism.[135]

Kelsen regarded Aquinas' *Summa Theologica* as one of "the classical examples of . . . coincidence of philosophical and political absolutism".[136] Kelsen, however, misread Aquinas. Saint Thomas rejected absolutist government and cautioned that the law should not try to prescribe every virtue or forbid every vice. The purpose of the human law is to promote the "common

---

[135] Ibid., 913–14.
[136] Ibid., 912.

good",[137] and that law should "lead men to virtue, not suddenly but gradually".[138] Otherwise, the law would be unenforceable, and the law itself would be "despised" and "greater evils" would result.[139]

Aquinas, here as elsewhere, writes from a realistic view of human nature. The human law is enacted for human beings, "the majority of whom are not perfect in virtue. Wherefore human laws do not forbid all vices, from which the virtuous abstain, but only the more grievous vices, from which it is possible for the majority to abstain; and chiefly those that are to the hurt of others, without the prohibition of which human society could not be maintained: thus human law prohibits murder, theft, and suchlike."[140]

"Human law", says Saint Thomas, ". . . does not lay upon the multitude of imperfect men the burdens of those who are already virtuous, viz., that they should abstain from all evil. Otherwise, these imperfect ones, being unable to bear such precepts, would break out into yet greater evils: thus it is written . . . (*Matth.* ix. 17) that if new wine, i.e., precepts of a perfect life, is put into old bottles, i.e., into imperfect men, the bottles break, and the wine runneth out, i.e., the precepts are despised, and those men, from contempt, break out into evils worse still."[141] The human law therefore " 'allows and leaves unpunished many things that are punished by Divine Providence.' "[142] "To believe it possible to know a universally valid truth", said John Paul II, "is in no way to encourage intoler-

[137] *S.T.*, I, II, Q. 96, art. 1.

[138] Ibid., art. 2.

[139] Ibid.

[140] Ibid.

[141] Ibid.

[142] Ibid., quoting from Saint Augustine, *On Free Will*, i, 5.

ance; on the contrary, it is the essential condition for sincere and authentic dialogue between persons."[143]

Contrary to Kelsen's position, which is dominant today, Aquinas' view of natural law in context offers a reasonable premise for limited government. "Philosophical relativism", by contrast, can offer no limits on the content of decisions made through the political process. Kelsen himself acknowledged that the laws of the Nazi and other totalitarian regimes, regardless of their content, were valid because they were duly enacted: "The legal order of totalitarian states authorizes their governments to confine in concentration camps persons whose opinions, religion, or race they do not like; to force them to perform any kind of labor, even to kill them. Such measures may be morally or violently condemned; but they cannot be considered as taking place outside the legal order of those states."[144] Thus, "from the point of view of the science of law, the law under the Nazi-government was law. We may regret it but we cannot deny that it was law."[145]

In later Questions we will discuss the application of Aquinas' analysis and the teaching of the Magisterium to specific issues. For the present, we merely note that a state organized according to the principles of Thomas Aquinas would bear no resemblance to the oppressive regime of an Ayatollah Khomeini. Saint Thomas urges on the legislator a prudent restraint. When such restraint is combined with his insistence that unjust laws are void, it becomes evident that he offers

---

[143] *F.R.*, no. 92.

[144] Hans Kelsen, *Pure Theory of Law* (1967), 40; see R. S. Clark, "Hans Kelsen's Pure Theory of Law", 22 *J. of Leg. Ed.* 170, 182 (1969).

[145] Hans Kelsen, *Das Naturrecht in der politischen Theorie* (F. M. Schmoetz, ed., 1963), 148, quoted in translation in F. A. Hayek, *Law, Legislation and Liberty* (vol. 2, *The Mirage of Social Justice*) (1976), 56.

a prescription not for oppression but for limited government and political freedom.

14. *Look. Isn't the bottom line the fact that the law should not legislate morality? Where do you get the right to impose your morality on me?*

All human law enforces a morality of some sort, as, for example, a law punishing embezzlement or providing tort damages for defamation. The question is therefore not whether the human law should enforce morality but rather which morality it will, and should, enforce.

Aquinas notes that "all acts of virtue are prescribed by the natural law."[146] But the human law cannot attempt to cover the entire field of virtue and vice. Human law is framed "for the common good of all the citizens".[147] It operates through "command, prohibition, permission and punishment".[148] Nevertheless, the law should not prescribe every virtue or forbid every vice lest by its unenforceability the law be "despised" and "greater evils" result.[149] On account of the limited reach of the human law with respect to virtue and vice, the divine law is necessary "for the directing of human conduct".[150]

Because the human law, as envisioned by Aquinas, cannot properly regulate the entire field of moral conduct, it would not be the law of George Orwell's *1984*. Nevertheless, although its scope is limited, it does have a significant role:

---

[146] *S.T.*, I, II, Q. 94, art. 3.
[147] *S.T.*, I, II, Q. 96, art. 1.
[148] *S.T.*, I, II, Q. 92, art. 2.
[149] *S.T.*, I, II, Q. 96, art. 2; see also Question 13 above.
[150] *S.T.*, I, II, Q. 91, art. 4; see Question 6 above.

The proper effect of law is to lead its subjects to their proper virtue: and since virtue is *that which makes its subject good*, it follows that the proper effect of law is to make those to whom it is given, good, either simply or in some particular respect. For if the intention of the lawgiver is fixed on true good, which is the common good regulated according to Divine justice, . . . the effect of the law is to make men good simply. If, however, the intention of the lawgiver is fixed on that which is not simply good, but useful or pleasurable to himself, or in opposition to Divine justice; then the law does not make men good simply, but in respect to that particular government.[151]

As Pope John Paul put it, "the most dangerous crisis which can afflict man [is] the *confusion between good and evil*, which makes it impossible to build up and to preserve the moral order of individuals and communities."[152] The morality (the virtue) of its citizens is a proper concern of the state because "the common good of the state cannot flourish, unless the citizens be virtuous, at least those whose business it is to govern. But it is enough for the community, that the other citizens be so far virtuous that they obey the commands of their rulers."[153] Despite the importance of virtue in the citizens, the role of the human law in enforcing virtue is limited. Saint Thomas said:

Now all the objects of virtues can be referred either to the private good of an individual, or to the common good of the multitude: thus matters of fortitude may be achieved either for the safety of the state, or for upholding the rights of a friend, and in like manner with the other virtues. But law . . . is ordained to the common good. Wherefore there is no virtue whose acts cannot be prescribed by the law. Neverthe-

---

[151] *S.T.*, I, II, Q. 92, art. 1.

[152] *V.S.*, no. 93.

[153] *S.T.*, I, II, Q. 92, art. 1.

less human law does not prescribe concerning all the acts of every virtue: but only in regard to those that are ordainable to the common good,—either immediately, as when certain things are done directly for the common good,—or mediately, as when a lawgiver prescribes certain things pertaining to good order, whereby the citizens are directed in the upholding of the common good of justice and peace. . . . Human law does not forbid all vicious acts, by the obligation of a precept, as neither does it prescribe all acts of virtue. But it forbids certain acts of each vice, just as it prescribes some acts of each virtue.[154]

Although the law enforces only some particular acts of virtue, a virtuous citizenry does promote the common good, and at least some acts—some practices—of every virtue can affect the common good. "There is no virtue whose act is not ordainable to the common good, . . . either mediately or immediately."[155] "Therefore," writes Peter Kreeft, "there are no 'victimless' crimes. Suicide, for instance, harms your friends, family, and society. Prostitution harms the institution of the family, thus all members of all families. Drugs harm the social body by harming the individual member of the body."[156] When we "disregard" the natural law, said Pope John Paul, "or even are merely ignorant of it, whether culpably or not, our acts damage the communion of persons, to the detriment of each".[157] However, there are some acts of virtues or vices that are so remote in their effect on the common good that, as a matter of prudence, the law should not require or prohibit them. It is unjust to cheat on a member of your own family in a private game of Monopoly. But the law, as a matter of pru-

---

[154] *S.T.*, I, II, Q. 96, art. 3.
[155] Ibid.
[156] Kreeft, *A Summa of the Summa*, 527, note 279.
[157] *V.S.*, no. 51.

dence, should not make it criminal to cheat in such a game, even though it could ultimately harm the common good if we became a nation of people habituated to cheating in private situations. To attempt to apply the coercive power of the human law to such situations would be counterproductive.

Saint Thomas emphasizes the limited role of the state in leading men to virtue "gradually". "Men who are well disposed", he wrote, "are led willingly to virtue by being admonished better than by coercion: but men who are evilly disposed are not led to virtue unless they are compelled."[158] The human law educates even in punishing: "From being accustomed to avoid evil and fulfill what is good, through fear of punishment, one is sometimes led on to do so likewise, with delight and of one's own accord. Accordingly, law, even by punishing, leads men on to being good."[159]

When the human law forbids murder, it enforces a moral judgment as to the right to life as well as to the common good. If the law were to withdraw its prohibition of killing, say, the unborn or the elderly, it would enforce a contrary moral judgment. Similarly, when the Civil Rights Act of 1964 forbade racial discrimination in restaurants and other public accommodations, it achieved a quiet revolution in public attitudes toward racial justice.[160] The prior segregationist laws had an opposite educative effect. In each case, the issue was not whether the law would enforce (and therefore promote by education) a certain moral position on race but which position it would enforce.

---

[158] *S.T.*, I, II, Q. 95, art. 1.

[159] *S.T.*, I, II, Q. 92, art. 2.

[160] See Charley Roberts, "The 1964 Civil Rights Act: Twenty-Five Years Later", *Los Angeles Daily Journal*, July 3, 1989, p. 1; Linda S. Greene, "Twenty Years of Civil Rights: How Firm a Foundation?" 37 *Rutgers L. Rev.* 707 (1985).

In Questions 6 through 14, we have examined Aquinas' position on various aspects of the human law. In the United States, the human law most often discussed in relation to natural law is the Constitution. Now that we have examined some aspects of the natural law, as explained by Aquinas, it will be useful to discuss that law in the context of the Constitution. Although the Constitution is the highest human law, it is still only human law. To what extent is the Constitution subject to the principles formulated by Aquinas with respect to the human law in general?

III

NATURAL LAW AND
THE HIGHEST HUMAN LAW

15. Isn't the job of a judge to apply the Constitution, as written, according to the intent of those who adopted it rather than according to his own view of what is useful or just?

The controversy as to how judges should interpret the Constitution is a debate over what would seem to be an obvious proposition, that a legal document ought to be interpreted according to the intent of its authors. In the interpretation of any legal document, whether a will, contract, statute, or constitution, the object should be to construe it according to the intent of the testator, contracting parties, legislature, or other originator. The framers of the United States Constitution labored with care over each phrase of that document. And they provided for change through the amending article.

All three branches of government—the legislative, the executive, and the judicial—have a duty to interpret and apply the Constitution within their jurisdictions.[1] But constitutional issues generally end up in court. If judges in constitutional cases are not bound to construe the Constitution according to the intent of those who drafted and adopted it, then it is difficult to see the purpose of having a constitution at all. As Thomas Jefferson put it, "Our peculiar security is in the possession of a written Constitution. Let us not make it a blank paper by construction."[2] Not all, of course, share Jefferson's view. "It is arrogant", said former Supreme Court Justice William Bren-

---

[1] See Louis Fisher, "The Curious Belief in Judicial Supremacy", 25 *Suffolk Univ. L. Rev.* 85 (1991).

[2] "Letter to Wilson C. Nicholas" (1803), in *The Jefferson Cyclopedia* (John P. Foley, ed., 1900), 190.

nan, "to pretend that from our vantage we can gauge accurately the intent of the Framers on application of principle to specific, contemporary questions."[3] Others deny that judges are obliged to follow the "original intent" even if they can ascertain it.[4]

Interpretivists, those who would hold a judge bound to interpret and follow the original intent, acknowledge that it is often difficult to determine the intended meaning of a constitutional provision or to apply that meaning to the problems of today. But they rightly insist that judges are bound to try to discover and apply that intent at least in its core principles.[5] In a letter to William Johnson in 1823, Jefferson said, "On every question of construction, [let us] carry ourselves back to the time when the Constitution was adopted, recollect the spirit manifested in the debates, and instead of trying what meaning may be squeezed out of the text, or invented against it, conform to the probable one in which it was passed."[6] We discern "original intent", says Robert Bork, "by asking what the words of the Constitution meant to reasonable men at the time of the ratification. In that inquiry, we have not only the text itself but the assistance of a great many secondary materials, such as the records of the Philadelphia Convention and the debates of the time."[7]

---

[3] William J. Brennan, "Construing the Constitution", 19 *U.C. Davis L. Rev.* 2, 4 (1985).

[4] See discussion of some of those views in Raoul Berger, "Activist Censures of Robert Bork", 85 *Northw. Univ. L. Rev.* 993 (1991).

[5] See, generally, Robert H. Bork, *The Tempting of America: The Political Seduction of the Law* (1990).

[6] Foley, *The Jefferson Cyclopedia*, 193.

[7] Hadley Arkes, Russell Hittinger, William Bentley Ball, and Robert H. Bork, "Natural Law and the Law: An Exchange", *First Things*, May 1992, pp. 45, 53.

Thomas Aquinas lived a few years before Judge Bork faced the Senate Judiciary Committee in 1987. But, as with other problems, Aquinas had something to say of relevance.

> It is better "that all things be regulated by law, than left to be decided by judges": and this for three reasons. *First*, because it is easier to find a few wise men competent to frame right laws, than to find the many who would be necessary to judge aright of each single case.—*Secondly*, because those who make laws consider long beforehand what laws to make; whereas judgment on each single case has to be pronounced as soon as it arises: and it is easier for man to see what is right, by taking many instances into consideration, than by considering one solitary fact.—*Thirdly*, because lawgivers judge in the abstract and of future events; whereas those who sit in judgment judge of things present, toward which they are affected by love, hatred, or some kind of cupidity; wherefore their judgment is perverted.[8]

Justice Joseph Story, who served on the Supreme Court of the United States from 1811 to 1845, spelled out some basic rules of construction that are relevant to constitutional interpretation even today:

> The first and fundamental rule in the interpretation of all instruments is, to construe them according to the sense of the terms, and the intention of the parties. . . .
>
> Where the words are plain and clear, and the sense distinct and perfect arising on them, there is generally no necessity to have recourse to other means of interpretation. It is only when there is some ambiguity or doubt arising from other sources that interpretation has its proper office. There may be obscurity as to the meaning, from the doubtful character of the words used, from other clauses in the same instru-

---

[8] *S.T.*, I, II, Q. 95, art. 1, quoting Aristotle, *Rhetoric*, i. 1.

ment, or from an incongruity or repugnancy between the words and the apparent intention derived from the whole structure of the instrument, or its avowed object. In all such cases interpretation becomes indispensable. . . .

In construing the Constitution of the United States, we are, in the first instance, to consider what are its nature and objects, its scope and design, as apparent from the structure of the instrument, viewed as a whole, and also viewed in its component parts. Where its words are plain, clear and determinate they require no interpretation; and it should, therefore, be admitted, if at all, with great caution, and only from necessity, either to escape some absurd consequence, or to guard against some fatal evil. Where the words admit of two senses each of which is conformable to common usage, that sense is to be adopted which without departing from the literal import of the words, best harmonizes with the nature and objects, the scope and design, of the instrument.[9]

It would be a mistake, however, to imagine that Story's canons, or any other rules of construction, ever could, or should, reduce interpretation to a merely mechanical process. Professor James McClellan, a definitive commentator on Story, wrote:

The conclusion seems inescapable that there will be moments when the Court is unable to pinpoint the proper constitutional ruling and will of necessity actually make the rule, even to the point of altering the Constitution. Such, it would seem, is a natural and inevitable consequence, given the fact we have a Constitution replete with nebulous phrases, the proper interpretation of which cannot always be determined by going back to contemporary construction or the debates

---

[9] Joseph Story, *Commentaries on the Constitution of the United States* (1891 ed.), Book III, nos. 400–444; Story's "Rules of Interpretation" constitute chap. V (nos. 397–456) of book III of his *Commentaries*.

of the federal and state conventions. In this sense the Constitution is, indeed, "what the judges say it is." Beyond this point, however, judicial constitution-making raises serious problems pertaining to democratic government. We may join the realists in snickering at the judges of the old school like Judge Story, who in their innocence and naiveté sincerely believed that they merely 'found' the law when deciding a case and left intact the original understanding of those who framed and ratified the Constitution. But if they did alter the Constitution, it was more likely by accident than design. . . . Agreed, judges make law, but is this any reason to recommend the practice as a general principle of judicial construction? When the rule *is* clear of doubt, is it not the task of the judge to 'find' the law and apply it to the case, as always? Before resorting to an individual interpretation, should not the judge make a sincere and honest attempt to discover the original intent?[10]

In the next Question we will discuss the judge's role in interpreting constitutional provisions that themselves are framed in general terms with a natural law content. Can a judge today interpret those provisions according to his own conception of natural law? Or is he required to follow the concepts—even the natural law concepts—of the Founders? The potential for judicial inventiveness is at its height with respect to such "natural law" provisions of the Constitution.

---

[10] James P. McClellan, *Joseph Story and the American Constitution* (1971), 114–15.

16. But aren't natural law concepts part of the Constitution itself?

Some provisions of the Constitution have natural law content.[11] Even with those, however, the principles enunciated by Justice Story[12] would require the judge or other interpreter to construe them, if possible, according to the intention of those who adopted them. Thus, the prohibition against ex post facto, or retroactive, laws was held in 1798 to forbid only penal legislation and not to prevent such laws that have only civil effect.[13]

Sometimes, however, a clear intent is not apparent. Or the judge must employ natural law reasoning to apply constitutional provisions to situations unknown to the Founders— for example, in deciding whether execution by lethal injection constitutes "cruel or unusual punishment" in violation of the Eighth Amendment.[14] The Story canons of construction

---

[11] For instance, the guarantees in the Fifth and Fourteenth Amendments against deprivation of life, liberty, or property "without due process of law"; the Fourteenth Amendment's command that no state shall "deny to any person within its jurisdiction the equal protection of the laws"; the Ninth Amendment's declaration that "the enumeration in the Constitution, of certain rights, shall not be construed to deny or disparage others retained by the people"; and the prohibition in Art. I, Sec. 10, of the enactment by any state of an "ex post facto law or law impairing the obligation of contracts".

[12] See Question 15 above.

[13] *Calder* v. *Bull*, 3 Dall. 386, 1 L. Ed. 648 (1798).

[14] One court, in upholding execution by lethal injection, said that the Eighth Amendment "embodies 'broad and idealistic concepts of dignity, civilized standards, humanity, and decency' ", and forbids "punishments which are incompatible with 'the evolving standards of decency that mark the progress of a maturing society' ". *Gray* v. *Lucas*, 710 F.2d 1048, 1058 (5th Cir. 1983).

would seem to require the judge at least to try to be faithful to the core principles that the Founders intended to embody.

The natural law issue arose in the 1987 nomination of Judge Robert Bork for the Supreme Court. Judge Bork drew criticism from members of the Senate Judiciary Committee because he denied the right of judges to use natural law concepts to expand the Constitution beyond its original intent with regard to the protection of unenumerated rights and other issues.[15] Four years later, committee members challenged Clarence Thomas on effectively the opposite ground, that he had endorsed the use of natural law by judges in constitutional adjudication.[16] Judge Bork acknowledges that "moral reasoning can make judges aware of complexities and of the likenesses and dissimilarities of situations, all of which is essential in applying the ratifiers' principles to new situations. . . . The role it has to play is assisting judges in the continuing task of deciding whether a new case is inside or outside an old principle."[17]

Bork rejects, however, the idea that natural law can be used, in effect, to amend the Constitution:

The formulation and expression of moral truths as positive law is, in our system of government, a system based on consent, a task confided to the people and their elected representatives. The judge, when he judges, must be, it is his sworn duty to be, a legal positivist. When he acts as a citizen, he, like all other citizens, must not be a legal positivist, but

---

[15] See the account of the Bork hearings in Ethan Bronner, *Battle for Justice: How the Bork Nomination Shook America* (1989), 217–306. See also Patrick B. McGuigan and Dawn M. Weyrich, *Ninth Justice: The Fight for Bork* (1990); Raoul Berger, "Activist Censures of Robert Bork", 85 *Northw. Univ. L. Rev.* 993 (1991).

[16] See Question 1 above.

[17] Robert H. Bork, "Natural Law and the Constitution", *First Things*, Mar. 1992, pp. 16, 17.

must seek moral truth. Otherwise, there is no way for anybody to say what the law should be, what should be enacted
and what repealed. Or, at least, there would be no way other
than to express one's personal interests, which no one with a
differing interest is likely to find in the least persuasive.[18] . . .
The highest political truth for a judge is the Constitution of
the United States, but if a statute does not contravene the
Constitution, it contains the "truth" the judge must apply,
because the people govern.[19]

Subject to the major reservation discussed in Question 17
below, Judge Bork is evidently correct in his view of the judge's
role. The nature of a constitution ought to require that even
the more adaptable provisions be interpreted at least with fidelity to the core principles the constitution originally embodied. Such fidelity leaves ample room for application of those
principles in light of modern knowledge. Interestingly, however, Judge Bork states that "the Constitution has nothing to
say about abortion, either way. That is a subject for moral debate and moral choice by the American people."[20] Since the
mid-nineteenth century, it has been known that abortion is
the taking of human life; without unduly expanding the judicial role, the courts ought to hold that the guarantees of the
right to life and the equal protection of the laws apply to the
unborn child, as they do to other human beings, regardless of

---

[18] Ibid., 19.

[19] Arkes, Hittinger, Ball, and Bork, "Natural Law and the Law", 45, 52;
see also the criticism of the Bork position in Russell Hittinger, "Liberal-
ism and the American Natural Law Tradition", 25 *Wake Forest L. Rev.* 429
(1990); William B. Ball, "The Tempting of Robert Bork: What's a Constitution without Natural Law?" *Crisis*, June 1990, p. 28; and Hadley Arkes,
Beyond the Constitution (1990).

[20] Arkes, Hittinger, All, and Bork, "Natural Law and the Law", 53.

the ignorance of the Founders as to the reality of life before birth.[21]

The history of the Fourteenth Amendment illustrates the potential consequences of judicial liberation from original intent in areas open to natural law interpretation.[22] The first eight amendments of the Bill of Rights were intended to protect the specified rights only against invasion by the federal government. The state governments were not bound by those provisions.[23] For protection of their rights against invasion by state governments, the people relied primarily on state constitutions.

The Fourteenth Amendment, adopted in 1868, was not intended to bind the states by the restrictions of the Bill of Rights.[24] The privileges-or-immunities clause of that amendment was intended to bind the states to protect certain basic rights, including the rights to life, property, personal security, and mobility. The due process clause was intended to guarantee only fair procedures and was not intended to empower courts to protect an open-ended catalogue of substantive rights. As Professor Raoul Berger explains, "The substantive rights were identified by the privileges or immunities clause; the equal protection clause was to bar legislative discrimination with respect

---

[21] See Robert M. Byrn, "An American Tragedy: The Supreme Court on Abortion", 41 *Fordham L. Rev.* 807 (1973).

[22] Sec. 1 provides, "No State shall . . . abridge the *privileges or immunities* of citizens of the United States; nor shall any State deprive any person of life, liberty, or property, without *due process* of law; nor deny to any person within its jurisdiction the *equal protection* of the laws" (emphasis added).

[23] *Barron* v. *Baltimore*, 32 U.S. (7 Pet.) 243 (1833).

[24] See Charles Fairman, "Does the Fourteenth Amendment Incorporate the Bill of Rights?" 2 *Stan. L. Rev.* 5, 135 (1949); Raoul Berger, *Government by Judiciary* (1977), 156, n. 95; Raoul Berger, *Death Penalties: The Supreme Court's Obstacle Course* (1982), 15.

to those rights; and the judicial machinery to serve them was to be supplied by nondiscriminatory due process of the several States."[25] The framers of the Fourteenth Amendment had the limited purpose "to secure familiar, 'fundamental rights,' and only those, and to guard them as of yore against deprivation except by (1) a nondiscriminatory law, and (2) the established judicial procedure of the State."[26]

Unfortunately, the Supreme Court, in 1873, virtually nullified the privileges-or-immunities clause in the *Slaughter-House Cases*.[27] Later, the Court changed the due process clause from a guarantee of fair procedure into a substantive restriction on state legislation. And the Court, contrary to the intent of the Fourteenth Amendment, has now construed the due process clause to incorporate virtually all the protections of the Bill of Rights, thus binding every state inflexibly by the Court's interpretations of those rights. This incorporation doctrine has effected the greatest change in the legal institutions of the nation since the Convention of 1787. It is the basis on which the states are inflexibly precluded from fashioning their own regulations regarding criminal procedure, pornography, prayer in public schools, and almost every aspect of life affected by the Bill of Rights. And it enabled the Supreme Court to discover in the "penumbras formed by emanations from" the Bill of Rights the constitutional right of privacy, which underlay the 1973 abortion ruling in *Roe* v. *Wade*.[28]

The incorporation doctrine's departure from the original intent of the Fourteenth Amendment has opened the way to

---

[25] Berger, *Government by Judiciary*, 18.

[26] Ibid., 19.

[27] 83 U.S. (16 Wall.) 36 (1873).

[28] *Griswold* v. *Conn.*, 381 U.S. 479, 484 (1965); *Roe* v. *Wade*, 410 U.S. 113 (1973).

expansion of protected rights according to the predilections of judges. Some judges even regard an obvious, explicit intent as not binding when it conflicts with evolving justice as interpreted by themselves. Justices William Brennan and Thurgood Marshall routinely opposed the imposition of the death penalty, "for whatever crime and under all circumstances", on the ground that it violates the Eighth Amendment's prohibition against "cruel and unusual punishments".[29] On the contrary, capital punishment is explicitly sanctioned by the Fifth Amendment, which declares, "No person shall be held to answer for a *capital*, or otherwise infamous crime, unless . . . ; nor shall any person be subject for the same offense to be twice put in jeopardy of *life* or limb; nor . . . be deprived of *life*, liberty, or property, without due process of law."[30] The specific recognition of the death penalty in the Fifth Amendment clearly establishes that the Eighth Amendment, adopted at the same time as the Fifth, does not prohibit that penalty.

Justice Brennan's argument to the contrary illustrates an improper use of natural law reasoning to attribute to the framers an intent directly contrary to their explicit intent:

> As I have said in my opinions, I view the Eighth Amendment's prohibition of cruel and unusual punishments as embodying to a unique degree moral principles that substantively restrain the punishments our civilized society may impose on those persons who transgress its laws. Foremost among the moral principles recognized in our cases and inherent in the prohibition is the primary principle that the State, even as it punishes, must treat its citizens in a manner consistent with their intrinsic worth as human beings. The calculated

---

[29] See *Gregg* v. *Georgia*, 428 U.S. 153, 229, 231 (1976) (dissenting opinions of Brennan and Marshall).

[30] Emphasis added.

killing of a human being by the State involves, by its very nature, an absolute denial of the executed person's humanity. The most vile murder does not, in my view, release the State from constitutional restraints on the destruction of human dignity. Yet an executed person has lost the very right to have rights, now or ever. For me, then, the fatal constitutional infirmity of capital punishment is that it treats members of the human race as nonhumans, as objects to be toyed with and discarded. It is, indeed, "cruel and unusual." It is thus inconsistent with the fundamental premise of the Clause that even the most base criminal remains a human being possessed of some potential, at least, for common human dignity.[31]

Note that Justice Brennan is not using natural law here as a standard higher than the Constitution itself. His analysis is on a lower level: What does the Eighth Amendment mean? His interpretation of it according to his version of natural law, in such open contradiction to the Fifth Amendment, would amount to a judicial amendment of the Constitution. Justice Brennan's approach is striking because it so clearly contradicts the very text of the Constitution. However, in recent decades especially, the Supreme Court has adopted the spirit of this latitudinarian approach to import various fundamental rights into the Constitution.[32]

Adaptation of constitutional provisions to modern circumstances is unavoidable, but even those provisions with a natural law content at least ought not to be construed to violate the plain meaning of the text and structure of the Constitution. "When the Court disregards the express intent and understanding of the Framers," said Justice John Marshall Harlan,

---

[31] William J. Brennan, "Construing the Constitution", 19 *U.C. Davis L. Rev.* 2, 13 (1985).

[32] See, for example, *Griswold v. Conn.*, 381 U.S. 479 (1965) (right to privacy); *Roe v. Wade*, 410 U.S. 113 (1973) (right to abortion).

"it has invaded the realm of the political processes to which the amending procedure was committed, and it has violated the constitutional structure which it is its highest duty to protect."[33]

17. *Do you seriously claim that a judge can properly use natural law to rule that a statute, or even part of the Constitution itself, is unjust and void?*

Yes. In the passage quoted at the end of the previous question, Justice Harlan said it is the "highest duty" of the Supreme Court to "protect" the "constitutional structure".[34] The protection of that structure is a high duty of the Court, but, in the nature of things, it cannot be its "highest duty". Judges are bound to follow the original intent, as far as it can be determined, and they have no right to amend the Constitution according to their own conception of natural law. But this restriction is subject to the fact that although it is the highest enacted law of the nation, the Constitution is itself a form of human law and is therefore subject to the higher standard of the natural law. That standard is supra-constitutional. It sets limits to what the legal system, however it is structured, can do even through constitutional provisions.

Judges should not tailor their interpretations of statutes to fit their own natural law views or other views as to what they

---

[33] *Oregon* v. *Mitchell*, 400 U.S. 112, 203 (1970) (Harlan concurring in part and dissenting in part); see discussion in Raoul Berger, "Lawrence Church on the Scope of Judicial Review and Original Intent", 70 *N. Car. L. Rev.* 113, 134 (1991).

[34] 400 U.S. at 203.

would have voted for had they been in the legislature. Instead, they should interpret a statute, as far as ascertainable, according to the intent of the enacting legislature. And if they disapprove of a statute or regard it as unjust, they should not distort the United States Constitution to find such a statute unconstitutional (or, in the opposite case, constitutional).

If a federal or state statute is unjust, it will be either unconstitutional or constitutional. If it is unconstitutional, it can be struck down on that ground, and the natural law will not be itself the basis of the decision. However, if an unjust law is constitutional—that is, it is permitted by the Constitution— or if the enactment of a just law is unjustly forbidden by the Constitution, then the natural law would come into play. The issue would be whether the Constitution itself is void, in that respect, because it is contrary to the higher law. Obviously, such a conclusion should be drawn only in extreme, intolerable cases and only as a last resort.

The first response, for example, to a proposal to authorize the intentional killing of innocent human beings should be to say that it would be not only unjust but also a violation of the Fifth and Fourteenth Amendments. That response would avoid the natural law question. *Roe* v. *Wade*, however, established such a right to kill as a constitutional right. Assuming that the Supreme Court is correct in its assertion that its decisions are the supreme law of the land,[35] the issue becomes whether the Constitution itself is subject to the higher law. Or if a constitutional amendment were adopted to authorize such killing or to require the confiscation without trial or compensation of the property of members of a particular race or religion or to reinstate slavery, would that constitutional amendment

---

[35] *Cooper* v. *Aaron*, 358 U.S. 1 (1958).

be valid? A natural law adherent should respond in the negative.[36] In whatever way the human law is imposed, whether by judicial decision, statute, or constitution, it remains, in the nature of things, subject to the higher natural law.[37]

The potential use of natural law to invalidate any federal or state law is very limited in this nation. The Constitution and the state constitutions incorporate natural law principles, such as due process and equal protection, so that laws contrary to those principles could be shown to violate the Constitution without any need for recourse to a supraconstitutional higher law. As the New York Court of Appeals said in *Wynehamer* v. *People*,[38] which struck down a state prohibition law as applied to existing stocks of liquor, "There is no process of reasoning by which it could be demonstrated that [the law] is void, upon principles and theories outside of the Constitution, which will not also, and by an easier induction, bring it in direct conflict with the Constitution itself." Similarly, in *Fletcher* v. *Peck*,[39] Chief Justice John Marshall, speaking for the Court, held that a state legislature was forbidden to rescind a previous land grant, "either by general principles, which are common to our free institutions, or by the particular provisions of the constitution of the United States".

The Supreme Court discussed the natural law issue in *Calder* v. *Bull*,[40] where it held that the prohibition of ex post facto laws,

---

[36] See the apparently contrary position of Supreme Court Justice Antonin Scalia, expressed in his response to questions following his May 2, 1996, address at the Gregorian University in Rome. 26 *Origins* (June 27, 1996), 82, 87–90.

[37] See *E.V.*, nos. 71–73.

[38] 13 N.Y. (3 Kern) 378, 392 (1856).

[39] 10 U.S. (6 Cranch) 87, 139, 3 L. Ed. 162 (1810).

[40] 3 Dall. at 387–89.

in Article I, Section 10, applied only to penal laws and did not protect property rights from retroactive interference. Justice Samuel Chase, in his opinion, stated that if a state legislature did enact a genuinely ex post facto law, it would be invalid even if it had not been prohibited by the Constitution of the United States or the constitution of the state:

> I cannot subscribe to the omnipotence of a State Legislature, or that it is absolute and without controul; although its authority should not be expressly restrained by the Constitution, or fundamental law of the State. . . . There are acts which the Federal, or State, Legislature cannot do, without exceeding their authority. There are certain vital principles in our free Republican governments, which will determine and over-rule an apparent and flagrant abuse of legislative power; as to authorize manifest injustice by positive law; or to take away that security for personal liberty, or private property, for the protection whereof the government was established. An *act* of the Legislature (for I cannot call it a law) contrary to the great first principles of the social compact, cannot be considered a rightful exercise of legislative authority. . . . A few instances will suffice to explain what I mean. A law that punished a citizen for an innocent action, or, in other words, for an act which, when done, was in violation of no existing law; a law that destroys, or impairs, the lawful private contracts of citizens; a law that makes a man a Judge in his own cause; or a law that takes property from A. and gives it to B.: It is against all reason and justice, for a people to entrust a Legislature with *such* powers; and, therefore, it cannot be presumed that they have done it. The genius, the nature, and the spirit, of our State Governments, amount to a prohibition of such acts of legislation; and the general principles of law and reason forbid them. . . . To maintain that our Federal, or State, Legislature possesses such powers, if they had not been expressly restrained; would, in my

opinion, be a political heresy, altogether inadmissible in our free republican governments.[41]

Justice James Iredell, however, rejected this natural law approach:

> If . . . the Legislature of the Union, or the Legislature of any member of the Union, shall pass a law, within the general scope of their constitutional power, the Court cannot pronounce it to be void, merely because it is, in their judgment, contrary to the principles of natural justice. *The ideas of natural justice are regulated by no fixed standard: the ablest and the purest men have differed upon the subject*; and all that the Court could properly say, in such an event, would be, that the Legislature (possessed of an equal right of opinion) has passed an act which, in the opinion of the judges, was inconsistent with the abstract principles of natural justice. There are then but two lights, in which the subject can be viewed: 1st. If the Legislature pursue the authority delegated to them, their acts are valid. 2d. If they transgress the boundaries of that authority, their acts are invalid.[42]

Justice Iredell's reluctance to apply natural law is understandable if that law has no objective content. And his approach has prevailed in the American courts. But even if the natural law were acknowledged as a higher standard, it ought not to provide judges a hunting license empowering them to impose their own morality to invalidate legislative decisions in genuinely debatable cases. One case, however, in which a supraconstitutional invocation of the natural law might have been appropriate is *Brown* v. *Board of Education*.[43] There is evidence

---

[41] 3 Dall. at 387–89.

[42] 3 Dall. at 399 (emphasis added); see discussion in Edward S. Corwin, "Natural Law and Constitutional Law", 3 *Nat. Law Inst. Proceedings* 47, 59–61 (1950); see also the Introduction to this book.

[43] 347 U.S. 483 (1954).

to support the conclusion that the Fourteenth Amendment was intended to allow officially segregated public schools.[44] If one accepted that conclusion and also found that public education today is sufficiently similar to that of 1868 to be governed by the intent of the Fourteenth Amendment on the subject, one could still argue that officially imposed racial segregation in schools (or elsewhere) is void because it is inherently unjust to an intolerable degree, so as to violate the supraconstitutional standard of the natural law. A human law, according to Aquinas, may be unjust as "contrary to human good" when "burdens are imposed unequally on the community".[45]

A similar approach would have been appropriate in the Dred Scott Case, in which the Supreme Court held that freed slaves and their free descendants could not be citizens and said that slaves were property rather than persons.[46] Even if the court there correctly interpreted the technical intent of the Constitution, the Constitution in that respect would be intolerably unjust in its attempt to break the inseparable connection that must exist, in any free and just society, between humanity and personhood.

Although the Constitution is the highest human law,[47] it must itself be subject to the higher law. If a constitutional amendment were adopted to require the disenfranchisement of persons of a certain race or religion, there would seem little doubt that a judge would have the right and the duty to declare the amendment itself unlawful and void. Nevertheless, this responsibility offers no warrant for "noninterpretive" judges to

---

[44] See Alexander Bickel, "The Original Understanding and the Segregation Decision", 69 *Harv. L. Rev.* 1 (1955).

[45] *S.T.*, I, II, Q. 96, art. 4; see Question 12 above.

[46] *Scott v. Sandford*, 60 U.S. (19 How.) 393, 15 L. Ed. 691, 709, 720 (1857).

[47] U.S. Constitution, art. VI, cl. 2.

roam at large over the constitutional landscape, acting as a continuing constitutional convention in disregard of the constitutional text and the evident intent of its framers.[48] Only rarely would a judge be entitled or obliged to rely on supraconstitutional principles to refuse to uphold or enforce an enacted law. As the German courts indicated after World War II, judges should take this step only when the conflict between the law or precedent and justice is "intolerable" or "unendurable".[49] Such a conflict could occur with respect to *Roe* v. *Wade*, because that ruling authorizes the execution of a certainly innocent human being. However, one need not reach that conflict on *Roe*, because the decision's denial of personhood to unborn human beings incorrectly interprets the Fourteenth Amendment.[50]

The United States Constitution is "the supreme law of the land".[51] But the ultimate supreme law is the law of God, including the natural law. It implies no disrespect for the Constitution to note that all forms of human law are subject to the higher law of God.

---

[48] See Berger, *Government by Judiciary*, 2.

[49] See Question 2 above.

[50] See Robert M. Byrn, "An American Tragedy: The Supreme Court on Abortion", 41 *Fordham L. Rev.* 807 (1973); Randall Hekman, "Judging: By What Standard?" 4 *Christian Leg. Soc. Q.* 19 (1983); Charles E. Rice, "Some Reasons for a Restoration of Natural Law Jurisprudence", 24 *Wake Forest L. Rev.* 539–68 (1989).

[51] U.S. Constitution, art. VI, cl. 2.

IV

THE REASONED FOUNDATION
OF THE NATURAL LAW

18. Back up a minute. You said before that Aquinas gives us sure answers to all sorts of questions on natural law. But haven't philosophers proven that we can't ever be sure of anything in the first place?

> "We can't be sure of anything!"
> "Are you sure of that?"
> "Of course I'm sure!"

This dialogue is not wholly imaginary. American schools at every level, including the university, have more than a few teachers, as well as students, who are certain that they cannot be certain of anything. An interesting question is why people pay tuition to study under professors who say that they do not know, and cannot know, anything. Of course, even an academic would concede the practical need to rely on sense impressions. Only a fool would ask for "proof" that the truck he sees is really bearing down on him. If he is sane, he will jump out of the way. He may be unsure that he really *knows* that the truck is there. But if he does not trust the evidence of his senses, he will be a dead academic.

The "great dividing line of all philosophies" runs between "the thought systems that hold that we can know things" and "those that say that we can know only our minds".[1] To see how this dividing line was drawn, we have to go back a few years. In the fourteenth century, William of Ockham (c. 1285–1349) asserted that "philosophy and theology are entirely separate. Contrary to St. Thomas, there is no region of overlap con-

---

[1] Paul H. Hallett, "The Great Divide", *National Catholic Register*, July 29, 1979, p. 4.

taining truths knowable both by reason and by revelation. Religion has no rational foundation but rests entirely on revelation. . . . William does not appear to have been inclined to religious skepticism. His denial of philosophical foundations for religion was intended to free theology from rationalist shackles. And . . . he was not a skeptic about the validity of human knowledge. Some Ockhamites, however, tended to draw skeptical inferences."[2]

Ockham's nominalism or, more precisely, conceptualism, "initiated a period of skeptical and critical philosophy which went far beyond Ockham's intentions. . . . His conceptualism had a lasting influence. . . . It is no exaggeration to say that the British Empirical philosophers from Hobbes to Hume owe their conceptualism to Ockham directly or indirectly."[3]

It would be a grave misinterpretation of [Ockham's] thought to imagine that there was in his mind any conflict between faith and reason, or revelation and philosophy. Ockham is perfectly safe in what he believes, only he does not *know* what he believes, nor does he need to know it. It is enough for him that probability stands in all cases on the side of faith and of revelation. . . . Of the rational understanding of faith attempted by Bonaventure, Albert the Great, Thomas Aquinas and their contemporaries, very little, if anything, was left after Ockham. . . . Faith was intact, but to follow Ockham was to give up any hope of achieving, in this life, a positive philosophical understanding of its intelligible meaning. In philosophy itself, . . . [Ockham] unleashed and encouraged forces which he himself could not possibly control after setting them free. In this sense, it can be said that the doctrine of Ockham marked a turning point in the history

---

[2] Wallace I. Matson, *A New History of Philosophy, Ancient and Medieval* (1987), 246, 248.

[3] Julius R. Weinberg, *A Short History of Medieval Philosophy* (1964), 265.

of philosophy as well as of theology. In theology his doctrine was paving the way to the "positive theology" of the moderns. In philosophy, it was paving the way to modern empiricism. In both cases it really was a *via moderna*: a modern way.[4]

One Fordham Jesuit said of today's students:

Blame it on William of Ockham! Television could not have so thoroughly corrupted the mind of a culture in one generation. It must have taken centuries. Thank God, they can't blame the Jesuits for William of Ockham. He died in the 14th century, nearly 200 years before we were founded. But he certainly left his mark on the modern mind with his nominalist philosophy. It is because of him that we feel that we never really know the nature of anything and therefore cannot grasp an objective standard of good and evil. With him starts the current that flows down through Hobbes, Locke, Hume, Bentham, and the whole contemporary crowd of subjectivists and emotivists, and leaves our kids unable to feel sure about the elementary difference between good and evil.[5]

In *Fides et Ratio*, John Paul said, " 'All human beings desire to know'; and truth is the proper object of this desire. . . . People cannot be genuinely indifferent to the question of whether what they know is true or not. If they discover that it is false, they reject it; but if they can establish its truth, they feel themselves rewarded. It is this that St. Augustine teaches when he writes: 'I have met many who wanted to deceive, but none who wanted to be deceived.' "[6] "[I]t was part of the original plan of the creation," said John Paul, "that reason should without

---

[4] Etienne Gilson, *History of Christian Philosophy in the Middle Ages* (1955), 498–99.

[5] Francis Canavan, S.J., "In the Midnight Hour", *National Catholic Register*, June 8, 1982, p. 4.

[6] *F.R.*, no. 25.

difficulty reach beyond the sensory data to the origin of all things: the Creator. But because of the disobedience by which man and woman chose to set themselves in full and absolute autonomy in relation to the One who had created them, this ready access to God the Creator diminished.[7]

Nevertheless, " 'Intelligence is not confined to observable data alone. It can with genuine certitude attain to reality itself as knowable, though in consequence of sin that certitude is partially obscured and weakened.' "[8]

René Descartes (1596–1650) sought to find a premise that was absolutely certain and could not be doubted. He proceeded by doubting everything, including his senses because they sometimes seemed to deceive him. Ultimately, he concluded that nothing was certain except the fact that he was thinking. From this he concluded that he himself existed. "Cogito ergo sum" "I think, therefore I am." "Since Descartes declared the only thing we can be sure of is our own existence as conscious beings—*cogito ergo sum*—modern philosophers have held with him that we know nothing but our own subjective states."[9] The root fallacy of Descartes was explained by Ralph McInerny:

> At the historical first step of the development of Modernity, in Descartes, the way in which doubt is cast on all judgments based on the senses in incoherent.
>
> Descartes' senses sometimes deceive him. So do mine. From that fact, Descartes wants to conclude that he can never rely on the senses with the certainty he wants. That is, he can always doubt what they report.
>
> Let us consider a standard case of being deceived by our

---

[7] *F.R.*, no. 22.

[8] *F.R.*, no. 82, quoting *Gaudium et Spes*, no. 15.

[9] Cornelius J. Hagerty, C.S.C., *The Problem of Evil* (1977), 24.

senses. The stick looks crooked in water. This can cause deception only if it is contrasted with a case where deception is excluded. Obviously it is presumed to be a straight stick which appears to be bent when seen in water.

It is when the stick is removed that we say, Good grief, it's straight. Because we say that, we take back what we said earlier about the crookedness of it when submerged.

Even to describe this simple case of deception, we have to take one of those judgments as certain. Unless we do, there is no contrast, no deception. . . .

[Descartes] must trust his senses in order to doubt them, so he cannot universally doubt them.

That is why this small point is indeed a big deal. It stops Modernity before it can get going. Once it gets going, it proceeds with a kind of inevitability toward the loss of the world. The only world left is one "we" fashion in our heads. Man becomes the measure of all things, of what is that it is, of what is not that it is not. That was the claim both Plato and Aristotle showed to be nonsense. It is still nonsense. The Classical view, and preeminently Thomism, is its antidote.[10]

The modern thinker, in the Descartes mold, begins and ends the thinking project in his own mind. Having concluded that all he can know is what is in his mind, he can never leave that mind. With no way of knowing the reality of what is outside his mind, he is reduced to spinning subjectivist, agnostic theories about what is going on outside. "They are the true eggheads, caught in an impenetrable solid shell around their heads."[11]

"Descartes . . . inaugurated the *great anthropocentric shift in philosophy*. 'I think therefore I am' . . . is the motto of modern

---

[10] Ralph McInerny, *A First Glance at St. Thomas Aquinas* (1990), 36–37. See also the discussion of Descartes in *L.F.*, no. 19.

[11] Carl Schmitt, of the Notre Dame Law School Class of 1993, made this point in an unpublished 1992 research paper.

rationalism. All the rationalism of the last centuries . . . can be considered a continuation and expansion of Cartesian positions. [Descartes] *distanced us from the philosophy of existence*, and also from the traditional approaches of Saint Thomas which lead to God who is 'autonomous existence.' . . . By making subjective consciousness absolute, Descartes moves instead toward . . . an Absolute [which] is not *autonomous existence*, but rather *autonomous thought*. Only that which corresponds to human thought makes sense. The objective truth of this thought is not as important as the fact that something exists in human consciousness. . . . Descartes turns his back on metaphysics and concentrates on the philosophy of knowledge. Kant is the most notable representative of this movement."[12]

Immanuel Kant (1724–1804) maintained that we cannot know the *noumena*—that is, things as they really are. Rather, we can only know the *phenomena*, the appearance of things.[13] This agnostic premise has come to dominate modern philosophy and law. Ayn Rand's comment on this aspect of the student riots of the 1960s, led by Mario Savio, is worth extended quotation:

> Mankind could not expect to remain unscathed after decades of exposure to the radiation of intellectual fission-debris, such as: "Reason is impotent to know things as they are— reality is unknowable—certainty is impossible—knowledge

---

[12] Pope John Paul II, *Crossing the Threshold of Hope* (1994), 51–52.

[13] See Immanuel Kant, *Critique of Pure Reason* (1961 ed.), chap. III, 257–75; see W. T. Jones, *Kant and the Nineteenth Century* (1975), which describes Kant's *Critique* as an effort by Kant to respond to the scepticism of David Hume by showing that "real knowledge of matters of fact is possible" (15). "Ultimately, however, Kant made many more concessions to antirationalism than he realized" (13). See also Etienne Gilson and Thomas Langan, *Modern Philosophy: Descartes to Kant* (1964), 264–68; George W. Rutler, *Christ and Reason: An Introduction to Ideas from Kant to Tyrrell* (1990), 1–29.

is mere probability—truth is that which works—mind is a superstition—logic is a social convention—ethics is a matter of subjective commitment to an arbitrary postulate"—and the consequent mutations are those contorted young creatures who scream, in chronic terror, that they know nothing and want to rule everything.

If [a] dramatist were writing a movie, he could justifiably entitle it "Mario Savio, Son of Immanuel Kant."

With rare and academically neglected exceptions, the philosophical "mainstream" that seeps into every classroom, subject and brain in today's universities, is: epistemological agnosticism, avowed irrationalism, ethical subjectivism. Our age is witnessing the ultimate climax, the cashing-in on a long process of destruction, at the end of the road laid out by Kant.

Ever since Kant divorced reason from reality, his intellectual descendants have been diligently widening the breach. In the name of reason, Pragmatism established a range-of-the-moment view as an enlightened perspective on life, context-dropping as a rule of epistemology, expediency as a principle of morality, and collective subjectivism as a substitute for metaphysics. Logical Positivism carried it farther and, in the name of reason, elevated the immemorial psycho-epistemology of shyster-lawyers to the status of a scientific epistemological system—by proclaiming that knowledge consists of linguistic manipulations. . . . As a result, a student came out of a modern university with the following sediment left in his brain by his four to eight years of study: existence is an uncharted, unknowable jungle, fear and uncertainty are man's permanent state, skepticism is the mark of maturity, cynicism is the mark of realism and, above all, the hallmark of an intellectual is the denial of the intellect.[14]

---

[14] Ayn Rand, "The Cashing-In: The Student Rebellion", *Objectivist Newsletter*, July–Aug. 1965, p. 33.

As the Party interrogator said to his victim in Orwell's *1984*:

> You believe that reality is something objective, external, existing in its own right. You also believe that the nature of reality is self-evident. When you delude yourself into thinking that you see something, you assume that everyone else sees the same thing as you. But I tell you, Winston, that reality is not external. Reality exists in the human mind and nowhere else. Not in the individual mind, which can make mistakes, and in any case soon perishes; only in the mind of the Party which is collective and immortal. Whatever the Party holds to be truth *is* truth.[15]

Universal scepticism is absurd. One who says we can never be certain of anything contradicts himself because he is certain of that proposition. If he says instead that he is not sure he can be sure of anything, he admits at least that he is sure he is not sure. Or some will say that all propositions are meaningless unless they can be empirically verified. But that statement itself cannot be empirically verified.

John Paul II, in *Fides et Ratio*, described the "threat of *scientism* . . . the philosophical notion which refuses to admit the validity of forms of knowledge other than those of the positive sciences; and it relegates religious, theological, ethical and aesthetic knowledge to the realm of mere fantasy."[16] He also criticized "*pragmatism*, an attitude . . . which . . . precludes . . . considerations or judgments based on ethical principles. The practical consequences of this . . . are significant . . . [T]here is growing support for a concept of democracy which is not grounded upon any reference to unchanging values: whether or not a line of action is admissable is decided by the vote of a parliamentary majority . . . [I]n practice, the great moral de-

---

[15] George Orwell, *1984* (1949), 252.
[16] *F.R.*, no. 88.

cisions of humanity are subordinated to decisions . . . by institutional agencies. Moreover, anthropology itself is severely compromised by a one-dimensional vision of the human being . . . which excludes the great ethical dilemmas and the existential analyses of the meaning of suffering and sacrifice, of life and death."[17]

Sir Alfred Jules Ayer, the founder of logical positivism, espoused "the principle of verification, according to which a statement intended to be a statement of fact is meaningful only if it's either formally valid, or some kind of observation is relevant to its truth or falsehood." Formal propositions, Ayer said, "like those of logic and mathematics, depend for their validity on the conventions of a symbol system". Ayer claimed that "to be significant a statement must be either, on the one hand, a formal statement, one that I should call analytic, or on the other hand empirically testable."[18] Ayer's principle, however, cannot withstand analysis:

> If all propositions must be verified in sense experience, then why not the principle of verification itself? The principle is a complex of meaning, no element of which is identified with sense experience. "Every meaningful proposition is verifiable in sense experience." The predicate, "sense experience," is not sensible; it is an abstract, intelligible content; it is not identified with any given sense experience. "Meaningful" is not a sense experience. What is the "meaning of meaning?" Whatever it might be, it cannot be identified and understood simply by pointing at something and punching it. The whole proposition might be said to stand for the totality of sense experiences and thus to symbolize them all.

---

[17] *F.R.*, no. 89.

[18] A. J. Ayer and F. C. Copleston, "Logical Positivism—A Debate", in *Philosophic Problems and Education* (Young Pai and Joseph T. Myers, eds., 1967), 103, 104, 105, 120.

If this is so, then there is a "meaning" beyond experience, and this "meaning" is *meaning itself.*[19]

Ayer died in 1989 at the age of seventy-eight. "Sir Alfred, an atheist, was so persuasive in argument, the story goes, that when the English writer Somerset Maugham lay dying, he got Sir Alfred to visit him and reassure him that there was no life after death. In 1988, Sir Alfred's heart stopped for four minutes at a hospital in London, and he wrote later that he had seen a red light and become 'aware that this light was responsible for the government of the universe'. The experience left his atheism unquenched, he wrote, but 'slightly weakened my conviction that my genuine death—which is due fairly soon—will be the end of me, though I continue to hope it will be.' "[20]

The short answer to the Question is: Yes, we can be absolutely sure of some things beyond the empirically verifiable. Those who claim otherwise not only contradict themselves but can offer no ultimate explanation of the meaning of life.

"The positions we have examined," said John Paul in *Fides et Ratio*, lead . . . to the nihilist interpretation, which is at once the denial of all foundations and the negation of all objective truth. Quite apart from the fact that it conflicts with the demands and the content of the word of God, nihilism is a denial of the humanity and of the very identity of the human being. . . .

"[T]he neglect of being inevitably leads to losing touch with objective truth and therefore with the very ground of human dignity. This in turn makes it possible to erase from the countenance of man and woman the marks of their likeness to God, and thus to lead them little by little either to a destructive will

---

[19] Frederick D. Wilhelmsen, *Man's Knowledge of Reality: An Introduction to Thomistic Epistemology* (1956), 50–51.

[20] *New York Times*, June 29, 1989, p. 12.

to power or to a solitude without hope. Once the truth is denied to human beings, it is pure illusion to try to set them free. Truth and freedom either go together hand in hand or together they perish in misery. . . .

"Our age has been termed by some thinkers the age of postmodernity. . . . One thing however is certain: the currents of thought which claim to be postmodern merit appropriate attention. According to some of them, the time of certainties is irrevocably past, and the human being must now live in a horizon of total absence of meaning, where everything is provisional and ephemeral. . . . [A] posivitist cast of mind continues to nurture the illusion that, thanks to scientific and technical progress, man and woman may live as a demiurge, single-handedly and completely taking charge of their destiny."[21]

19. *All right. So it doesn't make sense to say that we can't know anything. But what can we know and how do we know it?*

Let's start with the basics. Through the operation of his senses and his intellect, man can understand the essences or natures of material things. He can know that one thing is a pen and another is a wheelbarrow. He perceives individual things through his senses and imagination, and through his intellect he knows the essences of those things. "We have a faculty of intellect, called the active intellect, whose sole work is to throw light on the sensible image or phantasm to make the universal stand out from the particular as a spot-light makes one girl stand out from a chorus. This light, focused on the specific nature in the

---

[21] *F.R.*, no. 90–91.

phantasm, enables the intellect to concentrate on its proper object, the universal nature of the thing, to the disregard of the particularizing elements in it."[22] As Saint Thomas put it, "The active intellect . . . causes the phantasms received from the senses to be actually intelligible, by a process of abstraction."[23]

> Each person has his own intellect which has two functions: it abstracts essences from sense-perceived individuals; this abstracted essence is then intelligible; it is impressed on the passive intellect. On reflection the passive intellect understands that one essence belongs to many individuals, forming a class which can again be further unified by still more abstract ideas into wider classes. Abstraction terminates in the idea of being which includes God, the only self-existent being. "I am who am."[24]

"That things exist, therefore, is known neither by the intellect nor by the senses. This is true, but it is also profoundly irrelevant; strictly speaking, there is no such thing as a human intellect 'by itself'; nor is there such a thing as brute sensation 'by itself.' Man is neither one nor the other. He is both of them joined in that unity of being we call man. *It is only as a man — as a body-soul unity — that he knows things to exist, and he knows this truth as neither postulated nor demonstrated, but as evident.*"[25]

"Man's intellect, by its concepts, knows reality. The ideas are that *by which* reality is known; they are not that *which* is known."[26] Saint Thomas distinguishes three acts of the intel-

---

[22] Walter Farrell, *A Companion to the Summa* (1945), vol. I, 330–31.

[23] *S.T.*, I, Q. 84, art. 6.

[24] Hagerty, *The Problem of Evil*, 18.

[25] Wilhelmsen, *Man's Knowledge of Reality*, 30; see *S.T.*, I, Q. 75–102; Paul J. Glenn, *A Tour of the Summa* (1978), 60–84.

[26] Glenn, *A Tour of the Summa*, 72.

lect. The senses perceive an object. The intellect in its first act, of simple apprehension, forms the idea "dog", by which it knows what that object is. The intellect then proceeds to make a judgment: "Lassie is a dog." The third act of the intellect is discursive reasoning, as seen in the syllogism: "All dogs are mortal; Lassie is a dog; therefore Lassie is mortal."[27] Truth is the agreement or conformity of reality and the mind's judgment on reality.[28] If I look at Lassie and say, "Lassie is a dog", the statement is true. If I say "Lassie is a cat", the statement is false no matter how sincerely and strongly I believe Lassie to be a cat.

"Augustine says . . . 'that in which man excels irrational animals is reason, or mind, or intelligence, or whatever appropriate name we like to give it.' Therefore, reason, intellect, and mind are one power [of the soul]."[29] Saint Thomas distinguishes the speculative reason from the practical reason.[30] The object of the practical reason is the good, but the object of the speculative reason is being itself. The first principle of the speculative reason is the principle of contradiction (or noncontradiction), that a thing cannot both be and not be at the same time under the same aspect, or "that the same thing cannot be affirmed and denied at the same time".[31] This principle is self-evident. No rational person can doubt it. Related to the principle of contradiction are two other principles. First, the principle of the excluded middle: Either a thing is or it is not. Second, the principle of identity: A thing is what it is.

---

[27] See *S.T.*, I, Q. 85, art. 5; see also discussion in Vernon Bourke, ed., *The Pocket Aquinas* (1969), 3–5.

[28] See *S.T.*, I, Q. 16, art. 1.

[29] *S.T.*, I, Q. 79, art. 8.

[30] Ibid., art. 11.

[31] *S.T.*, I, II, Q. 94, art. 2.

This pen I am holding in my hand is a pen. It cannot be both a pen and not a pen in terms of the question of its pen-ness —that is, whether it is or is not a pen. The pen is also black, hard, cylindrical, five inches long, and so forth. Or it can also be a shovel if it is used to dig a hole, or a bridge if it is used by ants to get from one place to another. But these incidental qualities or functions relate to different aspects. They do not concern the essential question: Is it a pen? We know with absolute certainty that, in terms of its pen-ness, its character of being or not being a pen, it cannot be both a pen and not a pen. Or pursuant to the principle of identity, it is what it is —that is, a pen. Anyone who thinks that this item, in terms of its pen-ness, is both a pen and not a pen is unfit to carry on any rational discussion. And if he asks for proof, if he says, "Prove that this cannot be both a pen and not a pen", the answer is that there is no proof. As a self-evident proposition, the principle of contradiction is known beyond doubt to all rational beings.

The principle of contradiction "simply repeats the structure of being itself. 'Being is not nonbeing.' If being could both be and not be, what is it that is not? If it is, it is being; if it is not, it is nonbeing or nothing at all. The principle of contradiction is also the first principle in the order of demonstration or proof; every conclusion must issue eventually from being itself. If the conclusion to a process of reasoning can be shown to violate the principle of contradiction, then the conclusion declares something to exist that does not exist."[32]

The first self-evident principle of the practical reason is that "good is that which all things seek after."[33] This principle is the basis of the first, self-evident precept of the natural law, that

---

[32] Wilhelmsen, *Man's Knowledge of Reality*, 46.

[33] *S.T.*, I, II, Q. 94, art. 2.

"good is to be done and pursued, and evil is to be avoided."[34] In Question 6 above, we discussed the basic inclinations of human nature, which, in Aquinas' words, "are naturally apprehended by reason as being good".[35] In later Questions, we will examine the process by which one reasons from these inclinations to conclusions as to the goodness of particular actions.

This answer merely opens the subject of what and how we know so that we can move beyond the claim that we cannot ever really know anything. The rest of this book is a further exploration of what we can know and how we know it with respect to the natural law and its author.

---

[34] Ibid.
[35] Ibid.

V

THE REASONED FOUNDATION: MAN AS KNOWN THROUGH REASON TO BE SPIRITUAL AND IMMORTAL

20. What about man? As far as we can tell, he is just a body, a collection of atoms. Right?

Wrong. There are two realms of reality: the material and the spiritual. Material things are composed of tangible parts. A spiritual thing is "simple" in that it has no parts, no size, shape, or dimensions. Yet spiritual beings are just as real as the material. The reality of the spiritual is one of the least understood facts of life, especially among American students. Yet it is easy to prove.

If you are capable of doing spiritual things—that is, things that a merely material being cannot do—it follows that you must be spiritual. The question is not whether you have a soul. A soul is merely the life principle of a living thing. Every living thing has a soul. But the soul of the plant or the dog is material. "The soul of a plant and the soul of an animal are called material souls, not as though they were made of bodily stuff, but to indicate their *dependence* upon the bodily organism which they determine and actualize."[1] Our souls, however, are spiritual. We know they are because we can do spiritual things. The spiritual capabilities that prove we are spiritual are abstraction and reflection.

> If the human soul were a *material* substance, we could only think "material" thoughts; that is, we could only have what we call "sense-knowledge." We could know that this tree is green, and that barn is red; but we could not think about redness and greenness in the abstract; we could not speculate on the possible effect of the various colors on human emotions, as psychologists do. Again, we would know that this person attracted us, and that another person was re-

---

[1] Paul J. Glenn, *A Tour of the Summa* (1978), 60; see *S.T.*, I, Q. 75, art. 3.

pulsive to us; but we could never rise from the kindness of the one and the selfishness of the other, to theorize about goodness and badness in general. And so, because the soul can rise above mere sense-knowledge, and have immaterial thoughts, spiritual thoughts, the soul itself must be a spirit. "No effect can be greater than its cause."[2]

The clock on the wall and a penny have a characteristic in common. They are both round. The idea of roundness is an abstract idea. It—the idea of roundness—does not exist by itself in the material world. You can easily get a round ball. But, try as hard as you will, you will never find a "roundness" by itself in the material world. You can put a round ball in your locker, but you cannot put 'roundness' there in and by itself. Yet you know that you can think of roundness without visualizing any particular round thing. In thinking of roundness you are doing more than merely registering sense impressions. You are abstracting from your sense impressions a concept that does not exist by itself in the material world. Other examples of abstract ideas are truth, honesty, and love.

Every time you use a common noun to say what something is, you perform the spiritual activity of abstraction. I know that what I am writing on is a desk because it has the abstract quality of desk-ness, that which makes it a desk. Desks may differ in size, shape, and color, but I can tell the difference between a desk and a train because I have the abstract ideas of desk-ness and train-ness. If I call a desk a train, my statement is untrue because it does not conform to the reality that the item I am naming has the abstract qualities of desk-ness and does not have the abstract qualities of train-ness.

Our capacity for abstraction can be seen also in our ability

---

[2] Leo J. Trese, *Wisdom Shall Enter* (1954), 29.

to design. If you are going to build a house, the first thing you do is visualize it. It may have a swimming pool, an elevator, and so on. When you visualize that house, you form an idea of something that does not exist in the material world. Your concept of the house you want to build is an abstract idea. Birds, however, do not design their houses. They operate according to the instinct put in them by the Creator, who designed them. You will never see a couple of birds standing on a branch with a set of plans, visualizing the house they intend to build. Incidentally, the fact that designing something is a spiritual activity is one proof that God is spiritual because God designed us and the universe.[3]

The second capacity we have that proves that we are spiritual is that we can reflect on ourselves. In a sense, you can get outside of yourself and look back on yourself. This is reflection. You know that you can think about your entire self, your thoughts, your life history, whether we call this an examination of conscience or something else. A material thing cannot do that.

Our soul can turn completely around and look at itself; or, as the philosophers put it, our soul can "reflect on" itself. I can know something, and stand off and examine my knowledge. I can think, and in the very act of thinking, my mind can be scrutinizing the thinking process. I can choose to do something, and in the very act of making the choice, I can analyze the motives behind the choice. I can love, and still weigh and appraise my love in the very act of loving. This consciousness-of-self which we have—this ability to know, and at the same time to know *that* we know, is proof of the fact that our soul is not a material substance. Our soul could never look at itself, turn back upon itself, "reflect"

---

[3] See Questions 22 and 23 below.

upon itself, if it were made up of parts, as every material substance is.[4]

One way to illustrate the spiritual nature of reflection is to take a piece of paper and fold it over. The top half can "look" at the bottom half and vice versa. But because the paper is matter and is bound by its material dimensions, the paper cannot get outside of itself and "look" back on its entire self. Only a spiritual thing can reflect on itself. The fact that you can reflect on yourself proves that you are spiritual.

We know that our souls are spiritual because we can do spiritual things—that is, we can abstract and reflect. We know by observation that plants and animals, which cannot abstract and reflect, are material beings. Man, however, is a compound made of a material body and a spiritual soul.[5]

21. So what if man has a spiritual soul? What difference does that make?

A lot. Because you are spiritual, it follows that you are by nature immortal—that is, that your soul will never die. Of course, God could annihilate any created thing, including your soul. But we have God's word in revelation that he will not do that. What is important here is the fact that, by its very nature, your soul is immortal.

To prove that the soul is immortal and will never die we first have to understand what death is. Death is the breaking up of an entity into its component parts. In this sense, graduation brings about the "death" of the unit that was a championship

---

[4] Trese, *Wisdom Shall Enter*, 27–28.
[5] See *S.T.*, I, Q. 75–76; *E.V.*, no. 60.

football team. The death of a human being is the breaking up, the separation, of the component parts of that human being. Those component parts are the body and the soul—a material part and a spiritual part that itself has no parts.

The human being dies when the soul leaves the body. After the soul and body have separated, the death of the body occurs; the body decomposes, breaking up into its component parts. The determination as to whether a person has died is essentially a medical and scientific question.

The unifying concept here is that the death of anything is its breaking up into its component parts. But the human soul, being spiritual, has no parts, and therefore, by its nature, it will not die.[6] Father Trese summarized the point well:

> If the soul is a spirit, it must then be immortal, incapable of death. Because by definition a spirit is a simple substance, with no parts, no extension in space. (Part of my soul is not in my head, and part in my hands, and part in my feet. All of my soul is in every part of me, much as all of God is in every part of the Universe.)
>
> The soul being a simple substance, independent of the limitations of matter, it follows that there is nothing in the soul that can decompose, be destroyed, or cease to be. Death is the breaking up of a living organism into its component parts; but with the human soul, there just isn't anything "to break up." Thus our reason alone, even aside from God's divine revelation, tells us that our soul will never die.[7]

We know from observation that a dog cannot abstract and reflect. We are justified in concluding that the dog's soul is not a spiritual substance that would be "independent of the limitations of matter".[8] The soul of a dog, rather, is mate-

---

[6] See *S.T.*, I, Q. 75, art. 6.
[7] Trese, *Wisdom Shall Enter*, 29–30.
[8] Ibid.

rial, in that it is dependent on the material body of the dog for its existence and functioning. Because a dog has a material soul, wholly dependent on its material body, its soul will not survive the death of its body. A dog, therefore, is not by its nature immortal. "It is, then, clearly impossible for any operation of the brute animal's soul to be independent of its body. And from this it can be inferred with necessity that the soul of the brute perishes with the body."[9] The wise priest, however, was technically correct in reassuring the questioning boy, "Yes, you will have your dog with you in heaven if you want him." We will be perfectly happy in heaven, and, as a special act of providence, God could reunite the boy with his dog.[10] By its nature, however, the dog is not immortal.

Carl Becker asserted that in the light of "modern science" it is impossible "to regard man as the child of God for whom the earth was created as a temporary habitation. Rather we must regard him as little more than a chance deposit on the surface of the world, carelessly thrown up between two ice ages by the same forces that rust iron and ripen corn. . . . It has taken eight centuries to replace the conception of existence as [a] divinely composed and purposeful drama by the conception of existence as a blindly running flux of integrating energy."[11] On the contrary, however, as Saint Thomas put it, "the human soul is incorruptible."[12] Some day you will die and your body will decompose. But your soul will never die. Ultimately, as revelation tells us, you body will be reunited with your soul at

---

[9] Saint Thomas Aquinas, *Summa contra Gentiles* (James E. Anderson, transl., 1975), book II, chap. 82, p. 272.

[10] See Peter Kreeft, *Everything You Ever Wanted to Know about Heaven — But Never Dreamed of Asking* (1990), 45–46.

[11] Carl. L. Becker, *The Heavenly City of the Eighteenth Century Philosophers* (1932), 14.

[12] *S.T.*, I, Q. 75, art. 6.

the last judgment.[13] Having begun your life in your mother's womb, you will live on for all eternity.

So the "manufacturer's directions" provided in the natural law are not for a car with a useful life of five years or 50,000 miles. Rather, those directions provide guidance for a subject who will live forever. We should, therefore, consider whether our actions in the present life might affect our quality of life after death. Moreover, it makes a difference legally and politically whether the function of the state is to govern a collection of material individuals with no destiny beyond the grave or to establish a community for spiritual persons whose destiny transcends the state.

---

[13] See *S.T.*, Suppl., Q. 75; *V.S.*, no. 10.

VI

THE REASONED FOUNDATION:
GOD AS KNOWN
THROUGH REASON

22. Do you really claim that we can prove from reason alone that God exists?

Yes. This point merits extended attention. The natural law is almost meaningless apart from its lawgiver, who is God. But as soon as we introduce God into the discussion some people tend to switch off. Perhaps they have bought the Enlightenment notion that reason can know nothing about God and that all statements about religion are expressions of mere emotion. Of course, through the gift of faith we know that God exists. But is that merely a blind faith unsupported by reason? Obviously, our reason cannot of itself provide us with complete knowledge of God; if it could we would ourselves be God.[1] Nevertheless, through our reason we are able to gain some certain knowledge of God.[2] Not only that, but it is unreasonable not to believe in God.

"In . . . his Letter to the Romans, St. Paul . . . declares a profound truth: through all that is created the 'eyes of the mind' can come to know God. Through the medium of creatures, God stirs in reason an intuition of his 'power' and his 'divinity'. . . . Not only is it not restricted to sensory knowledge . . . but, by discoursing on the data provided by the senses, reason can reach the cause which lies at the origin of all perceptible reality."[3]

Saint Thomas spelled out five proofs from reason for the existence of God.[4] Briefly summarized, they are:

---

[1] See *S.T.*, I, Q. 88, art. 3.
[2] See generally, Edward D. O'Connor, C.S.C., *The Catholic Vision* (1992).
[3] *F.R.*, no. 22.
[4] See discussion in Peter Kreeft, *A Summa of the Summa* (1990), 53–70.

1. *Motion.* If the red lights flashed, the gates came down, and you stopped your car at the train crossing, what would your reaction be if only an empty freight car passed by? You would wonder what was making that freight car move. What is in motion must be put in motion by another and that by another again. This cannot go on to infinity. Therefore, at the head of the series of movers there must be a being that is itself unmoved and that is the source of all movement. This prime mover is God.

> The existence of God can be proved in five ways. The first and more manifest way is the argument from motion. It is certain, and evident to our senses, that in the world some things are in motion. Now whatever is in motion is put in motion by another, for nothing can be moved except it is in potentiality to that towards which it is in motion; whereas a thing moves inasmuch as it is in act. For motion is nothing else than the reduction of something from potentiality to actuality. But nothing can be reduced from potentiality to actuality, except by something in a state of actuality. Thus that which is actually hot, as fire, makes wood, which is potentially hot, to be actually hot, and thereby moves and changes it. Now it is not possible that the same thing should be at once in actuality and potentiality in the same respect, but only in different respects. For what is actually hot cannot simultaneously be potentially hot; but it is simultaneously potentially cold. It is therefore impossible that in the same respect and in the same way a thing should be both mover and moved, i.e., that it should move itself. Therefore, whatever is in motion must be put in motion by another. If that by which it is put in motion be itself put in motion, then this also must needs be put in motion by another, and that by another again. But this cannot go on to infinity, because then there would be no first mover, and, consequently, no other mover; seeing that subsequent movers move only inas-

much as they are put in motion by the first mover; as the staff moves only because it is put in motion by the hand. Therefore it is necessary to arrive at a first mover, put in motion by no other; and this everyone understands to be God.[5]

2. *Causation.* This proof depends on the self-evident principles that nothing can exist without a sufficient reason for its existence and that every effect must have a cause. It is impossible for a thing to be the efficient—that is, immediately effective—cause of itself; if it were, it would be prior to itself, which is impossible. Because every effect must have a cause, that cause in turn must be the effect of another cause, and so on. But the process cannot go on to infinity. There must be a first cause that is not caused by anything else and that contains in itself the sufficient reason for its existence. That first cause is God.[6] No one could ever borrow a book if each lender had to borrow it first from someone else ad infinitum.[7]

> The second way is from the nature of the efficient cause. In the world of sense we find there is an order of efficient causes. There is no case known (neither is it, indeed, possible) in which a thing is found to be the efficient cause of itself; for so it would be prior to itself, which is impossible. Now in efficient causes it is not possible to go on to infinity, because in all efficient causes following in order, the first is the cause of the intermediate cause, and the intermediate is

---

[5] *S.T.*, I, Q. 2, art. 3. See also Aristotle, *Physics*, book VII, chap. 1 (R. P. Hardie and R. K. Gage, transl.), in *Basic Works of Aristotle* (Richard McKeon, ed., 1941), 340.

[6] See Walter Farrell, *A Companion to the Summa* (1941), vol. 1, 34–35.

[7] See David R. Lang's account of the debate "Does God Exist?" between Peter Kreeft and Paul Breines at Boston College on Sept. 10, 1986, in *The Wanderer*, Oct. 23, 1986, p. 1.

the cause of the ultimate cause, whether the intermediate cause be several, or one only. Now to take away the cause is to take away the effect. Therefore, if there be no first cause among efficient causes, there will be no ultimate, nor any intermediate, cause. But if in efficient causes it is possible to go on to infinity, there will be no first efficient cause, neither will there be an ultimate effect, nor any intermediate efficient causes; all of which is plainly false. Therefore it is necessary to admit a first efficient cause, to which everyone gives the name of God.[8]

3. *Necessity or contingency.* This proof, too, depends on the self-evident principle of sufficient reason—that is, that whatever exists must have a sufficient reason for its existence. If there was ever a time when there was nothing, there could never be anything. From nothing, nothing can come. The film version of *The Sound of Music* had it right: "Nothing comes from nothing, nothing ever could." There must have always existed, from all eternity without any beginning, a necessary being, from whom beings that began to be received their existence. The existence of all other beings is contingent on the existence of this necessary being. If this always-existent being did not exist, neither could anything else exist. This necessary being is God. "The word, 'create', means 'to call into being from non-being,' that is, from 'nothingness.' To be created means not to possess in oneself the source, the reason of one's being, but to receive it 'from another.' He Who creates—the Creator—possesses existence in Himself and from Himself. To *be* pertains to His substance: His essence is *to be*. He is subsisting being. Precisely for this reason, He cannot not be; He is 'necessary being.' Differing from God who is 'necessary being,' the things which receive existence from Him, that is, creatures, are able not to be:

---

[8] *S.T.*, I, Q. 2, art. 3.

being does not constitute their essence; they are 'contingent' beings."[9]

> The third way is taken from possibility and necessity, and runs thus. We find in nature things that are possible to be and not to be, since they are found to be generated, and to corrupt, and consequently, they are possible to be and not to be. But it is impossible for these always to exist, for that which is possible not to be at some time is not. Therefore, if everything is possible not to be, then at one time there could have been nothing in existence. Now if this were true, even now there would be nothing in existence, because that which does not exist only begins to exist through something already existing. Therefore, if at one time nothing was in existence, it would have been impossible for anything to have begun to exist; and thus even now nothing would be in existence—which is absurd. Therefore, not all beings are merely possible, but there must exist something the existence of which is necessary. But every necessary thing either has its necessity caused by another, or not. Now it is impossible to go on to infinity in necessary things which have their necessity caused by another, as has been already proved in regard to efficient causes. Therefore we cannot but postulate the existence of some being having of itself its own necessity, and not receiving it from another, but rather causing in others their necessity. This all men speak of as God.[10]

4. *Perfection.* When we see things or other persons, we judge that they are more or less good, beautiful, kind, just, and so forth. But this judgment presupposes an absolute standard of perfection with which the less perfect are compared. This ab-

---

[9] Pope John Paul II, General Audience, Aug. 7, 1985, 20 *Talks of Pope John Paul II* (Pro Ecclesia, 509 Madison Ave., New York, N.Y. 10022), 51 (1985); *L'Osservatore Romano* (English ed.), Aug. 12, 1985, p. 5.

[10] *S.T.*, I, Q. 2, art. 3.

solute standard of perfection is God. Saint Thomas' explanation is clear and to the point:

> The fourth way is taken from the gradation to be found in things. Among beings there are some more and some less good, true, noble, and the like. But *more* and *less* are predicated of different things according as they resemble in their different ways something which is the maximum, as a thing is said to be hotter according as it more nearly resembles that which is hottest; so that there is something which is truest, something best, something noblest, and, consequently, something which is uttermost being; for those things that are greatest in truth are greatest in being, as it is written in [Aristotle's] *Metaph. ii.* Now the maximum in any genus is the cause of all in that genus; as fire, which is the maximum of heat, is the cause of all hot things. Therefore there must also be something which is to all beings the cause of their being, goodness, and every other perfection; and this we call God.[11]

5. *Design.* Whatever exhibits marks of design must be the work of an intelligent being. Nobody could possibly believe that his wrist watch just "fell together". On the contrary, it was obviously designed by an intelligent designer. How much more so with the human body, the world, and the universe. They all give evidence of an intelligent designer. The order of the universe, the workings of the human eye, and so forth, cannot believably be the product of chance or of some blind necessity in the nature of things. Their intelligent designer is God.

Whittaker Chambers, former senior editor of *Time* and a member of the Communist spy ring that included Alger Hiss, wrote:

---

[11] Ibid.

I date my break [from Communism] from a very casual happening. I was sitting in our apartment on St. Paul Street in Baltimore. It was shortly before we moved to Alger Hiss's apartment in Washington. My daughter was in her high chair. I was watching her eat. She was the most miraculous thing that had ever happened in my life. I liked to watch her even when she smeared porridge on her face or dropped it meditatively on the floor. My eye came to rest on the delicate convolutions of her ear—those intricate, perfect ears. The thought passed through my mind: "No, those ears were not created by any chance coming together of atoms in nature (the Communist view). They could have been created only by immense design." The thought was involuntary and unwanted. I crowded it out of my mind. But I never wholly forgot it or the occasion. I had to crowd it out of my mind. If I had completed it, I should have had to say: Design presupposes God. I did not then know that, at that moment, the finger of God was first laid upon my forehead.[12]

Saint Thomas argues to the same conclusion:

The fifth way is taken from the governance of the world. We see that things which lack intelligence, such as natural bodies, act for an end, and this is evident from their acting always, or nearly always, in the same way, so as to obtain the best result. Hence it is plain that not fortuitously, but designedly, do they achieve their end. Now whatever lacks intelligence cannot move towards an end, unless it be directed by some being endowed with knowledge and intelligence; as the arrow is shot to its mark by the archer. Therefore some intelligent being exists by whom all natural things are directed to their end; and this being we call God.[13]

---

[12] Whittaker Chambers, *Witness* (1952), 16.

[13] *S.T.*, I, Q. 2, art. 3. Saint Paul may have had the argument from design in mind when he said, "What may be known about God is manifest to them.

These are the five proofs advanced by Saint Thomas Aquinas to prove the existence of God. Two other proofs should be mentioned:

1. *The argument from conscience.* A notable statement of this proof was written by Cardinal John Henry Newman:

> If, as is the case, we feel responsibility, are ashamed, are frightened, at transgressing the voice of conscience, this implies that there is One to whom we are responsible, before whom we are ashamed, whose claims upon us we fear. If, on doing wrong, we feel the same tearful, broken-hearted sorrow which overwhelms us in hurting a mother; if, on doing right, we enjoy the same sunny serenity of mind, the same soothing satisfactory delight which follows on our receiving praise from a father, we certainly have within us the image of some person, to whom our love and veneration look, in whose smile we find our happiness, for whom we yearn, towards whom we direct our pleadings, in whose anger we are troubled and waste away. These feelings in us are such as require for their exciting cause an intelligent being; we are not affectionate towards a stone, nor do we feel shame before a horse or a dog; we have no remorse or compunction on breaking mere human law: yet, so it is, conscience excites all these painful emotions, confusion, foreboding, self-condemnation; and on the other hand it sheds upon us a deep peace, a sense of security, a resignation, and a hope, which there is no sensible, no earthly object to elicit. "The wicked flees when no one pursueth;" then why does he flee? whence his terror? Who is it that he sees in solitude, in darkness, in the hidden chambers of his heart? If the cause of these emotions does not belong to this visible world, the Object

---

For God has manifested it to them. For since the creation of the world his invisible attributes are clearly seen—his everlasting power also and divinity —being understood through the things that are made" (Rom 1:19–20).

towards which his perception is directed must be Supernatural and Divine; and thus the phenomena of Conscience, as a dictate, avail to impress the imagination with the picture of a Supreme Governor, a Judge, holy, just, powerful, all-seeing, retributive, and is the creative principle of religion, as the Moral Sense is the principle of ethics.[14]

2. *The argument from universal belief.* Like the argument from conscience, this proof is not conclusive. Rather, the existence of an almost universal belief in the existence of God strongly corroborates the conclusion that God exists. "The divine origin of this spirit of life explains the perennial dissatisfaction which man feels throughout his days on earth. Because he is made by God and bears within himself an indelible imprint of God, man is naturally drawn to God."[15] It is generally true that every people or tribe has had some kind of belief in a supreme being. With some exceptions, the human race as a whole has manifested a belief in the existence of God, despite wide variances in these beliefs. Such a belief, prevailing among men of all times and accepted by men of all degrees of ignorance or knowledge, cannot reasonably be accounted for except on the supposition that such a belief is a right conclusion of human reason. The universality of this belief cannot be explained as merely a result of fear, desire, or fraud. Rather, its universality among men is evidence of its reasonableness. "Throughout history even to the present day," said the Second Vatican Council, "There is found among different peoples a certain awareness of a hidden power, which lies behind the course of nature and the events of human life. At times, there is present even a recognition of a supreme being, or still more of a Fa-

---

[14] John Henry Newman, *Grammar of Assent* (1979 ed.) chap. 5, sec. 1, 101.
[15] *E.V.*, no. 35.

ther. This awareness and recognition results in a way of life that is imbued with a deep religious sense."[16]

The natural law is accessible to reason. And so is the fact of the existence of God as the author of that law.[17] Too often, we tend to assume that to believe in God is an exercise in witchcraft and that those who deny God are the reasonable people. In fact, as the proofs from reason for the existence of God indicate, belief in God is fully reasonable. Even more, it is wholly unreasonable not to believe in God. One who denies the existence of God must be prepared to say that an endless chain of movers is possible without a prime mover; that an infinite chain of causes is conceivable without an uncaused first cause; that something can come from absolutely nothing; that there is no ultimate and absolute standard of perfection; that the marvelous workings of the human brain, for example, can occur through blind chance without intelligent design; and that the universal testimony of man and of the human conscience is of little or no account.

23. What can we know through reason about God?

With our limited intellects we cannot know the infinite God fully. But we can prove certain attributes or perfections of God by reason. Significantly, the Catholic Church even affirms as a dogma this ability of reason to know God. In the words of Pope John Paul II:

---

[16] Second Vatican Council, *Declaration on the Relationship of the Church to Non-Christian Religions (Nostra Aetate)*, no. 2.

[17] See Ronda Chervin, *A Contemporary Look at Old Arguments for God's Existence*. Pamphlet no. 4004 (New Hope, Ky.: Faith Guild, 1993).

Divine Revelation is indeed at the basis of faith: of man's "I believe." At the same time, the passages of Sacred Scripture in which this Revelation has been consigned teach us that *man is capable* of knowing God by reason alone: he is capable of a *certain "knowledge" about God*, even though indirectly and not immediately. Therefore, alongside the "I believe" we find a certain "I know." This "I know" concerns the existence of God and even, to a certain extent, His essence.[18]

The First Vatican Council, in 1869–70, stated dogmatically: "Holy Mother Church holds and teaches that God, the origin and end of all things, can be known with certainty by the natural light of human reason from the things that he created."[19] That Council enumerated the attributes or perfections of God:

> The holy, Catholic, apostolic Roman Church believes and professes that there is one true and living God, the Creator and Lord of heaven and earth. He is almighty, eternal, beyond measure, incomprehensible, and infinite in intellect, will and in every perfection.
> Since he is one unique spiritual substance, entirely simple and unchangeable, he must be declared really and essentially distinct from the world, perfectly happy in himself and by his very nature, and inexpressibly exalted over all things that exist or can be conceived other than himself.[20]

One purpose of this book is to emphasize that the natural law is knowable to human reason. We can gain some appreciation of the power of right reason to know the truth with certainty if we examine the process by which we can know through reason even certain attributes of God himself. Among those attributes are the following:

---

[18] Pope John Paul II, General Audience, Mar. 20, 1985, *The Wanderer*, Apr. 11, 1985, p. 1.

[19] First Vatican Council, *Dogmatic Constitution on the Catholic Faith*, no. 2.

[20] Ibid., no. 1; John A. Hardon, S.J., *The Catholic Catechism* (1975), 55.

1. *Infinite.* God is without limit. He cannot be measured. As we saw before in the proofs of God's existence, God is the necessary being, the cause of all the universe. He is self-sufficient in that he has within himself the sufficient reason for his own existence. God is not dependent in any way on any other person or thing. It is impossible that this necessary and self-sufficient being could be limited in any way. If there were any perfection lacking to God, we would have to ask, "Where did that perfection come from, which God does not have?" If God were lacking in any perfection, he would not be the first and necessary cause of everything. "The Fathers of the Church", writes Father John Hardon, "furnished the vocabulary for this attribute. They speak of God as infinite, boundless, uncircumscribed. . . . Theologically, this goes beyond affirming that God has no limitations. It says that he has within himself the fullness of all perfection, whether knowledge or power or being."[21]

2. *One.* There is only one God. It is impossible that there could be more than one necessary, infinite being who is the cause of everything. If there were two "gods", each with jurisdiction over its own portion of reality, we would have to ask, "Who divided reality between them?" Ultimately, we have to come back to one first cause, one necessary and infinite being. Monsignor Paul Glenn summarized the teaching of Saint Thomas Aquinas on this point:

> God is infinite, and a plurality of infinities cannot be. If, by an impossible supposition, there were two infinite beings, "X" and "Y", then: either (a) "X" and "Y" would have identical perfections, and thus would actually be one being and not two; or (b) "X" would have its own perfections which "Y" would lack; thus neither being would be infinite, for

---

[21] Hardon, *The Catholic Catechism*, 56–57.

what lacks any perfection is, by that fact, finite or imperfect. Thus it is inconceivable that there should be more than one infinite being. That is to say, it is inconceivable that there should be more than one God.[22]

3. *Simple.* God is simple, which means in this sense that he has no parts. If God were composed of parts, we would have to ask, "Who put the parts together?"

> Since God is infinite and uncaused, it follows that he is *simple*, i.e., not composed of parts or elements. In other words, God is not a *composite* or *compounded* being. Every composite being is contingent upon the union of its parts and requires a uniting cause to bring these parts into union. But in God there is neither contingency nor subjection to causality. Again, the parts of a composite being are logically or naturally prior to their union; and there is nothing prior to the eternal God, the *necessary* First Cause. God, therefore, is *simple*. He has *no possessed parts or perfections*; His perfections are one with His undivided essence; all that God *has*, He *is*. Thus, properly speaking God does not *have* wisdom; God *is* Wisdom. Wisdom is one with the infinite essence of God, and hence God is Infinite Wisdom. Similarly, God is Infinite Justice, Infinite Mercy, Infinite Power, etc.[23]

4. *Spiritual.* God, as a simple being, is a spirit, for if God were material, he would be composed of parts, and, again, we would have to ask, "Where did the parts come from and who put the parts together?" Material parts by their nature are finite or limited. But a number of finite or limited parts cannot add up to an infinite or unlimited being. And we know that God, as the necessary, self-sufficient being, is infinite. "Since God

---

[22] Paul J. Glenn, *A Tour of the Summa* (1978), 12.
[23] Paul J. Glenn, *Apologetics* (1931), 59–60.

is simple, He is *spiritual*. For a real, subsistent being must be either bodily or spiritual. Now, a bodily being is always made of bodily parts, is contingent upon these parts and upon their union, is *composite*. But, as we have seen, God is not composite, but simple. He is therefore not bodily; it remains that He is spiritual. And being infinite in all perfection, He is a Spirit infinitely perfect."[24]

5. *Eternal.* As the necessary being, God must be eternal. If there was ever a time when there was nothing, there could never be anything. When we say that God is eternal, we mean that he always was and always will be. Time is the measure of change (or motion). But in God there is no change because he is infinite and perfect, self-sufficient and necessary. Therefore there is no measure of change—that is, there is no time—with respect to God. Rather, God is in that "now", without time, which we call eternity—that is, he is eternal.[25]

> Since God has no perfection distinct from His essence, His eternity is one with Himself. God is necessary being, un-caused, without beginning or end. His existence does not protract itself through successive moments, days, years, centuries; it is wholly present in a single unending *now*. For God there is no past, no future, but an all-embracing present, a single undying universal instant. The proof of God's eternity lies in the fact of His necessity. A necessary being must exist, and cannot be non-existent; existence belongs to its very essence. Obviously such a being is *always* a necessary being (else, it *began* to be necessary under action of some cause, and so is *contingent* and not necessary at all!); and be-

---

[24] Ibid., 60.
[25] See *S.T.*, I, Q. 10, art. 1, 2.

ing always necessary, it is always existent; in other words, it is *eternal*.[26]

6. *Personal.* God is personal. A person, in the classical definition, is an individual substance with intellect and will. We know God has the attributes of intellect and will because he designed and created the world. Designing is a spiritual act of the intellect and can be done only by a person.

> The intelligence of the First Cause of the universe can be deduced from the fact that in the universe there are intelligent beings; no effect can be essentially superior to its efficient cause. However, a more detailed and satisfying argument can be developed in the so-called teleological proof; there is a constant and universal manifestation of order in the world, an order characterized by such purposeful activity and harmonious design that it must be according to the plan of an intelligent designer. . . . The order and harmony and design of the world as a whole, as a complete thing, can never be adequately accounted for unless we admit that the ultimate efficient cause of that universe is intelligent.[27]

In Question 25, we will discuss the reality that the persons of the Trinity are relations rather than isolated individuals. In this question, however, we are merely concerned to note that we can know from reason that God is personal.

7. *Omnipresent.* God is present everywhere at all times. Because God is a spirit, he is not present in a place in the same way that a material body is present. Space and size are meaningless in relation to God. Rather, all of God is everywhere.

---

[26] Glenn, *Apologetics*, 64–65.
[27] James H. Dolan, S.J., *Theses in Natural Theology* (1952), 29.

God is the infinite, necessary first cause of everything. If there were a place where God is not, he would not be infinite. "God is present in every place, in every part of the existing universe. God is wholly and entirely present in every place, and this in such wise that He is not circumscribed or bounded by the boundaries of the place. God is wholly present in all the world and in all parts of the world, but he is in no wise identified with the world.—The proof of this lies in God's infinity. For the infinite must have limitless perfection—including the perfection of existence everywhere—and must be free from every limitation—such as being bounded or constrained within the limits of any place or places."[28]

8. *Omniscient.* God knows everything, past, present, and future. Nothing has happened, is now happening, or will or could happen in the future that is not dependent on the infinite power of the necessary being who is God. And God is not subject to the limitations of time. With reference to God's eternity, the whole of what we know as time is present. God knows whether we shall go to Chicago next year, whether we shall succeed in school, and whether we shall sin. "If there could be anything, actual or possible, hidden from God's knowledge, then God would not be infinite; He would be limited by the limitation of His knowledge. And if God were dependent upon the truth that He knows, His knowledge would be *contingent*, and, since God's knowledge is a substantial actuality which is one with the divine essence, God himself would be *contingent* and not *necessary*."[29] However, God's knowledge (or foreknowledge) of what we do does not deprive us of free will in doing it.[30] Saint

---

[28] Glenn, *Apologetics*, 66.

[29] Ibid., 67.

[30] On free will, see *C.C.C.*, nos. 1730–48.

Thomas affirms that "the will of God is the cause of things."[31] God allows us to participate in the causative aspects of his will by giving us free will and allowing us to will for ourselves and cause the actions that we do. God "suspends" his will by allowing us to exercise our free will. From our perspective we distinguish God's will from his knowledge. But his knowledge of what we will do is not causative: His knowledge does not force us to do anything nor does it predetermine our acts, although he knows what we will choose to do.

Although God knows whether we shall sin and whether we shall save our souls, our actions in this regard are not determined by God. They are, rather, the products of our own free choice.[32]

> *The human will in many actions enjoys a true freedom of choice.* . . . In many of our acts we have this clear consciousness of our freedom of choice: (1) Before the act; we are conscious of our deliberation about the reasons for or against a definite action; without freedom of choice, this deliberation would be absurd. (2) During the decision; we are conscious of free consent, and because of this we are careful, realizing we are assuming responsibility. (3) After the decision; we are conscious that we could have decided otherwise, and we blame or praise ourselves alone for any regret or credit accruing from the action. Unless our wills had a freedom of choice with regard to these actions, the deliberation, decision, and assumption of merit or demerit would be absurd.[33]

As Archbishop Fulton J. Sheen put it, "The simple words 'Thank you' will always stand out as a refutation of deter-

---

[31] *S.T.*, I, Q. 19, art. 4.
[32] See *C.C.C.*, nos. 1730–48.
[33] Joseph F. Sullivan, S.J., *General Ethics* (1931), 3.

minism, for they imply that something which was done could possibly have been left undone."[34]

9. *Omnipotent.* As the infinite being, God is all-powerful. There is nothing he cannot do. Could God make a rock so heavy he could not lift it? Could God make a square circle? These are contradictions in terms and cannot exist. They cannot even be conceived, let alone exist. All that can be done, God can do since he is in his very essence unlimited in his perfections, including his power. "To say that God is omnipotent is to say that He is *almighty* (i.e., all-mighty, all-powerful). God does not make any *effort* in accomplishing what He wills to do, nor is He limited to one work at a time, nor is He fatigued by His work, nor is His work built up, so to speak, bit by bit. God perfectly accomplishes what He wills to do by the eternal decrees of His perfect *will.* With God, to will and to perform is one and the same act. The proof of these assertions is found in God's infinite perfection. Infinite perfection includes boundless power, and excludes the imperfections of toil, effort, fatigue, successive partial accomplishment, etc."[35] Not only is God not dead. He is not even tired.

10. *All-perfect.* God as the infinite and necessary being is the source of all perfections. He therefore has the fullness of all perfections. He is all-good, all-just, all-merciful. Indeed, it is more correct to say not that God is good but that God is goodness. The perfections of God are of the very nature and substance of God. That is why we can say, "God is love. God is wisdom." "The perfection of God is infinite. . . . The totally self-sufficient essence must contain within itself every possible

---

[34] Fulton J. Sheen, *The Life of All Living* (1979), 23.

[35] Glenn, *Apologetics*, 68–69.

degree of every possible perfection, since in that self-sufficient, absolutely necessary nature a potency for perfection, or a potency for any further degree of perfection cannot be admitted."[36]

Our reason cannot give us a complete picture of God because human reason and human terms are limited. We do know from reason, however, that God exists and that he, the supreme being, is an infinitely perfect spirit with certain attributes. Of this we can be certain even without the aid of revelation. However, through revelation God has told us a great deal about himself.

---

[36] Dolan, *Theses in Natural Theology*, 42.

VII

REVELATION AS THE NECESSARY COMPLETION OF NATURAL LAW: WHAT GOD HAS TOLD US ABOUT HIMSELF AND ABOUT MAN

24. Why bring revelation or "religion" into this? All you will do is turn people off.

To this point this book has focused on the jurisprudence of Saint Thomas Aquinas and its reasoned foundations. That jurisprudence, however, can be adequately understood only in the context of the divine law made known to us by revelation.[1] What is generally known as Aquinas' *Treatise on Law*[2] is a comparatively brief part of his *Summa Theologica*, which is essentially a work of theology. And the *Treatise on Law* is less than half of Aquinas' formal treatment of law; it is followed by his discussion of the moral, ceremonial, and judicial precepts of the Old Testament.[3] Saint Thomas affirmed the divine law as a necessary complement to the natural law, and he relied on that divine law in his frequent references to Scripture.

Saint Thomas' emphasis on revelation provides a bridge to the interpretation of that revelation by the Magisterium, which integrates the work of Saint Thomas into its authoritative exposition both of the human person and of Christ as the moral norm. That work of the Magisterium is the subject of Questions 35 through 49 of this book. The intention here is merely to note the indispensability of revelation to the natural law teaching of Saint Thomas. As we shall see in later Questions, it is fully in accord with the spirit of his teaching for the natural law to find its completion and sublimation through the authoritative interpretation of revelation by the Magisterium.

This book is neither a catechism nor a theological treatise. But it will be useful to outline some particulars of what Saint

---

[1] See Question 6 above.
[2] *S.T.*, I, II, Q. 90–97.
[3] *S.T.*, I, II, Q. 98–108.

Thomas, as a Catholic, believed about the revelation provided by God. In Question 6 above, we listed the four reasons Saint Thomas gives for needing the divine law—that is, revelation —in addition to natural law and human law. This is a recurrent theme for Aquinas. In the very first question in the entire *Summa Theologica*, Saint Thomas, the great exponent of reason, asks "whether, besides Philosophy, any Further Doctrine is Required". He answers Yes in a passage important enough to quote in full:

> It was necessary for man's salvation that there should be a knowledge revealed by God, besides philosophical science built up by human reason. Firstly, indeed, because man is directed to God, as to an end that surpasses the grasp of his reason: "The eye hath not seen O God, besides Thee, what things Thou hast prepared for them that wait for Thee." (*Isa.* lxiv. 4). But the end must first be known by men who are to direct their thoughts and actions to the end. Hence it was necessary for the salvation of man that certain truths which exceed human reason should be made known to him by divine revelation. Even as regards those truths about God which human reason could have discovered, it was necessary that man should be taught by a divine revelation; because the truth about God such as reason could discover, would only be known by a few, and that after a long time, and with the admixture of many errors. Whereas man's whole salvation, which is in God, depends upon the knowledge of this truth. Therefore, in order that the salvation of men might be brought about more fitly and more surely, it was necessary that they should be taught divine truths by divine revelation. It was therefore necessary that, besides philosophical science built up by reason there should be a sacred science learned through revelation.[4]

---

[4] *S.T.*, I, Q. 1, art. 1.

We need revelation so we can know readily and with certainty what the natural law requires in specific cases. Revelation provides certainty in areas where we, in our fallen state, could attain the truth only with difficulty "and with the admixture of many errors".[5] Some truths disclosed in revelation are beyond the power of unaided reason to discern. But there is nothing in revelation inconsistent with reason. And it makes sense to rely on what God has explicitly revealed.

We must avoid the error of "fideism" (faith without reason), but it is equally important to avoid the opposing error of "rationalism" (reason without faith).[6] Faith and reason are complementary. And, as the First Vatican Council (1869–70) definitively put it, "although faith is above reason, yet there can never be any real disagreement between faith and reason, because it is the same God who reveals mysteries and infuses faith and has put the light of reason into the human soul. Now God cannot deny himself any more than the truth can ever contradict the truth."[7]

Through reason we can know the existence and attributes of God, the immortality of the soul, the principles of the natural law, and other basic truths. Beyond this knowledge, we accept what God has told us explicitly, through our exercise of the gift of faith. "Man is able to recognize good and evil thanks to that discernment of good from evil which he himself carries out by his reason, in particular by his reason enlightened by Divine Revelation and by faith, through the law which God

---

[5] Ibid.

[6] Pope John Paul II, *Address to Eighth International Thomistic Congress*, Sept. 13, 1980, *L'Osservatore Romano* (English ed.), Oct. 20, 1980, p. 9; see General Audience, July 17, 1985, *20 Talks of Pope John Paul II* 43 (1985); *F.R.*, nos. 52, 55.

[7] First Vatican Council, *Constitution on Faith*, chap. 4; John F. Clarkson, S.J., et al., eds., *The Church Teaches* (1973), 33.

gave to the Chosen People, beginning with the commandments on Sinai."[8] In *Veritatis Splendor*, John Paul said, "The attempt to set freedom in opposition to truth, and indeed to separate them radically, is the consequence, manifestation and consummation of *another more serious and destructive dichotomy, that which separates faith from morality*."[9] Faith was defined by the First Vatican Council as "a super-natural virtue" through which, "with the inspiration and help of God's grace, we believe that what he has revealed is true—not because its intrinsic truth is seen with the natural light of reason—but because of the authority of God who reveals it, of God who can neither deceive nor be deceived."[10] The virtue of faith is "essentially a gift of God".[11] Faith is "the power to know God as he has revealed himself".[12] It is our response to God's revelation of himself to us.[13]

"Faith is . . . an obedient response to God. This implies that God be acknowledged in his divinity, transcendence and supreme freedom."[14] " 'The obedience of faith' . . . must be given to God as he reveals himself. By faith man freely commits his entire self to God, making 'the full submission of his intellect and will to God who reveals,' and willingly assenting to the Revelation given by him. Before this faith can be exercised, man must have the grace of God to move and assist him."[15] Before he became Pope, John Paul II wrote: "Faith . . .

---

[8] *V.S.*, no. 44.

[9] Ibid., no. 88.

[10] First Vatican Council, *Constitution on Faith*, chap. 3; Clarkson et al., *The Church Teaches*, 28–29.

[11] Ibid.

[12] John A. Hardon, S.J., *The Catholic Catechism* (1975), 33.

[13] See *C.C.C.*, nos. 142–34.

[14] *F.R.*, no. 13.

[15] Second Vatican Council, *Dogmatic Constitution on Divine Revelation* (*Dei*

is not merely the response of the mind to an abstract truth. . . . 'The obedience of faith' is not bound to any particular human faculty but relates to man's whole personal structure and spiritual dynamism. Man's proper response to God's self-revelation consists in self-abandonment to God. This is the true dimension of faith, in which man does not merely accept a particular set of propositions, but accepts his own vocation and the sense of his existence."[16]

Pope John Paul II said:

[Saint Thomas Aquinas] emphasizes the *supernatural* value of faith: it transcends the natural intellect as a light infused by God for knowing truth, which surpasses the possibilities and demands of pure reason. Nevertheless, it is not a matter of an *irrational* act, but of a vital synthesis in which the main factor is doubtless the divine, which moves the will to adhere to the truth revealed by God, Lord of intelligence, absolutely infallible and holy. However, the act of faith also includes a certain *reasonableness*, both in the believer's reference to the historical evidence of relative *fact*, as well as in the correct understanding of the metaphysical and theological presupposition that God can neither deceive nor be deceived. Faith moreover has its own *rationality* or intellectuality in that it is an act of the human intellect and, in its own way, is an exercise of thought, in the search as well as in assent. Thus an act of faith comes from the free choice of the rational and conscious person . . . which is based on a reason of the greatest persuasive force, that is, God's own

Verbum), no. 5; quoting from Rom 16:26 and First Vatican Council, *Dogmatic Constitution on the Catholic Faith*, chap. 3.

[16] Karol Wojtyla, *Sources of Renewal* (1972), 20. Statements of Cardinal Wojtyla before he became Pope John Paul II are not authoritative papal statements. When such statements are quoted here and in later Questions in this book, it is for the light they can shed on the subjects under discussion. On the nature of faith, see *V.S.*, nos. 88–89; *F.R.*, nos. 13, 16–35.

authority as Truth, Goodness, Holiness, which are identical with His subsistent Being. The ultimate grounding of faith, which is the basis of all anthropology and Christian ethics, is the *summa et prima Veritas*, God as infinite Being, of which Truth is merely another name. Therefore human reason is not negated or degraded by the act of faith, but achieves its greatest intellectual heights in the humility with which it acknowledges and accepts God's infinite greatness.[17]

Faith "entails an act of trusting abandonment to Christ, which enables us to live as he lived . . . in profound love of God and of our brothers and sisters."[18] "Reason . . . is not asked to pass judgement on the contents of faith, something of which it would be incapable . . . Its function is rather to find meaning, to discover explanations which might allow everyone to come to a certain understanding of the contents of faith. . . . The fundamental harmony between the knowledge of faith and the knowledge of philosophy is once again confirmed. Faith asks that its object be understood with the help of reason; and at the summit of its searching reason acknowledges that it cannot do without what faith presents."[19] [T]here is a profound and indissoluble unity between the knowledge of reason and the knowledge of faith."[20] Saint Thomas "began a new era in moral theology", said John Paul II, "because he succeeded in incorporating classical ethical thought into a new Christian anthropology and in inculturating moral science within a theological vision."[21] As Saint Thomas maintains, the

---

[17] Pope John Paul II, *Address to International Study Congress on St. Thomas Aquinas*, Sept. 29, 1990; 36 *The Pope Speaks* 78, 79–80 (1991).

[18] *V.S.*, no. 88.

[19] *F.R.*, no. 42.

[20] Ibid., no. 16.

[21] Pope John Paul II, *Address to Congress of the International Thomas Aquinas Society*, Sept. 28, 1991; 37 *The Pope Speaks* 52, 53 (1992).

natural law can be known by reason without the aid of explicit revelation. However, revelation is itself a gift complementing reason and facilitating our accurate perception of the natural law. Given the reality of God as the giver of the natural law, it would make no sense to rule out his revelation as a source of knowledge and understanding of that law. "*[W]hen the sense of God is lost, there is also a tendency to lose the sense of man*, of his dignity and his life."[22] And some acquaintance with the content of the revelation on which Saint Thomas relied is essential if we are to understand his treatment of natural law and the completion of his work by the Magisterium. That is why, even at the risk of "turning people off", we cannot coherently discuss the natural law without reference to the explicit revelation provided by the author of that law.

25. *All right. Revelation might have some bearing on the natural law. So let's start at the top. What does it tell us about God himself?*

Christ revealed to us that in one God there are three divine Persons. "I and the Father are One."[23] "Go therefore, and make disciples of all nations, baptizing them in *the name* of the Father, and of the Son, and of the Holy Spirit."[24] In the Old Testament, too, we see the combination of oneness and plurality in God. Thus Genesis says, "Let *us* make man to *our* image and likeness"; but then it says, "And God created man

---

[22] *E.V.*, no. 21; see also *E.V.*, no. 36.

[23] Jn 10:30.

[24] Mt 28:19 (emphasis added).

to *his* own image and likeness; to the image of God *he* created him."[25]

The Trinity is a supernatural mystery, beyond human understanding.[26] But that does not mean that it is inconsistent with reason. Rather, our intellects simply do not have the power to comprehend this mystery. Although we cannot understand the Trinity, the first seven councils held by the Church defined certain outlines of the mystery.[27] In approaching the Trinity the distinction between person and nature must be understood. You are a person; your nature is human. Person refers to who you are. Nature refers to what you are. Who you are is John Smith. What you are is a human being—that is, you have a human nature. Each person has one nature. This is how it is with man. With God, however, there are three divine Persons in the one divine nature. It is important to avoid the notion that God the Father came first, the Son came second, and the Holy Spirit came third. Instead, the first, second, and third Persons of the Trinity are all eternal and all are fully God. Each Person in the Trinity is distinct from the others, and each possesses the divine nature totally.[28] The three distinct divine Persons possess the one divine nature; they know with the same intellect, and they love with the same will. Though distinct, they are not three isolated entities. Rather, "relation in God . . . is the divine essence itself."[29]

God has—or, more properly, is—a social life. The life of the three Persons in the Trinity is a life of relation and activity.

---

[25] Gn 1:26, 27 (emphasis added).

[26] On the Trinity generally, see *C.C.C.*, nos. 232–67.

[27] Hardon, *The Catholic Catechism*, 53–54.

[28] See *S.T.*, I, Q. 29, art. 4; Q. 30, art. 4; Q. 39, art. 2.

[29] *S.T.*, I, Q. 29, art. 4; see also *S.T.*, I, Q. 28, art. 2, and *C.C.C.*, nos. 252, 255.

All three are equally one God, although we attribute to the Father the work of creation, to the Son the work of redemption, and to the Holy Spirit the work of sanctification. "And yet what one does, All do; where One is, All are."[30] The life of the Trinity is a ceaseless activity of knowledge and love. According to Cardinal Joseph Ratzinger:

> In the one and indivisible God there exists the phenomenon of dialogue, the reciprocal exchange of word and love. . . . St. Augustine once enshrined this idea in the following formula: "He is not called Father with reference to himself but only in relation to the Son; seen by himself he is simply God." Here the decisive point comes beautifully to light. "Father" is purely a concept of relationship. Only in being for the other is he Father; in his own being-in-himself he is simply God. . . . In this idea of relativity in word and love, . . . Christian thought discovered the kernel of the concept of person, which describes something other and infinitely more than the mere idea of the "individual."[31]

The Second Vatican Council declared that "the Lord Jesus, when praying to the Father 'that they may all be one . . . even as we are one' (*Jn.* 17:21–22), has opened up new horizons closed to human reason by implying that there is a certain parallel between the union existing among the divine persons and the union of the sons of God in truth and love. It follows, then, that if man is the only creature on earth that God has wanted for its own sake, man can fully discover his true self

---

[30] Leo J. Trese, *The Faith Explained* (1965), 29–30 (1991 ed., 26).

[31] Cardinal Joseph Ratzinger, *Introduction to Christianity* (1990), 131–32; see Questions 35–37 below for a discussion of some implications of this concept of person as relation.

only in a sincere giving of himself."[32] In loving one another, we emulate the essential activity of God himself.

The doctrine of the Trinity is thus, in effect, a social and moral teaching. It shows that the basic human inclination to live in relation to others in community[33] leads man not only to act in accord with his nature but to model his life on the divine Persons of the Trinity:

> Practically speaking, the Trinity affords a sublime lesson to Christians on the meaning of selfless charity. It is all too possible to conceive charity as an external rule imposed from the outside, as though sharing what belongs to us personally were some grudging concession to the demands of social existence. It is possible to think that human fulfillment consists in *self*-satisfaction, with only so much given to others as the "law," human or divine, requires in order to meet the requirements of communal living.
>
> What a different understanding charity acquires when viewed from the vantage point of the love that obtains among the persons who form the Godhead! God, as we have seen, is the necessary being who cannot not exist, who therefore must be. Since God is triune love, then love cannot not exist, it therefore must be. In God, this necessity is of the essence of his being. The three persons cannot not be joined together in perfect unity. In similar fashion, speaking analogously, this necessity to love belongs to the essence of our created being. Unlike God, we can be so jealous of our individual liberty as not to share what we possess with others in the human family. But then we do violence to our humanity, modeled after the Trinity. So far from being an alien imposition on our nature, what we call the "command" to love our neigh-

---

[32] Second Vatican Council, *Pastoral Constitution on the Church in the Modern World (Gaudium et Spes)*, no. 24.

[33] *S.T.*, I, II, Q. 94, art. 2.

bor is actually the profoundest human need. It is a positive hunger of the spirit to exercise its freedom, by freely giving of ourselves, as persons, in order to benefit other persons and, in the process, contribute toward the formation of the earthly counterpart of the triune heavenly community.[34]

"The Church", in the words of John Paul II, "receives 'the meaning of man' from divine revelation. 'In order to know man, authentic man in his fullness, one must know God,' said Pope Paul VI, and he went on to quote St. Catherine of Siena, who in prayer expressed the same idea: 'In your nature, O eternal Godhead, I shall know my own nature.' "[35] In later Questions, we will explore some further implications of the Trinity for "the meaning of man".[36] For the moment let us merely note that our Creator is not some abstract force; nor is he an isolated, unapproachable figure. Rather, we are created in the image and likeness of a triune God whose very essence is relation and love.

26. But why were human beings created in the first place?

It would be less than prudent to entrust your car to a mechanic who had not yet figured out why cars are made and what their ultimate purpose is. Nor would it make sense to entrust the ordering of law and society to people who admit that they do not know the purpose of human existence. Therefore, an understanding of why and for what purpose man was created, which Saint Thomas treats in the first part of the *Summa Theologica*,

---

[34] Hardon, *The Catholic Catechism*, 66–67.

[35] *C.A.*, no. 55; quoting from homily of Pope Paul VI at the final public session of the Second Vatican Council, Dec. 7, 1965.

[36] See Questions 35–37 below.

is essential if we are to understand his later treatment of law, including the natural law.[37]

God created, out of nothing, three levels of beings: first, the purely material, such as rocks, trees, animals; second, man, who is composed of matter and spirit, body and soul; and third, angels, who are pure created spirits. According to Saint Thomas, it is "more probable . . . that the angels were created at the same time as corporeal creatures".[38]

Angels are persons, with intellects and wills. God created them out of love so that they could choose to love him and share in the life of the Trinity in perfect happiness forever. Love is an act of the will, and the power to love includes the power to refuse to love. Some angels, out of the sin of pride, refused to acknowledge that God alone is God; they refused to love him and obey him. That was the first sin, the beginning of hell.

> [Hell] is, essentially, the eternal separation of a spirit from Almighty God. Later on, when the human race would sin in the person of Adam, God would give the human race a second chance. But there was no second chance for the sinning

---

[37] On the creation generally, see *C.C.C.*, nos. 279–324.

[38] *S.T.*, I, Q. 61, art. 3. The existence of angels is an article of faith that all Catholics must believe. See Hardon, *The Catholic Catechism*, 84; see also Dan 7:10; Mt 18:10. "That each of us has an individual guardian angel is not a matter of faith, but it is the commonly held belief of all Catholics"; Trese, *The Faith Explained* (1959), 41 (1991 ed., 35). According to Saint Thomas, "By free-will man can avoid evil to a certain degree, but not in any sufficient degree; forasmuch as he is weak in affection towards good on account of the manifold passions of the soul. Likewise, universal natural knowledge of the law, which by nature belongs to man, to a certain degree directs man to good, but not in a sufficient degree; because in the application of the universal principles of law to particular actions man happens to be deficient in many ways. . . . (*Wis.* ix. 14). . . . Thus man needs to be guarded by the angels." *S.T.*, I, Q. 113, art. 1. On angels, see *C.C.C.*, nos. 328–36.

angels. Because of the perfect clarity of their angelic minds and the unhampered freedom of their angelic wills, even the infinite mercy of God could find no excuse for the sin of the angels. They understood (to a degree that Adam never did) what the full consequence of their sin would be. With them there was no "temptation," in the sense in which we ordinarily understand the word. Theirs was what we would call a cold-blooded sin. By their deliberate and fully aware rejection of God, their wills were fixed against God, fixed forever. For them there was no turning back; they did not want to turn back. Their choice was made for eternity. There burns in them an everlasting hatred for God and all His works.[39]

In addition to the angels and the material world and universe, God created man.[40] It is an article of faith that "the entire human race is descended from one man and one woman. Adam and Eve were the first ancestors of every human being."[41] The theory of evolution maintains that man has evolved from lower forms of life. Evolution is the development of parts, however, and the spiritual soul could not possibly evolve because it has no parts. Theoretically, the body of man could have evolved from lower forms of matter. But, still, God would have had to create the matter on which that evolutionary process worked. Science can tell us nothing about the ultimate origin of matter. It is theoretically possible that God created matter in such a way that it would evolve into the human body. However, the spiritual soul could not evolve. At some point in the evolutionary process, if any, God would have had to infuse the spiritual

---

[39] Trese, *The Faith Explained* (1965), 34–35 (1991 ed., 30).

[40] On the creation of man in the image and likeness of God, see *C.C.C.*, nos. 355–84; see also *E.V.*, no. 34.

[41] Trese, *The Faith Explained*, 47 (1991 ed., 40); see also Clarkson et al., *The Church Teaches*, 150–51; see also *C.C.C.*, nos. 355–84.

soul of man into that evolving matter. Only when the matter was infused with a spiritual soul would man exist.

If the evolution of the body were ever proven to be a fact, it would not disturb our faith, for the creative power of God would still be necessary to explain the origin of matter and of the spiritual soul, which could not evolve from matter. Pope Pius XII, in his encyclical *Humani Generis*, in 1950, declared:

> The Teaching Authority of the Church does not forbid that, in conformity with the present state of human sciences and sacred theology, research and discussions on the part of men experienced in both fields, take place with regard to the doctrine of evolution, insofar as it inquires into the origin of the human body as coming from pre-existent and living matter, for Catholic Faith obliges us to hold that souls are immediately created by God. However this must be done in such a way that the reasons for both opinions, that is, those favorable and those unfavorable to evolution, be weighed and judged with the necessary seriousness, moderation, and measure, and provided that all are prepared to submit to the judgment of the Church, to whom Christ has given the mission of interpreting authentically the Sacred Scriptures and of defending the dogmas of Faith. . . .
>
> When, however, there is a question of another conjectural opinion, namely polygenism, the children of the Church by no means enjoy such liberty. For the faithful cannot embrace that opinion which maintains either that after Adam there existed on this earth true men who did not take their origin through natural generation from him as from the first parent of all, or that Adam represents a certain number of first parents.[42]

In his October 22, 1996, address to the Pontifical Academy of Sciences, Pope John Paul II said:

---

[42] Pope Pius XII, *Humani Generis* (1950), nos. 36–37.

Today, nearly half a century after the publication of [*Humani Generis*], new knowledge leads to the recognition of the theory of evolution as more than a hypothesis. . . . A theory's validity depends on whether or not it can be verified; it is constantly tested against the facts; wherever it can no longer explain the latter, it shows its limitations and unsuitability. It must then be rethought. . . .

And, to tell the truth, rather than *the* theory of evolution, we should speak of *several* theories of evolution. On the one hand, this plurality has to do with the different explanations advanced for the mechanism of evolution, and on the other, with the various philosophies on which it is based. Hence the existence of materialist, reductionist and spiritualist interpretations. What is to be decided here is the true role of philosophy and, beyond it, of theology.

The church's magisterium is directly concerned with the question of evolution for it involves the conception of man: Revelation teaches us that he was created in the image and likeness of God. . . .

St. Thomas observes that man's likeness to God resides especially in his speculative intellect, for his relationship with the object of his knowledge resembles God's relationship with what he has created . . .

It is by virtue of his spiritual soul that the whole person possesses such a dignity even in his body. Pius XII stressed this essential point: If the human body take its origin from pre-existent living matter, the spiritual soul is immediately created by God. . . .

Consequently, theories of evolution which . . . consider the spirit as emerging from the forces of living matter or as a mere epiphenomenon of this matter are incompatible with the truth about man. Nor are they able to ground the dignity of the person.[43]

---

[43] 26 *Origins* (Dec. 5, 1996), 414, 415.

The theory of evolution of the body is not proven.[44] In answer to the question of "whether the production of the human body is fittingly described in Scripture", Aquinas said:

> Some have thought that man's body was formed first in priority of time, and that afterwards the soul was infused into the formed body. But it is inconsistent with the perfection of the production of things, that God should have made either the body without the soul or the soul without the body, since each is a part of human nature. This is especially unfitting as regards the body, for the body depends on the soul, and not the soul on the body.[45]

In any event, it is certain that the human soul could not have evolved. Each human soul results from a specific act of creation by God. Your remote ancestor was most assuredly not a chimpanzee. On the contrary, "man is created in the image and likeness of God (*Gn.* 1:26). . . . All human beings are one because they come from a single father, Adam, and a single mother, Eve . . . (*Gn.* 3:20). . . . Both aspects, the divine dignity of the human race and the oneness of its origin and destiny, are definitively sealed in the figure of the second Adam, Christ: the Son of God died for all, to unite everyone in the definitive salvation of divine filiation. And so the common dignity of all men appears with total clarity."[46] The promulgation of that message is the work of the Magisterium, as discussed in Questions 37 through 49 below.

But now we have to proceed to the next inquiry: On what terms and conditions did God create man and how did man

---

[44] See discussion in Hardon, *The Catholic Catechism*, 91–102.

[45] *S.T.*, I, Q. 91, art. 4; see also John Young, "The Abolition of Adam", *Position Paper 226*, Oct. 1992, p. 310.

[46] Cardinal Joseph Ratzinger, *Address* to Consistory of the College of Cardinals, Apr. 4, 1991, "The Problem of Threats to Human Life", *L'Osservatore Romano* (English ed.), Apr. 8, 1991, p. 2; 36 *The Pope Speaks* 332–33 (1991).

live up to the bargain? Man's failure to do so is what we know as original sin.

27. *What does original sin have to do with our understanding of natural law?*

A realistic view of the natural law, especially as expounded by Saint Thomas, is impossible without considering man's fall from grace through original sin.[47] God created man for the same reason he created angels: to share in the life of the Trinity, in perfect happiness, for all eternity. The first human beings, Adam and Eve, were created with three levels of gifts. The first was the natural. They were given their human nature in all its ordinary characteristics—body, soul, intellect, will. Second were the preternatural gifts, unusual natural perfections including infused knowledge (they did not have to study); freedom from disease, suffering, and death; and the gift of integrity, which means that they were not subject to the conflict we experience between our natural urges and our reason; they had extraordinary will power and control of their passions and senses.

The third level of gifts given by God to Adam and Eve was the supernatural, the power to rise above their nature so as to share in the social life of the Trinity. If you were able to give your dog, Wrecks, the power to share in the social life of your family, to converse at the dinner table, to say "Please pass the salt", to read the newspaper, you would be giving him a supernatural gift, raising him above his nature. With his own power, Wrecks is absolutely incapable of raising himself to this level.

---

[47] On original sin, see *C.C.C.*, nos. 385–421.

Similarly, there is no way that man, a created being, could raise himself, by his own power, to the level of participation in the social life of the Creator, the Trinity. Yet God conferred this supernatural gift on man. At the end of their lives on earth, Adam and Eve would not have died. They would have been taken to heaven to participate, in eternal happiness, in the life of God himself.[48]

As with the angels, all that was necessary for Adam and Eve to gain eternal happiness was for them to choose to love God, which includes the choice to obey him. "And the Lord God commanded the Man thus: 'From every tree of the garden you may eat; but from the tree of knowledge of good and evil you must not eat; for the day you eat of it, you must die.' "[49] Adam and Eve disobeyed. "Man's first sin was pride", says Saint Thomas.[50] The important question is not whether there really was an apple from which Eve took the first bite. Rather, the essential point is that those real people, Adam and Eve, made a conscious, deliberate choice to disobey God. This is what we call original sin, the first sin of the human race. Adam and Eve immediately lost their preternatural and supernatural gifts.[51]

Adam was the representative of the entire human race to come. Had Adam been faithful, we would have inherited those preternatural and supernatural gifts. Instead, the original sin of Adam, the first human being, "is communicated to all men by propagation not by imitation".[52] As a result, we come into this life without the supernatural gift of sanctifying grace; we

---

[48] See Clarkson et al., *The Church Teaches*, 162–63, quoting the description of the elevation and fall of man from a schema of the First Vatican Council.

[49] Gen 2:15–17.

[50] *S.T.*, II, II, Q. 163, art. 1

[51] See *S.T.*, II, II, Q. 164.

[52] Council of Trent, *Decree on Original Sin*, no. 2; Clarkson et al., *The Church Teaches*, 159.

have no right to heaven and no way to get there except for the fact that Christ has restored this opportunity for eternal happiness.

We come into the world subject to death and suffering. And we lack the integrity and self-control that were given to Adam and Eve; instead we have an inclination to evil, which we call concupiscence.[53] "Before the fall, Adam enjoyed the gift of integrity. . . . After the fall, Adam lost this gift for himself and his posterity, since even those who have been regenerated in baptism are plagued by an interior struggle with their unruly desires and hearts."[54]

Aquinas describes this consequence of original sin: "Besides the natural and the human law it was necessary for the directing of human conduct to have a Divine law" because, among other reasons, "of the uncertainty of human judgment", which is a consequence of original sin.[55] He further notes that the general principles of the natural law can be "blotted out from men's hearts, . . . in the case of a particular action, in so far as reason is hindered from applying the general principle to a particular point of practice, on account of concupiscence or some other passion. . . . But as to the other, i.e., the secondary precepts, the natural law can be blotted out from the human heart . . . by vicious customs and corrupt habits, as among some men, theft, and even unnatural vices, as the Apostles states (*Rom.* I), were not esteemed sinful."[56]

It is not unjust that we come into the world without the preternatural and supernatural gifts lost by Adam. Justice is

---

[53] On concupiscence in the context of original sin and the Ninth Commandment, see *C.C.C.*, nos. 2514–16.

[54] Hardon, *The Catholic Catechism*, 101.

[55] *S.T.*, I, II, Q. 91, art. 4; see Question 6 above.

[56] *S.T.*, I, II, Q. 94, art. 6; see also *S.T.*, I, II, Q. 77, art. 2.

giving a person that to which he is entitled. But we had no right to those gifts. As creatures, we had no claim on God to share eternally in the life of the Trinity; nor were we entitled to the preternatural gifts; nor even to be created at all. Suppose your father were told by his father that he would give him ten million dollars if he would refrain from drinking alcoholic beverages until his twenty-first birthday. If your father refrained from drinking and received that money, you, as his descendant, would be a wealthy person today. If, however, your father took a drink the night before his twenty-first birthday, you in turn would not have the wealth you would have inherited if he had lived up to the bargain. However, your grandfather, in withholding the money from his son, your father, did no injustice. His son had no right to that money because he did not fulfill the condition. And you, the grandchild, have no right to that money either. Your grandfather did not treat you unjustly in refusing to pay to his son the money that the son failed to earn. So it is with original sin. We have no right to the preternatural and supernatural gifts, and it is not unjust when, as a result of the sin of Adam, we come into the world without those gifts.

Man's "history of sin begins when he no longer acknowledges the Lord as his Creator and himself wishes to be the one who determines, with complete independence, what is good and what is evil. 'You will be like God, knowing good and evil.' (Gen 3:5)."[57]

Original sin is truly sin, the breaking of the sinner's relation with God.[58] Actual sin, whether mortal or venial, is the sin we ourselves commit. With the exception of the Blessed Virgin Mary, all human persons since Adam and Eve were conceived

---

[57] *V.S.*, no. 102.

[58] Second Vatican Council, *Pastoral Constitution on the Church in the Modern World* (*Gaudium et Spes*), no. 13.

with original sin. "The story of original sin and its part in the life of every human being born into the world offers the key to the answering of many problems facing us in the twentieth century as well as at the dawn of civilization. Why sickness and suffering? Why cannot we just let children 'express themselves' and grow up 'naturally'? Why do men have to fight against sin and temptation instead of 'coasting along' through life? The answer to all those questions will not be difficult to fathom if we realize the teaching of the Catholic Church on original sin."[59]

"[I]t was part of the original plan of the creation that reason should without difficulty reach . . . to the origin of all things: the Creator. But because . . . man and woman chose to set themselves in full and absolute autonomy in relation to the One who had created them, this ready access to God the Creator diminished."[60] As a result of original sin, "[m]an's capacity to know the truth is also darkened, and his will to submit to it is weakened. Thus, giving himself over to relativism and skepticism (cf. Jn 18:38), he goes off in search of an illusory freedom apart from truth itself."[61]

The reality of original sin, however, is not cause for despair. Quite the contrary. "The Fall is a view of life", wrote G. K. Chesterton. "It is not only the only enlightening but the only encouraging view of life. It holds . . . that we have misused a good world, and not merely been entrapped into a bad one. It refers evil back to the wrong use of the will, and thus declares that it can eventually be righted by the right use of the will.

---

[59] Edward J. Hayes, Paul J. Hayes, and James J. Drummey, *Catholicism and Reason* (1973), 175.

[60] *F.R.*, no. 22.

[61] *V.S.*, no. 1.

Every other creed except that one is some form of surrender to fate."[62]

An important final point: Saint Thomas states that "the first man sinned chiefly by coveting God's likeness, as regards knowledge of good and evil, according to the serpent's instigation, namely that *by his own natural power he might decide what was good, and what was evil* for him to do; or again that he should of himself foreknow what good and what evil would befall him. Secondarily, he sinned by coveting God's likeness as regards his own power of operation, namely that *by his own natural power he might act so as to obtain happiness*."[63] The philosophy of the Enlightenment rejects objective standards of goodness, so that man will decide on his own what is good and bad. It attempts to construct a happy society without reliance on the objective natural law, the divine law, and the grace of God. This "new" idea, however, is no more than a rerun of the Genesis script.

---

[62] Gilbert K. Chesterton, *The Thing* (1957 ed.), 227.

[63] *S.T.*, II, II, Q. 163, art. 2 (emphasis added).

VIII

THE CENTRALITY OF CHRIST

28. Where does Christ fit into the natural law picture?

Christ is the link between observance of the law of God, including the natural law, and salvation. Without Christ, there is no hope of sharing, after death, in the eternal happiness of the Trinity. With Christ, there is the surety that observance of the natural law does more than promote a tolerable community life and personal happiness on earth. Because of Christ, observance of the natural law becomes an element in a personal choice with eternal consequences. The jurisprudence of Saint Thomas is ultimately pointless apart from Jesus Christ.

After the Fall, God could have left mankind in its fallen state. But in his mercy and love, he promised man a second chance for eternal life. However, because God is also infinitely just, reparation was necessary. Reparation for the sin of man, of course, should be made by man. But the gravity of an offense is aggravated by the dignity and office of the person offended.[1] Remember how the assassination of President John F. Kennedy shocked the world; the gravity of the offense was increased by the dignity and stature of the victim. But sin is an offense against God. Because God is infinite, the offense of man was infinite, and, in justice, a reparation of infinite value was required. No mere man, or number of men, could make up for it on behalf of all mankind because man is finite.[2] Who could make infinite reparation to God but God himself? The result is that God himself, the second Person of the Trinity, took on human nature so that he, as man, could make reparation for the sins of man and so that, as God, his reparation

---

[1] See *S.T.*, I, II, Q. 73, art. 9.

[2] See Saint Thomas Aquinas, *Summa contra Gentiles* (Charles J. O'Neil, transl., 1975), book IV, chap. 54, p. 228.

would be sufficient satisfaction for the infinite offense against God. The second Person of the Trinity was God from all eternity. But, at the time of the Annunciation,[3] when the Angel Gabriel informed the Blessed Mother that she was to be the mother of God, and she accepted, God the Son became man. This is called the Incarnation, meaning that God the Son took on human nature.[4]

The purpose of the Incarnation was redemption. If you pawn a watch, you can redeem it later by paying a price for it. So it is with Christ. As God and man, he redeemed us, he "bought us back" by satisfying the infinite justice of God, and he restored to us the gift of eternal life, which each of us can accept by loving and obeying God. Or we can reject it by sin.

The union of a divine nature and a human nature in the one divine person, Christ, is called the hypostatic union.[5] This important doctrine, defined by the Council of Chalcedon in 451, was well summarized by Father Hardon:

> The doctrine of Chalcedon is the Church's final classic expression of faith on the person of Christ. It placed the capstone on Nicea, Constantinople, and Ephesus. Ever since, all papal and conciliar teaching has merely refined and clarified the dogmatic essentials formulated by the end of the fifth century.

What are these essentials?

— that Christ assumed a real and not just an apparent body. He was born of a woman, from whom he received a truly human nature.

---

[3] Lk 1:26–38.

[4] On the Incarnation generally, see *S.T.*, III, Q. 1–26; see also *C.C.C.*, nos. 422–83.

[5] See *S.T.*, III, Q. 2.

— that in becoming man, he assumed not only a body but also a rational soul, with intellect and will. Christ therefore had a divine and human mind, a divine and human will.

— that the two natures in Christ are united to form one individual. Christ is one person, the second person of the Trinity.

— that in Christ each of the two natures remains unimpaired, they are not confused or changed in their respective properties; nor are they divided or separated, as though merely co-existing side by side.

— that in becoming man, Christ was and remains true God, one in nature with the Father. When St. Paul speaks of God "emptying himself" to become man, this does not mean that God somehow ceased to be God.

— that even as man, Christ is absolutely sinless. He not only did not sin, but he could not sin because he was God. Only in the spurious supposition that Christ has two persons is sin conceivable, since the human person might then commit sin, while the divine person would be perfectly holy. Since Christ was utterly sinless, he was also free from concupiscence or unruly passions, and also free from such effects of concupiscence as positive ignorance or error.

— that Mary is consequently not only Mother of Christ but Mother of God, since he was "born of Mary" in time who is begotten of the Father in eternity.

— that, since the Savior was one person, whatever he did (or does) was (and is) done simultaneously by both natures, although in different ways. When Christ talked and walked and ate and slept and died, it was the God-man who did all these things. When he worked the miracles of healing disease, calming the storm at sea, and raising the dead, it too was the God-man who did all these things. Now at the right hand of his Father, it is the same God-man who is our heavenly high priest and who on the last day will come to judge the living and the dead.[6]

Jesus Christ is truly God and man.[7] "To the question 'Who are you?' Christ would have but one answer. He is the divine Second Person of the Blessed Trinity, God the Son, the Word. But to the question, 'What are you?' Christ our Lord would have two answers, for He has two natures; He is God and He is man."[8]

Pope Saint Pius X, in 1907, formally condemned the proposition that "Christ did not always have the consciousness of his messianic dignity."[9] Christ knew he was God and never had an identity crisis. However, "the one person could operate, really and truly, in both natures. If Our Lord wanted to lift a load, He could have lifted it either by the effortless fiat of the divine will or by the hard effort of the human muscles."[10]

Christ had two intellects and two wills. The human intellect and will were always in proper subjection to the divine intellect and will. Presumably, he chose to learn how to drive a nail as any other boy would learn it; presumably, he hit his thumb on occasion.[11] But he always possessed the divine power; the fact that he chose to suffer and to die for us on Calvary is a mea-

---

[6] John A. Hardon, S.J., *The Catholic Catechism* (1975), 140–41.

[7] See *S.T.*, III, Q. 31–59.

[8] Frank J. Sheed, *Theology and Sanity* (1978), 162.

[9] Pope St. Pius X, *Lamentabili Sane* (1907).

[10] Sheed, *Theology and Sanity*, 166.

[11] See Leo J. Trese, *The Faith Explained* (1965), 80–81 (1991 ed., 67); *S.T.*, III, Q. 9–12.

sure of his love for us. Through the Passion of Christ, Saint Thomas says, "man knows thereby how much God loves him, and is thereby stirred to love him in return."[12]

Every act of a divine person is of infinite value. It was not necessary for the divine person, Christ, to go through what he went through in order to redeem us. Saint Thomas notes that, "by suffering out of love and obedience, Christ gave more to God than was required to compensate for the offense of the whole human race."[13] The smallest act on Christ's part would have been infinitely valuable and sufficient. Instead, he chose to live among us, to become like us in all things except sin, and to suffer and die, in his human nature, for us.[14] In so doing, he demonstrated the infinite love of God for his creatures. Saint Alphonsus Liguori, himself a lawyer, wrote:

> Jesus Christ could easily have obtained for us salvation without suffering. Would it not have sufficed for him to have offered to his eternal Father one single prayer for the pardon of man? For this prayer, being of infinite value, would have been sufficient to save the world, and infinite worlds besides. Why, then, did he choose for himself so much suffering, and a death so cruel . . . ? To what purpose so much cost in order to save man? . . . Because Jesus loved us so much, he desired to be loved very much by us; and therefore he did everything he could, even unto suffering for us, in order to

---

[12] *S.T.*, III, Q. 46, art. 3.

[13] *S.T.*, III, Q. 48, art. 2; see also *S.T.*, III, Q. 46, art. 4.

[14] See *S.T.*, III, Q. 46, art. 12: "The Lord of glory is said to be crucified, not as the Lord of glory, but as a man capable of suffering. . . . As is said in a sermon of the Council of Ephesus, 'Christ's death being, as it were, God's death'—namely, by union in Person—'destroyed death; since He who suffered was both God and man. For God's Nature was not wounded, nor did it undergo any change by those sufferings.' "

conciliate our love, and to show that there was nothing more that he could do to make us love him.[15]

The lawgiver of the natural law, therefore, is not some impersonal traffic cop lurking behind a billboard to catch us in a speed trap. Rather, he loves us very much and wants us freely to choose to love him by choosing to do good. He gave us the natural law to facilitate that choice on our part. But, as a result of original sin, "the human capacity to know the truth was impaired by an aversion to the One who is the source and origin of truth. . . . The eyes of the mind were no longer able to see clearly: reason became more and more a prisoner to itself. The coming of Christ was the saving event which redeemed reason from its weakness, setting it free from the shackles in which it had imprisoned itself."[16]

Christ, however, is not merely a lawgiver and teacher. Rather, as both God and man, he is himself the norm who shows to man what it means to be human.[17] "People today need to turn to Christ once again in order to receive from him the answer to their questions about what is good and what is evil."[18] It is "Christ the new Adam, in the very revelation of the mystery of the Father and of his love, [who] fully reveals man to himself and brings to light his most high calling."[19] As Pope John Paul II put it in his first encyclical, *Redemptor Hominis*, in 1979, "How precious must man be in the eyes of the Creator, if he 'gained so great a Redeemer,' and if God 'gave His

---

[15] Saint Alphonsus Liguori, *The Passion and the Death of Jesus Christ* (1927), chap. II, sec. 3, 33–34.

[16] *F.R.*, no. 22.

[17] See Question 35 below.

[18] *V.S.*, no. 8.

[19] Second Vatican Council, *Pastoral Constitution on the Church in the Modern World (Gaudium et Spes)*, no. 22.

only son' in order that man 'should not perish but have eternal life.' "[20] However, "[t]o imitate and live out the love of Christ is not possible for man by his strength alone. . . . Love and life according to the Gospel . . . are possible only as a result of a gift of God who heals, restores and transforms the human heart by his grace."[21] "Saint Augustine . . . admirably sums up this Pauline dialectic of law and grace: 'The law was given that grace might be sought; and grace was given, that the law might be fulfilled.' "[22]

29. I respect Christ as a good man and a great teacher. But how could it be reasonable to conclude that he is God? And who cares? What difference does it make for the natural law whether Christ is or is not God?

Saint Thomas asserted that the natural law is knowable through reason. But he also affirmed the necessity of the divine law of revelation. And he accepted, with respect to "faith and good morals",[23] the teaching authority of the Church founded by Christ. The affirmation of the divinity of Christ is an essential element in Saint Thomas' "big picture", of which the natural law is a part.[24] It is not the purpose of this discussion to examine in detail the proofs for the divinity of Christ. Rather it

---

[20] Pope John Paul II, *The Redeemer of Man* (*Redemptor Hominis*) (1979), no. 10; see 24 *The Pope Speaks* 94, 110 (1979).

[21] *V.S.*, nos. 22–23; see also *V.S.*, no. 21.

[22] *V.S.*, no. 23, quoting *De Spiritu et Littera*. On grace, generally, see *C.C.C.*, nos. 1996–2005; see also *V.S.*, no. 21.

[23] Saint Thomas Aquinas, *Quaestiones Quodlibetales*, III, Q. 4.

[24] See Saint Thomas' discussion of the Incarnation and the divinity and humanity of Christ in *S.T.*, III, Q. 1–26, 31–59.

will be useful to note some reasons for concluding that belief in the divinity of Christ is fully in accord with reason.

First, Christ claimed to be God, the author of the natural law. "Before Abraham came to be, I am."[25] Given this claim, there are only three possibilities: He is God; or he knew he was not God when he claimed to be God, in which case he was a liar; or he thought he was God when he really was not, in which case he was insane. One thing that cannot rationally be said about Christ is that he was a good man and a great teacher but not God. He claimed to be God. If he is not God, he is a liar or insane.

Second, Jesus Christ fulfilled the Old Testament prophecies concerning the messiah. "These prophecies were fulfilled in no one but Christ, and he fulfilled them perfectly."[26] Christ himself made prophecies about future events, and these prophecies were fulfilled. "I tell you now before it comes to pass, so that when it comes to pass you may believe that I am he."[27]

Third, the divinity of Christ is proven by his miracles. "Christ worked miracles in order to confirm His doctrine, and in order to show forth His Divine power."[28]

> Recall a few of his miracles: At Capharnaum a house was so full of people a paralytic had to be lowered through the roof to attract attention. Seeing his faith, Jesus forgave his sins, upon which Pharisees and doctors of the law charged him with blasphemy. In reply, Jesus cured the paralytic by a

---

[25] Jn 8:56–59; see also Mk 14:61–64.

[26] Edward J. Hayes, Paul J. Hayes, and James J. Drummey, *Catholicism and Reason* (1973), 49; Gn 49:10; Is 11:1–2, 7:14, 35:5–6, 53, 50:6, 53:7; Micah 5:1; Ps 2:17, 41:10, 72:10; Zech 11:12–13.

[27] Jn 13:19; see Mt 20:18–19; 26:34; Lk 21:24; Jn 13:21–26.

[28] *S.T.*, III, Q. 43, art. 3.

word and ordered him to carry his bed. He fed five thousand men in a desert by multiplying five loaves and two fishes. Consider the number of witnesses of this miracle and their enthusiasm: They tried to make him their king. He raised from the dead the twelve year old daughter of Jairus, who had just died; the widow's son of Naim, who was being carried to the cemetery; and Lazarus of Bethany, who had been buried four days. Everyone who witnessed these events called them miracles. Even the chief priests and Pharisees gathered in council said after he raised Lazarus: "What do we, for this man doth many miracles?"[29]

Saint Thomas tells us that "the miracles which Christ worked were a sufficient proof of His Godhead in three respects. *First*, as to the very nature of the works, which surpassed the entire capability of created power, and therefore could not be done save by Divine power. . . . *Secondly*, as to the way in which He worked miracles—namely, because he worked miracles as though of His own power, and not by praying, as others do. . . . *Thirdly*, from the very fact that He taught that He was God; for unless this were true, it would not be confirmed by miracles worked by Divine power."[30] The greatest miracle worked by Christ was his own Resurrection. As Saint Thomas notes, "Our belief in Christ's Godhead is confirmed by His rising again."[31] Moreover, "Christ rose by His own power. . . . The Divine power is the same thing as the operation of the Father and the Son; accordingly these two things are mutually con-

---

[29] Cornelius J. Hagerty, *The Divinity of Christ* (undated), 3–4, quoting Jn 11:41; see Hayes, Hayes, and Drummey, *Catholicism and Reason* (1973), 61–66.

[30] *S.T.*, III, Q. 43, art. 4 (emphasis added).

[31] *S.T.*, III, Q. 53, art. 1.

sequent, that Christ was raised up by the Divine power of the Father, and by His own power."[32]

Today's jurisprudence of the Enlightenment regards religious beliefs and statements as inherently irrational. To the extent that it acknowledges any concept of natural law, that jurisprudence isolates it from any relation to God. It is useful, in answer to this Question and the next, to note some reasons for concluding that Saint Thomas' essential belief in the Incarnation and divinity of Christ is in accord with—and supported by—reason. As discussed in Question 22 above, it is unreasonable not to believe in the existence of God. Similarly, although faith is a gift, it is fair to say that it is unreasonable not to believe in the divinity of Christ.

What difference does it make for the natural law whether Christ is God? All the difference in the world, literally. The natural law comes from God. And if Christ is who and what he claims to be, he is the author of that law and the arbiter of its meaning through his vicar on earth. So it was important for us to dwell in this Question on the reasonableness of belief in the divinity of Christ. And it is worthwhile to move on to examine, in the next Question, the Resurrection as a historical event and as the definitive proof of that divinity.

30. Why bring the Resurrection of Christ into a book on natural law?

God is the author of the natural law. If Christ is God, any reasonable examination of the natural law must consider what Christ tells us about the law, of which he is the author. The

---

[32] Ibid., art. 4.

Resurrection is the definitive proof that Christ is God. "The Resurrection of the Crucified proved that he was really I AM, the Son of God."[33]

> The Resurrection was first of all *the confirmation of all that Christ had "done and taught."* It was the Divine seal stamped on his words and life. He himself had indicated to his disciples and adversaries this definitive *sign* of his truth. . . . If this word and promise of his are revealed as true, then all his other words and promises possess the power of truth that does not pass away, as he himself had proclaimed. . . . No stronger, more decisive and more authoritative proof than the resurrection from the dead could have been imagined or asked for. All the truths, including those most impenetrable to the human mind, find their justification, even from the rational point of view, in the fact that the risen Christ gave the definitive proof, promised beforehand, of his divine authority. Thus the *truth of Christ's divinity itself is confirmed by the Resurrection.*[34]

Pope John Paul II described the Resurrection as, "in the first place, *a historical event.* It took place *in a precise context of time and place*"[35] However, John Paul continued, "while the resurrection is an event determined according to time and place, *nevertheless it transcends and stands above history.* . . . Christ's Resurrection is the greatest Event *in the history of salvation*, and indeed, we can say in the history of humanity, since it gives definitive meaning to the world. The whole world revolves around the Cross, but *only in the Resurrection does the Cross reach its full significance of salvific Event.* The Cross and Resurrection constitute

---

[33] Pope John Paul II, General Audience, Mar. 8, 1989, 24 *Talks of Pope John Paul II* (Pro Ecclesia, 509 Madison Ave., New York, N.Y. 10022) 15 (1989).

[34] Ibid.

[35] Pope John Paul II, *Weekly Catechesis*, Mar. 1, 1989, 24 *Talks of Pope John Paul II*, 13 (1989).

the one paschal mystery in which the history of the world is centered."[36]

We sometimes overlook the fact that the Resurrection was a historical event, just as much as the signing of the Declaration of Independence and the Japanese attack on Pearl Harbor. Through our faith we know with absolute certainty that Christ rose from the dead. But we can give support to that conclusion by analyzing the Resurrection as history. If you were to convince a jury that Christ really rose, you would have to answer several questions:

1. Did Christ die?

2. Was he buried?

3. Was the tomb empty on Easter?

4. Where did the body go? There are only two alternatives: Somebody took it. Or Christ rose from the dead. If we exclude all the possibilities of the body's having been taken, we have to conclude that he rose.

5. Who could have taken the body? The realistic possibilities are:

    a. The Jews

    b. The Romans

    c. The disciples of Christ

---

[36] Ibid., 13–14; see also Saint Thomas' discussion of the Resurrection in *S.T.*, III, Q. 53–56. On the death and Resurrection of Christ, see *C.C.C.*, nos. 595–658.

When we exclude these three possibilities and realize that there are no other realistic explanations, we have to conclude that Christ rose from the dead.

6. But was not the Resurrection a figment of the disciples' imagination and were not the appearances of Christ after his Resurrection mere hallucinations?

The answers to the above questions can be summarized as follows:[37]

1. *Did Christ die?* There is no doubt that Jesus Christ was crucified. His crucifixion is confirmed by non-Christian sources such as Tacitus, Pliny the Younger, and Josephus. If Christ had not been crucified, the references in the Gospels and Epistles to his crucifixion would have been immediately contradicted by his enemies. The crucifixion of Christ, in light of his miracles and his claim to be God, was a major public event of the time.

Proof that Christ died is found in the nature of crucifixion itself. This was a common mode of Roman execution, and the procedures governing it were well settled in Roman law and military practice. Dr. Pierre Barbet, in his book *A Doctor at Calvary*, examines the medical aspects of the agony in the garden, the scourging, the crowning of Christ with thorns, his carrying of his cross, the method of crucifixion, and the

---

[37] See, generally, John Henry Newman, *Witnesses of the Resurrection, Position Paper 172* (April 1988); Karl Adam, *The Son of God* (1934); William D. Edwards, Wesley J. Gabel, and Floyd E. Hosner, "On the Physical Death of Jesus Christ", 255 *J. Am. Med. Assn.* 1455 (Mar. 21, 1988); J. N. D. Anderson, "The Resurrection of Jesus Christ", 3 *Christian Lawyer* 10 (1970); Thomas McGovern, "The Resurrection: Objective Fact or Pious Delusion", *Homiletic & Pastoral Review*, June 1990, p. 14.

methods used by the Roman soldiers to verify the deaths of those crucified.[38] The soldiers were duty bound, under possible penalty of their own deaths, to make absolutely certain that each crucified person died. In light of Barbet's analysis and in light of everything we know about the ritual of crucifixion, it is utterly unreasonable to believe that a crucified person could survive. This certainty is confirmed in Christ's case by the fact that his was a most noteworthy execution, and large crowds were watching to see whether he would perform a miracle at the last moment to escape. And he was placed in the arms of his mother and was buried by her and his friends in a cold, airless tomb. Would his mother and those others who love him have entombed him if there had been the slightest sign that he was still alive? Finally, at that time Christ's enemies made no claims that he did not die. It contradicts the evidence to believe that Christ did not die.

2. *Was he buried?* This question can be answered briefly. The tomb was a short distance from the place of execution. Joseph of Arimathaea received permission to take the body after Christ's death had been verified, the body was entombed, and the Romans set a guard over the tomb. Nobody at the time or since has seriously questioned the fact that Christ was buried in that tomb.

3. *Was the tomb empty on Easter?* Of course it was. If the body had still been there, the Jewish leaders would have produced it to refute the preaching and claims of the Christians.

4. *Where did the body go?* If Christ did not rise from the dead, somebody must have taken his lifeless body from the tomb.

---

[38] See Pierre Barbet, *A Doctor at Calvary* (1963).

If we exclude all realistic possibilities that someone took the body, we must conclude that Christ rose under his own power.

5. *Did someone take the body?*

a. *Did the Jews take the body?* Certainly not. It was completely against their interest to do so.

b. *Did the Romans take the body?* They had no more reason than the Jews to take the body. The claims of Christ not only were contrary to the beliefs and material interests of the Jews but were regarded by the Romans as contrary to the interest of the Empire. Neither the Jews nor the Romans would have done anything that would support the claim that Christ had risen.

c. *Did the apostles or other disciples of Christ take the body?* To answer, we have to answer two further questions: How could they have taken it? And if they took the body, how can we explain the transformation of the apostles and their willingness to die for their belief in the Resurrection?

How could the apostles have taken the body? The tomb was guarded by Roman soldiers who could pay with their own lives for dereliction of duty. The only way the apostles could have obtained the body was by bribery or by force. With respect to bribery, where would these poor men have gotten the money? And how much money could induce a Roman soldier to hand over the body and thereby risk serious and possibly capital punishment? We are not certain how many guards there were, but all of them would have had to have been bribed. Nor is it possible that the apostles could have overpowered the guards and taken the body by force. The tomb was about a quarter of a mile from Herod's palace. Any attempt to overpower the guards would have been heard. And do you really believe that the untrained apostles would have been able to overcome the trained and armed soldiers on guard?

The Jewish leaders bribed the soldiers to say that "his disciples came by night and stole him while we were sleeping."[39] But if the soldiers were asleep, how could they have known that the disciples stole the body? Moreover, if the apostles stole the body and therefore knew that the claimed Resurrection was a fraud, would they have been willing to give up their lives for that claim? We know that most of the apostles died as martyrs and that all of them were willing to suffer martyrs' deaths. We can be sure that they must have been offered bribes to renounce and "expose" Christianity, and they must have known that they faced virtually certain death if they refused to recant and if they continued to preach. Yet none of them recanted, and all of them continued to preach the risen Christ even at the price of their lives. It is a psychological impossibility that they would have so acted if they had known the Resurrection was a fraud. The transformation of the apostles into heroic champions and martyrs for the faith makes it wholly unreasonable to believe that they took the body of Christ. The later conduct of the apostles and other disciples of Christ is explainable only on the grounds that they believed that they had seen the risen Christ; that belief could not have existed if they had taken the body. It remains to be asked whether they actually did see what they thought they saw.

6. *Did the apostles and disciples merely imagine that they had seen Christ? Were the appearances of Christ mere hallucinations?* The fact that someone dies for his professed belief does not prove the truth of that belief. But it makes it entirely credible that he believes what he says. So we are certain that the apostles believed that they had seen the risen Christ. Next we should ask whether the experiences they believed they had were the

---

[39] Mt 28:15.

sort about which they could have been mistaken. The answer is No. It is incredible that they could have been mistaken in thinking that Christ walked and talked with them, took food from them, ate part of it and gave the rest back to them, cooked fish for breakfast on the shore, a breakfast which the apostles themselves consumed. And so on. Thus, it is wholly unreasonable to think that the apostles did not believe that they saw what they were certain they saw or that they could have been mistaken in that belief.

Could Christ's appearances have been hallucinations? Certain characteristics of hallucinatory experiences are not found in this case. Hallucinations commonly occur in high-strung people; but there is no reason to believe that all the people who saw Christ were of this type. Hallucinations are individualistic phenomena; it is highly unlikely that two people will have identical hallucinations. But Christ is recorded as appearing to 500 people on one occasion and on other occasions to smaller groups of various sizes. Commonly, hallucinations concern some expected event, but the evidence is convincing that the disciples were not expecting Christ to rise from the dead. In addition, the alleged hallucinations of Christ occurred at widely different times and in varied circumstances. And Christ's conduct at the time of his appearances was tangible—for example, he asked for food, ate some, and gave the rest back to the apostles; you cannot hallucinate a bite out of a hamburger. Also, if the appearances were hallucinations, why did they suddenly stop after forty days, at the time of the Ascension? And, finally, if the appearances of Christ were hallucinations, how do you explain the empty tomb? If the appearances of Christ were not real, where was his body?

If Christ did not really rise from the dead, the transformation of the apostles and the spread and endurance of the Church in spite of persecution would be a greater miracle than the Resurrection itself. A fair-minded jury examining the facts ought to conclude that the Resurrection of Christ is as much a fact of history as is George Washington's crossing of the Delaware.

If we were discussing any other historical event, there would be no serious challenge to the reality of its occurrence. But because it concerns Christ, the factual evidence of the Resurrection is rejected by some in favor of an absolute refusal to believe that such a miracle could occur. In fact, the Resurrection is confirmation of the reality that Christ is God.

IX

THE ROLE OF THE CATHOLIC CHURCH AS AUTHORITATIVE INTERPRETER OF THE NATURAL LAW

31. Suppose you are right and Christ is God, the Author of the natural law. So what? How do we know what he wants us to do?

This book examines the natural law jurisprudence of Aquinas as it is integrated into the teaching of the Magisterium. Saint Thomas not only affirmed the natural moral law but also accepted the teaching authority of the Catholic Church on issues of morality as well as of faith.

Jesus Christ did not come on earth for a few years, die, and fade away. He founded a Church that, among her other functions, has the mission of defining for us the applications of the natural law[1] and completing our understanding of that law in the context of Christ and the relational nature of the human person.[2] The Church is "the Mystical Body of Christ. . . . We must accustom ourselves to see Christ Himself in the Church. For it is indeed Christ who lives in the Church, and through her teaches, governs, and sanctifies; and it is also Christ who manifests Himself in manifold guise in the various members of His society."[3] "Believing in the Church," said Pope John Paul II, "stating in regard to her the yes of acceptance in faith, is *a logical consequence of the entire Creed, and particularly of our profession of faith in Christ, the God-man.*"[4]

---

[1] See discussion in John A. Hardon, S.J., *The Catholic Catechism* (1975), 206–53.

[2] See Questions 35–37 below.

[3] Pope Paul VI, *Ecclesiam Suam* (1964), nos. 30, 35, quoting Pope Pius XII, *Mystici Corporis* (1943), 10 *The Pope Speaks* 253, 262, 264 (1965). On the origin and mission of the Church, see *C.C.C.*, nos. 758–810; *V.S.*, nos. 21, 25.

[4] Pope John Paul II, General Audience, July 24, 1991, 37 *The Pope Speaks* 20 (1992). See also *V.S.*, no. 7.

Where is the Church founded by Christ? It stands to reason that four characteristics or marks would have to be found in any organization claiming to be the Church founded by Christ: That Church must be one, holy, catholic, and apostolic.[5]

1. The Church must be *one*. Obviously Christ must have founded only one Church because if there were more than one, they would inevitably contradict one another. Is the Eucharist truly the body of Christ? Can a marriage be terminated by divorce? Conflicting answers on these and similar questions cannot both be right. And God, who is all-truth, cannot affirm the truth of that which is false. So the Church founded by Christ must be one Church, united in teaching, leadership, and worship. The words of our Lord reinforce this conclusion. "And other sheep I have that are not of this fold. Them also I must bring, and they shall hear my voice, and there shall be one fold and one Shepherd."[6] Or again: "Holy Father, keep in thy name those whom thou hast given me, that they may be one even as we are."[7] The Catholic Church, among all others, is uniquely one in belief, leadership, and worship.

2. The Church must be *holy*. Christ's purpose in redeeming us was to bring us closer to God—that is, to make us holy. The Church founded by Christ must of its nature draw people closer to God and tend to sanctify them. The Catholic Church is holy in the means she provides to sanctify her members through her doctrine and teachings, the Mass, and the sacraments; and she is holy in the sanctification and reformation of their lives that

---

[5] *C.C.C.*, nos. 811, 812–70.

[6] Jn 10:16.

[7] Jn 17:11.

her members can attain—and many have attained—through the means provided by the Church. The holiness of the Church does not imply that individual members of the Church are all holy. The Church survives in spite of her members and leaders, not because of them.[8]

3. The church must be *catholic*. This word, with a small *c*, means universal. The Church founded by Christ is for all men, in every place, and at all times, without distinction based on race, sex, age, nationality, wealth, or otherwise. "And this Gospel of the kingdom shall be preached in the whole world, for a witness to all nations."[9] "Go into the whole world and preach the Gospel to every creature."[10] "You shall be witnesses for Me in Jerusalem and in all Judea and Samaria and even to the very ends of the earth."[11] The Catholic Church is preeminent among all Christian religions in its universality of time and place. She alone among them has existed in every age from the time of Christ, and no other church so fully embraces the people of every continent and nation.

4. The Church must be *apostolic*. Any church claiming to be the one founded by Christ must, of course, trace its history in unbroken continuity to the apostles. "And I say to thee, thou art Peter, and upon this rock I will build My Church, and the gates of hell shall not prevail against it."[12] "All power in heaven and on earth has been given to Me. Go, therefore, and make disciples of all nations, baptizing them in the name

---

[8] See discussion in Hardon, *The Catholic Catechism*, 214–17.

[9] Mt 24:14.

[10] Mk 16:15.

[11] Acts 1:8.

[12] Mt 16:18.

of the Father, and of the Son, and of the Holy Spirit, teaching them to observe all that I have commanded you; and behold, I am with you all days, even unto the consummation of the world."[13]

The apostolic character of the Catholic Church is evident. She alone can trace her lineage through the popes back to Peter, the first pope, appointed by Christ himself. The Lutheran church was founded by Martin Luther in 1524, the Episcopalian, or Anglican, by Henry VIII in 1534, the Methodist Episcopal by John Wesley in 1739, the Baptist (American) by Roger Williams in 1639, the Quaker by George Fox in 1647, and so on.[14] In the words of Cardinal James Gibbons:

> The Catholic Church can easily vindicate the title of Apostolic, because she derives her origin from the apostles. Every Priest and Bishop can trace his genealogy to the first disciples of Christ with as much facility as the most remote branch of a vine can be traced to the main stem. All the Catholic Clergy in the United States, for instance, were ordained only by Bishops who are in active communion with the See of Rome. These Bishops themselves received their commissions from the Bishop of Rome. . . . Like the Evangelist Luke, who traces the genealogy of our Savior back to Adam and to God, we can trace the pedigree of Pius IX [now John Paul II] to Peter and to Christ. There is not a link wanting in the chain which binds the humblest Priest in the land to the Prince of the Apostles. . . . Count over the Bishops from the very See of St. Peter, and mark, in this list of Fathers, how one succeeded the other. This is the rock against which the proud gates of hell do not prevail.[15]

---

[13] Mt 28:18–20.
[14] See Cardinal James Gibbons, *The Faith of Our Fathers* (1982), 34.
[15] Ibid., 35–36.

Note, incidentally, that the image of the "gates" implies that hell, rather than the Church, is on the defensive.[16] It is the Church that advances, on the offensive, and overcomes.

The Catholic Church, declared the Second Vatican Council, "is the sole Church of Christ which in the Creed we profess to be one, holy, catholic, and apostolic. . . . This Church, constituted and organized as a society in the present world, subsists in the Catholic Church, which is governed by the successor of Peter and by the bishops in communion with him. Nevertheless, many elements of sanctification and of truth are found outside its visible confines."[17]

God wants every human being to be saved and to enjoy eternal happiness with him in heaven. Christ has redeemed us by providing us with an opportunity to regain the gift of supernatural life that Adam and Eve lost for us. That supernatural gift is sanctifying grace, and the only way we can obtain it is by baptism.[18] As the Second Vatican Council said:

> This holy Council . . . teaches that the Church, a pilgrim now on earth, is necessary for salvation: . . . Christ . . . himself explicitly asserted the necessity of faith and baptism (*cf. Mk. 16:16; Jn. 3:5*), and thereby affirmed at the same time the necessity of the Church which men enter through baptism as through a door. Hence, they could not be saved who, knowing that the Catholic Church was founded as necessary by God through Christ, would refuse either to enter it or to remain in it.[19]

---

[16] See Mt 16:18.

[17] Second Vatican Council, *Dogmatic Constitution on the Church* (*Lumen Gentium*), no. 8.

[18] On baptism generally, see *C.C.C.*, nos. 1213–84.

[19] Second Vatican Council, *Dogmatic Constitution on the Church* (*Lumen Gentium*), no. 14.

The Council, however, recognized that others who are not formally baptized in the Church are nevertheless linked to her and share in her benefits.[20] Baptism of blood is one form of baptism that substitutes for sacramental baptism by water.[21] "Even without baptism, anyone who suffers martyrdom for the sake of Christ is certain of his eternal reward."[22] Baptism of desire, the third form of baptism, was described by the Second Vatican Council as follows:

> Those who, through no fault of their own, do not know the gospel of Christ or his Church, but who nevertheless seek God with a sincere heart, and, moved by grace, try in their actions to do his will as they know it through the dictates of their conscience—those too [may] achieve eternal salvation. Nor shall divine providence deny the assistance necessary for salvation to those who, without any fault of theirs, have not yet arrived at an explicit knowledge of God, and who, not without grace, strive to lead a good life. Whatever good or truth is found amongst them is considered by the Church to be a preparation for the Gospel and as given by him who enlightens all men that they may at length have life.[23]

In his 1990 encyclical, *The Mission of the Redeemer*, Pope John Paul II said:

> The universality of salvation means that it is granted not only to those who explicitly believe in Christ and have entered the Church. . . . Today, as in the past, many people

---

[20] Ibid., nos. 15–17.

[21] *C.C.C.*, no. 1258.

[22] Leo J. Trese, *The Faith Explained* (1965), 329 (1991 ed. 276); see *S.T.*, III, Q. 66, art. 11, 12.

[23] Second Vatican Council, *Dogmatic Constitution on the Church* (*Lumen Gentium*), no. 16; see *S.T.*, III, Q. 66, art. 11, 12; see *C.C.C.*, nos. 1258–60; *V.S.*, no. 3.

do not have an opportunity to come to know or accept the Gospel revelation or to enter the Church. The social and cultural conditions in which they live do not permit this, and frequently they have been brought up in other religious traditions. For such people, salvation in Christ is accessible by virtue of a grace which, while having a mysterious relationship to the Church, does not make them formally part of the Church, but enlightens them in a way which is accommodated to their spiritual and material situation. This grace comes from Christ; it is the result of His sacrifice and is communicated by the Holy Spirit. It enables each person to attain salvation through his or her free will. . . . This applies not only to Christians, but to all people of good will in whose hearts grace is secretly at work.[24]

God wants all men to be saved. The Catholic Church reminds those who have been baptized that their inclusion in the Church is not due to their own merits. Rather, the baptized "should humbly recognize their chosen position and gratefully live up to the covenant to which they have been called. Otherwise what began as a sign of God's special favor on earth may end as a witness to his justice in the life to come."[25]

How do we know what Christ wants us to do? One of the main functions of the Church is to teach the Truth, who is Christ, not only on faith but on questions of morals including the natural law. She claims this right to teach through her foundation in Christ, who is "the Lord of history. . . . Jesus Christ is the eternal truth which was revealed in the fullness of time. It was precisely in order to transmit the Good News

---

[24] Pope John Paul II, *The Mission of the Redeemer (Redemptoris Missio)* (1990), no. 10, 36 *The Pope Speaks* 138, 143 (1990).

[25] Hardon, *The Catholic Catechism*, 236.

to all peoples that he founded His Church with the specific mission to evangelize: 'Go into the whole world and proclaim the Gospel to every creature.' (Mk. 16:15)."[26]

32. *I still don't get it. If the natural law is knowable through reason, where does the Catholic Church get the right to tell me what it means? Isn't my reason as good as the Pope's?*

Your I.Q. may be even higher than the Pope's. But that is not the point. As the Second Vatican Council declared, "The task of giving an authentic interpretation to the word of God, whether in its written form or in the form of Tradition, has been entrusted to the living teaching office of the Church alone. Its authority in this matter is exercised in the name of Jesus Christ."[27] The Church teaches on matters of faith and morals. The teaching Church consists of the Pope and the bishops in union with the Pope.[28]

In 1870, the First Vatican Council dogmatically affirmed the papal authority as an article of faith:

The Roman Pontiff has . . . the full and supreme power of jurisdiction over the whole Church, not only in matters that

---

[26] Pope John Paul II, *Address to Bishops of Latin America*, Oct. 12, 1992; 38 *The Pope Speaks* 84–85 (1993).

[27] Second Vatican Council, *Dogmatic Constitution on Divine Revelation* (*Dei Verbum*), no. 10. On the Church as "mother and teacher", see *C.C.C.*, nos. 2030–51; see also *V.S.*, no. 27; *F.R.*, nos. 49–63.

[28] See Second Vatican Council, *Dogmatic Constitution on the Church* (*Lumen Gentium*), nos. 22–25; *C.C.C.*, nos. 880–92, 935–39.

pertain to faith and morals, but also in matters that pertain to the discipline and government of the Church throughout the whole world. . . . The Roman Pontiff, when he speaks *ex cathedra*, that is, when, acting in the office of shepherd and teacher of all Christians, he defines, by virtue of his supreme apostolic authority, doctrine concerning faith or morals to be held by the universal Church, possesses through the divine assistance promised to him in the person of St. Peter, the infallibility with which the divine Redeemer willed his Church to be endowed in defining doctrine concerning faith or morals; and . . . such definitions of the Roman Pontiff are therefore irreformable because of their nature, but not because of the agreement of the Church.[29]

[This infallible teaching power] means simply that the Church (either in the person of the Pope, or of all the bishops together under the Pope) cannot make a mistake when she solemnly proclaims that a certain matter of belief or of conduct has been revealed by God and must be followed by all. . . . Certainly Jesus would not be with His Church if He allowed His Church to fall into error concerning the essentials of salvation. The Catholic knows that the Pope can sin, like any other human being. The Catholic knows that the Pope's personal opinions enjoy only as much standing as the Pope's human wisdom may give them, but the Catholic also knows that when the Pope, as the head of Christ's Church, publicly and solemnly proclaims that a certain truth has been revealed by Christ, either personally or through His Apostles, Peter's successor cannot be in error. Jesus would not establish a Church which could lead men astray.[30]

---

[29] First Vatican Council, *The First Dogmatic Constitution on the Church of Christ*, chaps. 3 and 4, in John F. Clarkson, S.J., et al., eds., *The Church Teaches* (1973), 94, 99, 102; see *S.T.*, Suppl. Q. 40, art. 6.

[30] Trese, *The Faith Explained* (1965), 167–68 (1991 ed., 141).

The Second Vatican Council declared that the infallibility that Christ promised to his Church resides not only in the Pope when he is speaking *ex cathedra* but also "in the body of bishops when, together with Peter's successor, they exercise the supreme teaching office".[31]

> Although the bishops, taken individually, do not enjoy the privilege of infallibility, they do, however, proclaim infallibly the doctrine of Christ on the following conditions: namely, when, even though dispersed throughout the world but preserving for all that amongst themselves and with Peter's successor the bond of communion, in their authoritative teaching concerning faith and morals, they are in agreement that a particular teaching is to be held definitively and absolutely. This is still more clearly the case when, assembled in an ecumenical council, they are, for the universal Church, teachers of and judges in matters of faith and morals, whose decisions must be adhered to with the loyal and obedient assent of faith.[32]

"The universal Church", wrote Saint Thomas, "cannot err, since she is governed by the Holy Ghost, Who is the Spirit of truth: for such was Our Lord's promise to His disciples (*Jo.* xvi.13): 'When He, the Spirit of truth, is come, He will teach you all truth.' "[33] Notice, however, that every exercise of the power to teach infallibly requires the assent of the Pope. It was to Peter and his successors that Christ gave the keys of the kingdom of heaven.

Teachings of the Church that are not necessarily infallible are nonetheless authoritative. These exercises of the ordinary

---

[31] Second Vatican Council, *Dogmatic Constitution on the Church* (*Lumen Gentium*), no. 25.

[32] Ibid.

[33] *S.T.*, II, II, Q. 1, art. 9; see *C.C.C.*, nos. 85–100.

Magisterium (or teaching authority, from the Latin word *magister*, teacher) must be accepted by Catholics in the formation of their consciences.

> Bishops, who teach in communion with the roman Pontiff, are to be revered by all as witnesses of divine and Catholic truth; the faithful, for their part, are obliged to submit to their bishops' decision, made in the name of Christ, in matters of faith and morals, and to adhere to it with a ready and respectful allegiance of mind. This loyal submission of will and intellect must be given, in a special way, to the authentic teaching authority of the roman Pontiff, even when he does not speak *ex cathedra* in such wise, indeed, that his supreme teaching authority be acknowledged with respect, and that one sincerely adhere to decisions made by him, conformably with his manifest mind and intention, which is made known principally either by the character of the documents in question, or by the frequency with which a certain doctrine is proposed, or by the manner in which the doctrine is formulated.[34]

It is not legitimate to practice a "cafeteria Catholicism" by picking and choosing among the teachings of the Church. As Saint Thomas said:

> Whoever does not adhere, as to an infallible and Divine rule, to the teaching of the Church, which proceeds from the First Truth manifested in Holy Writ, has not the habit of faith, but holds that which is of faith otherwise than by faith. . . . Now it is manifest that he who adheres to the teaching of the Church, as to an infallible rule, assents to whatever the Church teaches; otherwise, if, of the things taught by the Church, he holds what he chooses to hold, and rejects what he chooses to reject, he no longer adheres to the teaching of

---

[34] Second Vatican Council, *Dogmatic Constitution on the Church* (*Lumen Gentium*), no. 25.

the Church as to an infallible rule, but to his own will. . . . Therefore it is clear that such a heretic with regard to one article has no faith in the other articles, but only a kind of opinion in accordance with his own will.[35]

Saint Thomas was insistent on the obligation to follow the teachings of the Church: "In those matters which pertain to faith and good morals, . . . as Augustine says in *De Doctrina Christiana* III: 'Everyone should consult the rule of faith which he gets from the clearer texts in the Scriptures and from the authority of the Church.' Therefore, no one who assents to the opinion of any teacher in opposition to the manifest testimony of Scripture or in opposition to what is officially held in accordance with the authority of the Church can be excused from the vice of being in error."[36] Pope John Paul II is evidently of the same mind. In his September 16, 1987, address to the bishops of the United States assembled in Los Angeles, he said that "there is a tendency on the part of some Catholics to be selective in their adherence to the Church's moral teachings. It is sometimes claimed that dissent from the *Magisterium* is totally compatible with being a 'good Catholic' and poses no obstacle to the reception of the Sacraments. This is a grave error that challenges the teaching office of the Bishops of the United States and elsewhere."[37]

Everyone has a pope, in the sense that everyone recognizes an authoritative interpreter on moral questions. If that interpreter is not the real Pope, it will be a pope of the individual's own selection: Ann Landers, CBS News, the majority of the Supreme Court, or the individual himself. The institution of

---

[35] *S.T.*, II, II, Q. 5, art. 3.

[36] Saint Thomas Aquinas, *Quaestiones Quodlibetales* (Alfred Freddoso, transl., unpublished), III, Q. 4, art. 10.

[37] 32 *The Pope Speaks* 378, 381 (1987); see also *V.S.*, nos. 113, 116.

the papacy is a gift of God, permitting us to be certain that the teachings we follow are God's own truth. "Everyone can see to how many fallacies an avenue would be opened up and how many errors would become mixed with the truth, if it were left solely to the light of reason of each to find it out, or if it were to be discovered by the private interpretation of the truth which is revealed. And if this is applicable to many other truths of the moral order, we must pay attention all the more to those things which appertain to marriage where the inordinate desire for pleasure can attack frail human nature and easily deceive it and lead it astray."[38] In his *Spiritual Exercises*, Saint Ignatius Loyola wrote:

> If we wish to be sure that we are right in all things, we should always be ready to accept this principle: I will believe that the white that I see is black, if the hierarchical Church so defines it. For, I believe that between the Bridegroom, Christ our Lord, and the Bride, His Church, there is but one spirit, which governs and directs us for the salvation of our souls, for the same Spirit and Lord, who gave us the Ten Commandments, guides and governs our Holy Mother Church.[39]

If the natural law is given to man by God so that he will know how to act so as to achieve salvation, it would seem reasonable to conclude that God would also provide a visible interpreter to decide disputed applications of that law. The power of the Church is not limited to "matters strictly religious", as Pius XII put it, but rather "the whole matter of the natural law, its foundation, its interpretation, its application, so far as their moral aspects extend, are within the Church's power."[40]

---

[38] Pope Pius XI, *Casti Connubii* (1931), III.

[39] Saint Ignatius Loyola, *Spiritual Exercises* (1964 ed.), 141.

[40] Pope Pius XII, *Allocution Magnificate Dominum* (1954), 1 *The Pope Speaks*

The Church is not the arbiter of the natural law in the sense that Paris clothing designers might be the arbiters of fashion, determining that whatever they decree will be the fashion norms for the year. The Church does not invent "the moral norm. . . . The Church is in no way the author or the arbiter of this norm. In obedience to the truth which is Christ . . . the Church interprets the moral norm and proclaims it to all people of good will."[41] The Church is the authoritative interpreter of that norm; in this sense she could be called the visible arbiter of it in that she has authority to settle conclusively disputes that might arise as to the meaning of the natural law. The "truth" of the "universal and permanent moral norms . . . of the moral law . . . unfolds down the centuries: the norms expressing that truth remain valid in their substance, but must be specified and determined . . . in the light of historical circumstances by the Church's Magisterium, whose decision is preceded and accompanied by the work of interpretation and formulation characteristic of the reason of individual believers and of theological reflection."[42] The Catholic Church has repeatedly and formally staked her claim as the authoritative interpreter of the natural law:

> What concerns morality can also be the object of the authentic *Magisterium* because the Gospel, being the word of Life, inspires and guides the whole sphere of human behavior. The *Magisterium*, therefore, has the task of discerning by means of judgments normative for the consciences of believers those acts which in themselves conform to the demands of faith and foster their expression in life and those which,

---

375, 380 (1954). See also Second Vatican Council, *Declaration on Religious Liberty (Dignitatis Humanae)*, no. 14; see *C.C.C.*, nos. 2032–40.

[41] *V.S.*, no. 95.

[42] Ibid., no. 53.

on the contrary, because intrinsically evil, are incompatible with such demands. By reason of the connection between the orders of creation and redemption, and by reason of the necessity, in view of salvation, of knowing and observing the whole moral law, the competence of the *Magisterium* also extends to that which concerns the natural law.

Revelation also contains moral teachings which *per se* could be known by natural reason. Access to them, however, is made difficult by man's sinful condition. It is a doctrine of Faith that these moral norms can be infallibly taught by the *Magisterium*.[43]

The *Code of Canon Law* asserts that "to the Church belongs the right always and everywhere to announce moral principles, including those pertaining to the social order, and to make judgments on any human affairs to the extent that they are required by the fundamental rights of the human person or the salvation of souls."[44]

"The Church has no philosophy of her own nor does she canonize any one particular philosophy in preference to others . . . Rather, it is the Magisterium's duty to respond clearly and strongly when controversial philosophical opinions threaten right understanding of what has been revealed, and when false and partial theories which sow the seed of serious error, confusing the pure and simple faith of the People of God, begin to spread more widely. . . . This discernment, however, should not be seen as primarily negative. . . . On the contrary, the

---

[43] Congregation for the Doctrine of the Faith, *Instruction on the Ecclesial Vocation of the Theologian* (1990), 35 *The Pope Speaks* 388, 393–94 (1990). See discussion in Charles E. Rice, "The Pope as Interpreter of the Natural Law", *Social Justice Review*, Mar./Apr. 1991, p. 39.

[44] *Code of Canon Law* (1983), Canon 747, Sec. 2; see discussion in Russell Hittinger, "The Problems of the State in *Centesimus Annus*", 15 *Ford. Int'l. Law J.* 953, 980 (1991–92).

Magisterium's interventions are intended above all to prompt, promote and encourage philosophical inquiry."[45]

The guidance of the Church, then, is essential if men are to achieve a consistently correct observance of the law written in their nature. In giving this direction, the Church is not merely seeking to persuade. Rather, although she desires that men should be convinced of the reasonableness of her position, she is expounding the law. More precisely, she is teaching the Truth, who is a person, Christ. And she teaches that truth by the direct authority of that divine person. For this reason, when the authentic teaching voice of the Church, whether the Pope or the bishops in communion with him, pronounces authoritatively on a matter of natural moral law, the pronouncement's binding force is not limited by the persuasiveness of the arguments advanced:

> The Church [acts], not indeed like some private guide or adviser, but by virtue of the Lord's command and authority. Therefore, when it is a question of instructions and propositions which the properly established Shepherds, (that is, the Roman Pontiff for the whole Church and the bishops for the faithful entrusted to them) publish on matters within the natural law, the faithful must not invoke that saying (which is wont to be employed with respect to opinions of individuals): "the strength of the authority is no more than the strength of the arguments." Hence, even though to someone, certain declarations of the Church may not seem proved by the arguments put forward, his obligation to obey still remains.[46]

If the papal teaching need not be accepted by a Catholic unless he is personally convinced of the soundness of the Pope's

---

[45] *F.R.*, nos. 49, 51.

[46] Pope Pius XII, *Allocution Magnificate Dominum* (1954), 1 *The Pope Speaks* 375, 380 (1954).

reasoning, then "the Holy Father is being regarded as nothing more than a wise and morally sensitive man, who deserves to be listened to only because of his human qualifications."[47] The Pope teaches not a philosophy but Christ, and he teaches not as a philosopher but as the Vicar of Christ.[48]

It would be a mistake to regard the Church's claim to be interpreter of the natural law as a matter of concern only for Catholics. The principles of the natural law are not sectarian dogmas. They arise from human nature generally. Although they are accessible to reason, those principles find their completion only through their integration by the Magisterium into the law of Christ. It is Christ who shows us that the human person "can fully discover his true self only in a sincere giving of himself".[49] As completed by this "law" of the person, the natural law is simply the story of how things work, whether those things are individual persons, society, or the state. The natural law is therefore a concern of persons of all creeds. And the Magisterium speaks in the interest of all citizens when it insists that "the person represents the ultimate end of society."[50]

Every society, like every man, has to have a god. There has to be an ultimate authority. If it is not the real God, speaking through his vicar on earth, it will be a god of man's own making. This may be man himself, the consensus, the courts— whatever. Ultimately, in the absence of an external interpreter, that moral authority will center in the state, which already pos-

---

[47] Cardinal Patrick O'Boyle, "Instruction on the Catholic Conscience" (Oct. 9, 1968), *Catholic Standard* (Washington, D.C.), Oct. 10, 1968.

[48] This point will be discussed more fully in Question 35 below.

[49] Second Vatican Council, *Pastoral Constitution on the Church in the Modern World* (*Gaudium et Spes*), no. 24.

[50] *C.C.C.*, no. 1929.

sesses the coercive power. And if the state recognizes no higher authority than itself, its law will inevitably tend toward utilitarian oppression. Because an interpreter is needed, the claim of the Catholic Church—that the authoritative interpreter is the Pope as the Vicar of Christ, who is God—merits consideration. If not the Pope, who else could adequately serve as the visible moral authority?

33. How can it be right *for the Pope to tell me what the natural law means? Don't I have to follow my own conscience?*

Yes, but . . .

Your conscience is the judgment of your reason on the moral rightness or wrongness of a particular act. It is an action of the intellect, making a judgment: "This is good" or "This is bad". That judgment may be influenced by emotion, but it is still a judgment of your intellect.[51] "The judgment of conscience is a practical judgment . . . which applies to a concrete situation the rational conviction that one must love and do good and avoid evil. This first principle of practical reason is part of the natural law. . . . But whereas the natural law discloses the objective and universal demands of the moral good, conscience is the application of the law to a particular case . . . an inner dictate for the individual, a summons to do what is good in this particular situation. Conscience thus formulates *moral obligation* in the light of the natural law. . . . 'Conscience is not an indepen-

---

[51] See *S.T.*, I, Q. 79, art. 13; *S.T.*, I, II, Q. 19, art. 5, 6. On the morality of human actions and conscience generally, see *C.C.C.*, nos. 1749–1802; see also *V.S.*, nos. 54–64.

dent and exclusive capacity to decide what is good and what is evil. Rather there is profoundly imprinted upon it a principle of obedience vis-à-vis the objective norm.' "[52] "[M]any of the problems of the contemporary world stem from a crisis of truth. . . . '[O]nce the idea of a universal truth about the good knowable by human reason, is lost, inevitably the notion of conscience also changes. Conscience is no longer considered in its prime reality as an act of a person's intelligence, the function of which is to apply the universal knowledge of the good in a specific situation and thus to express a judgment about the right conduct to be chosen here and now. Instead, there is a tendency to grant to the individual conscience the prerogative of independently determining the criteria of good and evil and then acting accordingly. Such an outlook is quite congenial to an individualist ethic, wherein each individual is faced with his own truth different from the truth of others.' "[53]

Your conscience is not infallible. As with other operations of your intellect, the judgment of your conscience may be objectively wrong.[54] But your subjective culpability will depend on whether you have fulfilled three duties with respect to your conscience:

1. *Form your conscience.* As with other judgments you make, your first duty with respect to your conscience is to form it correctly. "Although each individual has a right to be respected in his own journey in search of the truth, there exists a prior moral obligation, and a grave one at that, to seek the truth and to adhere to it once it is known. As Cardinal John Henry Newman,

---

[52] *V.S.*, nos. 59–60 quoting the encyclical *Dominum et Vivificantem* (1986); see *C.C.C.*, nos. 1777–82.

[53] *F.R.*, no. 98, quoting *V.S.*, no. 32.

[54] See *C.C.C.*, no. 1786.

that outstanding defender of the rights of conscience, forcefully put it: 'Conscience has rights because it has duties.' "[55] "Parallel with our duty to obey conscience is the obligation to educate it. Otherwise, if we do wrong in ignorance, we may not be free from blame. True, the conscience is not infallible, but, like other faculties of the spirit, it requires development and careful training as a delicate instrument for knowing the laws of God."[56] If you were deciding what grade of oil to put in your car, you would form that judgment by consulting the manufacturer's directions. So, in deciding whether an action is moral or not, your first duty is to form that judgment by consulting the directions of your own manufacturer. Our Manufacturer speaks to us through the natural law and the teachings of his Church. The Church teaches the truth of what it means to be a person; "she teaches *who* man *is*, created by God in Christ, and therefore what his true good is."[57] "The competence of the Magisterium . . . extends to that which concerns the natural law. . . . It is a doctrine of faith that these moral norms can be infallibly taught by the Magisterium."[58]

2. *Follow your conscience if it is clear.* Your second duty is to follow your judgment as to the rightness or wrongness of an act if that judgment is clear and free from doubt. "A human being must always obey the certain judgment of his conscience."[59]

---

[55] *V.S.*, no. 34, quoting Newman's *Letter to the Duke of Norfolk*; see *C.C.C.*, nos. 1783–85; *F.R.*, no. 25.

[56] Hardon, *The Catholic Catechism*, 293; see *V.S.*, no. 64; *E.V.*, no. 24.

[57] Pope John Paul II, *Address to International Congress on Moral Theology*, Apr. 10, 1986, 31 *The Pope Speaks* 175, 178 (1986).

[58] Congregation for the Doctrine of the Faith, *Instruction on the Ecclesial Vocation of the Theologian* (1990), 35 *The Pope Speaks* 388, 393–94 (1990); see Question 32 above. See also *V.S.*, no. 64.

[59] *C.C.C.*, no. 1800.

"We are obliged always to act on the dictates of a conscience that is certain. It must be obeyed even though objectively it may be false, because conscience is the nearest available norm we have for knowing what is right and wrong, and the criterion by which God will judge the human soul."[60] If you are objectively wrong in your judgment, however, you may be culpable for failing to form your conscience properly.[61]

3. *Never act on a doubtful conscience.* "On the other hand, we may never act with a doubtful conscience. So that unless the mind clearly says that a prospective action is permissible, we may not do it. Otherwise, we should be saying equivalently, 'This may be good or bad, offensive or pleasing to God. But I do not care, and will do it anyway.' If the mind is in doubt, therefore, we must either refrain from taking action or resolve the doubt."[62] If you are in doubt as to whether the action is right and you choose to do it anyway, you are choosing to do what you know may be wrong. But you know you will not do wrong if you do not do the act. If in doubt, do not do it. Take the safer course. The *Catechism of the Catholic Church* offers rules to help us resolve such doubt:

> 1787. Man is sometimes confronted by situations that make moral judgments less assured and decision difficult. But he must always seriously seek what is right and good and discern the will of God expressed in divine law.
> 1788. To this purpose, man strives to interpret the data of experience and the signs of the times assisted by the virtue of prudence, by the advice of competent people, and by the help of the Holy Spirit and his gifts.

---

[60] Hardon, *The Catholic Catechism*, 292; see *S.T.*, I, II, Q. 19, art. 5; see *V.S.*, nos. 62–63; *C.C.C.*, no. 1790.

[61] See *C.C.C.*, nos. 1791–92.

[62] Hardon, *The Catholic Catechism*, 292; see *S.T.*, I, II, Q. 19, art. 6.

1789. Some rules apply in every case:

— One may never do evil so that good may result from it;

— the Golden Rule: 'Whatever you wish that men would do to you, do so to them.'

— charity always proceeds by way of respect for one's neighbor and his conscience: "Thus sinning against your brethren and wounding their conscience . . . you sin against Christ." Therefore "it is right not to . . . do anything that makes your brother stumble."

If a Catholic's conscience, for example, judges merely that the practice of contraception is permissible but not mandatory —that is, that he may practice contraception but is not required to do so—he can follow his conscience and the teaching of the Church. If his conscience judges that contraception is mandatory for him—that is, that he must practice contraception— only then would his conscience collide with the teaching of the Church. Where, however, there is a clear teaching of the Church, such as that on contraception, abortion, or extramarital sex, it would be virtually impossible for a believing Catholic to think beyond any doubt that the prohibited action was mandatory for him.

Because conscience is fallible, the role of the teaching Church is important in providing a sure guide as to what is objectively right and wrong.[63]

---

[63] See Question 46 below for an extended discussion by Cardinal Joseph Ratzinger of erroneous theories on conscience that stem from the Enlightenment philosophy.

34. But is there really a right or wrong that is the same for everybody? Doesn't it depend on the person and the situation?

The reality of objective right and wrong—that some things are good or bad regardless of how we personally view them—is rooted in the nature of things. Saint Thomas said that "things prescribed by divine law are right, not only because they are put forth by law, but also because they are in accord with nature. . . . It is natural for man to be a social animal. . . . So, the things without which human society cannot be maintained are naturally appropriate to man. Examples . . . are: to preserve for each man what is his own and to refrain from injuries. . . . Man is naturally ordered to God as his end. Therefore, the things by which man is brought to the knowledge and love of God are naturally right, but whatever things have the contrary effect are naturally evil for man."[64]

Saint Thomas' view, however, does not prevail today. "The world of Descartes now holds, in economics, politics, education, theology, and elsewhere that the rational is the real, that which man's mind decrees to be the valid symbols becomes thereby reality. The roots of this are in *Genesis* 3:5—man's will to be his own god, knowing or determining for himself what constitutes good and evil, reality and non-reality."[65] Anna Quindlen, a *New York Times* columnist, illustrates the point. In criticizing the obscenity prosecution of those who publicly ex-

---

[64] Saint Thomas Aquinas, *Summa contra Gentiles* (Vernon J. Bourke, transl., 1975), book III, chap. 129, pp. 162–64. See also *C.C.C.*, nos. 1750–56; *V.S.*, no. 84.

[65] Rousas John Rushdoony, "The Cartesian Heresy", 287 *Chalcedon Report* 16, 17 (June 1989).

hibited the homoerotic photographs of Robert Mapplethorpe, Quindlen reduced the issue to a matter of personal preference: "You don't like Federal funding for this stuff? That's O.K.; the Stealth bomber offends my esthetic sensibilities. You say potato; I'll say pohtato [sic]. . . . And you can buy anchovies and do whatever you want in your house, too." René Descartes could have written her punch line: "The board of standards resides within our own skulls."[66]

Many appear to believe that nothing is wrong "for you" unless you "feel" it is wrong. If we were to ask an average high school student, even one who does not favor it, what he (or she) thinks about abortion, he would likely say that, although not personally approving of abortion, he cannot say it is always wrong for everyone else. Perhaps without realizing it, he would deny the reality of objective and inherent standards of good, rooted in the nature of things.

He would deny in the abortion case a principle that we all apply in our everyday actions. For example, suppose you see your friend, Freddy, with the hood of his car up, holding a can of oil in one hand and a can of molasses in the other, and you ask, "What are you doing?" Freddy answers, "Trying to decide whether to put oil or molasses in my car." If you were a real friend of Freddy, how would you respond? Would you say "Freddy, how do you *feel* about it?" No, you would say, "Freddy, you should do good by your car. And the good is that which is in accord with the nature of the thing. Oil is good for cars. Molasses isn't." "Yeah, but this is a Chevy." "Freddy, it doesn't make any difference. Cars are all the same." "Is that right? Well, who are you to tell me what to do with my car?" "If you don't believe me, Freddy, look in the glove compart-

---

[66] *New York Times*, Apr. 22, 1990, p. E27; see the discussion of nihilism in *F.R.*, nos. 46 and 90.

ment at the manufacturer's directions." (That is, by analogy, what the natural law and the Ten Commandments are—a set of manufacturer's directions.) So Freddy looks at the owner's manual and sees, in red letters on page 10, "Use oil—do not use molasses." Freddy says, "That's what it says, all right. But wait a minute. Whose car is this? It's my car. [It's my body, etc.] They can't push me around. I'll do what I want with *my* car." So Freddy puts in the molasses. He is sincere. He is liberated. He is pro-choice. And he is a pedestrian. Why? Because, whether we are talking about automobiles, human beings, or society, the natural law is the story of how things work. If we so violate the nature of a car by feeding it molasses, the car will not achieve its purpose. It will not work. Similarly, the intentional killing of an innocent human being, as in abortion and euthanasia, is always objectively wrong as a violation of natural justice as well as of the revealed word of God. And, regardless of the motive or other subjective dispositions of the killer, it is always harmful to the common good of society as well as to the victim and the killer himself.[67]

It is important to keep in mind here the distinction between objective wrong and subjective culpability. We generally have neither the right nor the ability to judge the subjective moral culpability of anyone. But the existence or lack of subjective culpability cannot change the objective character of the act.[68]

As Saint Thomas tells us, "If . . . we consider one action in the moral order, it is impossible for it to be morally both good

---

[67] See Charles E. Rice, "Some Reasons for a Restoration of Natural Law Jurisprudence", 24 *Wake Forest L. Rev.* 539 (1989); Robert P. George, "Proportionalism and the Catholic Moral Tradition", 70 *U. of Detroit Mercy L. Rev.* 1 (1992).

[68] See *V.S.*, nos., 70, 78–82; see discussion in Question 3, above, and Question 37, below; see also *C.C.C.*, nos. 1750–61.

and evil."[69] Looked at from the aspect of its moral quality, "the same act cannot be both good and evil."[70] Keeping this objective view of good and evil in mind, we know that we do no favor, for instance, to the person contemplating abortion when we encourage her to decide according to her feelings. It is a lie to pretend that abortion can ever be anything but an objective evil. We cannot throw rocks at her whatever she decides. Her subjective disposition is for resolution between herself and God. But we lie to her if we pretend that her contemplated action can ever be anything but an objective evil. It does violence to her nature as well as to her unborn child. And a society that tolerates it does violence to itself.[71]

In sum, there is an objective morality that is the same for everybody. The Magisterium provides guidance as to the content of that morality when it teaches the truth about what it means to be a human person in light of the person of Christ.[72]

---

[69] *S.T.*, I, II, Q. 20, art. 6.

[70] Ibid. See William E. May, "The Teaching of Theologians from St. Thomas Aquinas until Vatican Council II on the Existence of Moral Absolutes", 28 *Faith and Reason* 139 (1992).

[71] See Charles E. Rice, "Some Reasons for a Restoration of Natural Law Jurisprudence", 24 *Wake Forest L. Rev.* 539, 563 (1989).

[72] See Questions 35–37 below.

X

THE MAGISTERIUM: INDISPENSABLE INTERPRETER FOR THE COMMON GOOD

35. So you treat the Magisterium, the teaching authority of the Church, as sort of a "superteacher" of natural law philosophy. Right?

Wrong. The Church does not "teach" natural law. She proclaims Christ.[1] This is so because it is Christ who shows man what it means to be man. "Jesus' way of acting and his words, his deeds and his precepts constitute the moral rule of Christian life. Indeed, his actions, and in particular his Passion and Death on the Cross, are the living revelation of his love for the Father and for others. This is exactly the love that Jesus wishes to be imitated by all who follow him. . . . [T]he Christian faith . . . is not simply a set of propositions to be accepted with intellectual assent. Rather, faith is a lived knowledge of Christ, a living remembrance of his commandments, and a *truth to be lived out*."[2] "In reality," said the Second Vatican Council, "it is only in the mystery of the Word made flesh that the mystery of man truly becomes clear. For Adam, the first man, was a type of him who was to come, Christ the Lord. Christ the new Adam, in the very revelation of the mystery of the Father and of his love, fully reveals man to himself and brings to light his most high calling."[3]

In his address to the Fourth General Conference of the Latin American Bishops in Santo Domingo on the 500th anniversary of Columbus' discovery of America, Pope John Paul II said, "Our task is to make the truth about Christ and the truth

---

[1] See *C.C.C.*, nos. 1691–98, affirming Christ as "the way, and the truth, and the life" (no. 1698).

[2] *V.S.*, no. 20.

[3] Second Vatican Council, *Pastoral Constitution on the Church in the Modern World* (*Gaudium et Spes*), no. 22; see *F.R.*, no. 60.

about mankind penetrate more deeply into all strata of society and transform them. . . . Evangelizing means proclaiming a person, Christ. Indeed, 'there is no true evangelization if the name, the teaching, the life, the promises, the kingdom and the mystery of Jesus of Nazareth, the Son of God, are not proclaimed.' "[4]

The Church is still the essential interpreter of the application of the natural law to particular cases. But the Magisterium goes further. It incorporates the natural law into *lex Christi*, the law of Christ.[5] Joseph Costanzo, S.J., explained

---

[4] Pope John Paul II, *Address to Bishops of Latin America*, Oct. 12, 1992, 38 *The Pope Speaks* 84, 87–88 (1993); quoting from Pope Paul VI, Apostolic Exhortation, *Evangelization in the Modern World* (*Evangelii Nuntiandi*), Dec. 8, 1975, no. 22.

[5] The *Catechism of the Catholic Church*, issued in 1992, affirms the natural law in the context of Christ:

1953. The moral law finds its fullness and its unity in Christ. Jesus Christ is in person the way of perfection. He is the end of the law, for only he teaches and bestows the justice of God: "For Christ is the end of the law, that every one who has faith may be justified" (Rom 10:4).

1955. The "divine and natural" law (*Gaudium et Spes*, no. 89) shows man the way to follow so as to practice the good and attain his end. The natural law states the first and essential precepts which govern the moral life. It hinges upon the desire for God and submission to him, who is the source and judge of all that is good, as well as upon the sense that the other is one's equal. Its principal precepts are expressed in the Decalogue. This law is called "natural," not in reference to the nature of irrational beings, but because reason which decrees it properly belongs to human nature: "Where then are these rules written, if not in the book of that light we call the truth? In it is written every just law; from it the law passes into the heart of the man who does justice, not that it migrates into it, but that it places its imprint on it, like a seal on a ring that passes onto wax, without leaving the ring." (St. Augustine, *De Trin.* 14, 15, 21).

"The natural law is nothing other than the light of understanding

this unique role of the Magisterium in the context of Paul VI's 1968 encyclical on birth control, *Humanae Vitae*:

> All referrals to the natural moral law in *Humanae Vitae* are, as in every Church document, not to a theory of natural law that is explicitly and exclusively identified with a particular system of philosophical speculation in the history of moral philosophy but pointedly to the existential natural law that is an integral constituent of evangelical morality, the *lex Christi*, by which man, through the redemptive merits of Christ and by the grace of God, may attain eternal life situated as he is from the moment of his being in the *de facto* supernatural status. That is why every mention of it is always in conjunction with the supernatural. It is *the* natural law (unlike that of the philosophers) which is within the scope of the commission of Christ to Peter and his successors to teach, interpret, and transmit to the faithful to the end of time without error. This may explain why in none of the Church

---

placed in us by God; through it we know what we must do and what we must avoid. God has given this light or law at the creation" (St. Thomas Aquinas, *Dec. praec.* 1).

1959. The natural law, the Creator's very good work, provides the solid foundation on which man can build the structure of moral rules to guide his choices. It also provides the indispensable moral foundation for building the human community. Finally, it provides the necessary basis for the civil law with which it is connected, whether by a reflection that draws conclusions from its principles, or by additions of a positive and juridical nature.

1960. The precepts of natural law are not perceived by everyone clearly and immediately. In the present situation sinful man needs grace and revelation so moral and religious truths may be known "by everyone with facility, with firm certainty and with no admixture of error" (Pius XII, *Humani generis* [1950]). The natural law provides revealed law and grace with a foundation prepared by God and in accordance with the work of the Spirit.

See also *C.C.C.*, nos. 1950–52, 1954, 1956–58.

official and authoritative documents, papal and conciliar, do we ever find a systematic corpus of natural law doctrine formulated, much less the development of argumentation as to its existence, the demonstration of its general and particular principles, and the rationale vindicating the application of the principle to a particular moral act. Put into perspective, *Humanae Vitae* propounds a doctrinal teaching which is of the natural moral law but whose certain discernment and unambiguous formulation derive principally from the abiding assistance of the Holy Spirit that has sustained the constant and universal teaching of the Church on the moral principles on marriage as they are existentially integral to the evangelical morality, the *lex Christi*, and subsequently on the unique charism of the papal magisterium which has applied those moral principles to specific acts of conjugal relations. It is as Vicar of Christ, "by virtue of the mandate entrusted to Us by Christ" as successor to Peter and not as a venerated and world-renowned moralist, that Pope Paul VI teaches in *Humanae Vitae*.[6]

In *Humanae Vitae* itself, Paul VI gave this description of his encyclical:

[It is] a teaching founded on the natural law, illuminated and enriched by divine revelation. No believer will wish to deny that the teaching authority of the Church is competent to interpret even the natural moral law. It is, in fact, indisputable, as our predecessors have many times declared, that Jesus Christ, when communicating to Peter and to the Apostles His divine authority and sending them to teach all nations His commandments, constituted them as guardians and authentic interpreters of all the moral law, not only, that is, of the law of the Gospel, but also of the natural law, which

---

[6] Joseph F. Costanzo, *The Historical Credibility of Hans Küng* (1979), 339; quoting from *Humanae Vitae*, no. 6.

is also an expression of the will of God, the faithful fulfillment of which is equally necessary for salvation.[7]

Note here that the Church teaches the natural law not
merely as a philosophy but as "an expression of the will of
God". The Church honors Saint Thomas Aquinas, in John
Paul II's words, as *"Doctor Humanitatis"*.[8] "The Church has
often made reference to the Thomistic doctrine of natural law,
including it in her own teaching on morality."[9] But the Magisterium does not teach the philosophy or theology of Aquinas.
Rather, it teaches Christ. "Christian faith immerses human
beings in the order of grace, which enables them to share in
the mystery of Christ, which in turn offers them a true and
coherent knowledge of the Triune God. In Jesus Christ, who
is the Truth, faith recognizes the ultimate appeal to humanity. . . . This truth, which God reveals to us in Jesus Christ,
is not opposed to the truths which philosophy perceives. On
the contrary, the two modes of knowledge lead to truth in all
its fullness. . . . This unity of truth, natural and revealed, is
embodied in a living and personal way in Christ, as the apostle
reminds us: 'Truth is in Jesus.'"[10] In his 1991 social encyclical, *Centesimus Annus*, John Paul went beyond Aquinas' explicit
position by indicating that human personhood intrinsically involves relation to others in that "it is through the free gift

---

[7] Pope Paul VI, *Humanae Vitae* (1968), no. 4.

[8] Pope John Paul II, *Address to International Study Congress on St. Thomas
Aquinas* (1990), 36 *The Pope Speaks* 78 (1991); see also Pope John Paul II, *Ad-
dress to Congress of the International Thomas Aquinas Society* (1991), 37 *The Pope
Speaks* 52 (1992); the importance of Saint Thomas is emphasized in Pope Leo
XIII's encyclical, *Aeterni Patris* (1879), which is reprinted in Saint Thomas
Aquinas, *Summa Theologica* (Benziger Bros., ed. 1947), vol. 1, vii.

[9] *V.S.*, no. 44, see also, *F.R.*, 43, 57, 78.

[10] *F.R.*, nos. 33–34.

of self that man truly finds himself."[11] Natural law is mentioned in that encyclical only obliquely.[12] But the encyclical
integrates the natural law of Saint Thomas into its analysis of
the law of Christ and the law of the human person that arises
from his creation in the image and likeness of God and his
redemption by Jesus Christ. As John Paul said, "The Church
promotes . . . a true culture of peace . . . *by preaching the truth
about the creation of the world*, which God has placed in human
hands so that people may make it more fruitful and more perfect through their work; and *by preaching the truth about the
redemption*, whereby the Son of God has saved mankind and at
the same time has united all people, making them responsible
for one another. Sacred Scripture continually speaks to us of
an active commitment to our neighbor and demands of us a
shared responsibility for all of humanity."[13] The bottom line
is that moral issues cannot be fully resolved through philosophical abstractions and reasoning apart from the realities of
creation and redemption.

In his statement on the publication in 1992 of the *Catechism
of the Catholic Church*, Cardinal Joseph Ratzinger acknowledged
that the catechism is "really a book of morals". He went on
to say:

> [But] it is something more. It deals with the human person,
> but in the conviction that the human-question cannot be
> separated from the God-question. . . . In the catechism . . .
> everything that is said about our moral conduct can there-
> fore be said only from God's viewpoint, from the viewpoint
> of that God who revealed himself in Jesus Christ. . . . With
> the faith of the Church as its point of departure, the cate-

---

[11] *C.A.*, no. 41.
[12] See Question 38 below.
[13] *C.A.*, no. 51.

chism tells us that happiness can be had only with others, in responsibility for the whole of humanity. However, the communion of human beings with one another and responsibility towards others can in turn ultimately be had only in communion with God and in responsibility before God. . . . For the human person, happiness is love. In this sense the catechism morality is an instruction on what love is. In this regard it tells us that the essence of true love became visible in the person of Jesus Christ, in his words as well as in his life and death. It also tells us that the ten commandments are only an explanation of love's ways; that we read them correctly only if we read them in Jesus Christ. . . . In fact, the catechism's morality has its starting point in what the Creator has placed in the heart of every person: the need for happiness and love. Here we also clearly see what is meant by God's likeness: human beings are like God because they can love and are capable of truth. Moral behaviour is therefore, in the deepest sense of the word, a behaviour with creation as the standard. If Catholic moral tradition and—in line with it—the catechism too speak of the nature of the human being, the natural law and behavior according to nature, it does not mean a supposed biologism, but behaviour that begins from what the Creator has placed in our being. As a consequence, the heart of all morality is love, and by always following this direction we inevitably find ourselves encountering Christ, the love of God made man.[14]

The Magisterium's emphasis on teaching Christ involves no diminution of its regard for Saint Thomas as "a sure guide in theological and philosophical disciplines".[15] In his 1990 address to the International Study Congress on Aquinas, John

---

[14] *L'Osservatore Romano* (English ed.), Dec. 16, 1992, p. 4. On the dignity of the human person, see *C.C.C.*, nos. 1699–1715; see also nos. 355–68.

[15] Pope John Paul II, *Address to International Thomistic Congress*, *L'Osservatore Romano* (English ed.), Oct. 20, 1980, pp. 9, 10.

Paul II praised Saint Thomas for his "precise affirmation of the *dignity of human nature*; his concept of the *healing and elevation of mankind* to a higher level of greatness which took place as a result of the Incarnation of the Word; his precise formulation of the *perfecting nature of grace*, as a key principle of the view of the world and the ethics of human values developed in the *Summa*; and the importance which he attributed to *human reason* in knowing the truth and in treating moral and socio-ethical questions".[16] The Pope invited his listeners to "foster in every way possible the constant and deeper study of the philosophical, theological, ethical and political doctrine which St. Thomas has left as a heritage to the Catholic schools and which the Church has not hesitated to make her own, especially in that which regards the nature, capacity, perfectibility, vocation and responsibility of the human being in both the personal and social spheres, as is also pointed out in the directives of the Second Vatican Council".[17]

In sum, the Church is not a "superteacher" of natural law philosophy. She incorporates the teaching of Saint Thomas into her teaching of Christ. And her proclamation of Christ is neither academic nor defensive. In his 1990 encyclical, *The Mission of the Redeemer*, Pope John Paul II described the present as a " 'new springtime' of Christianity" and said that "God is opening before the Church the horizons of a humanity more fully prepared for the sowing of the Gospel. . . . No believer in Christ, no institution of the Church can avoid this supreme duty: to proclaim Christ to all peoples."[18]

---

[16] *The Pope Speaks* 78 (1991).

[17] Ibid., 80–81.

[18] Pope John Paul II, *The Mission of the Redeemer (Redemptoris Missio)* (1990), nos. 2, 3; 36 *The Pope Speaks* 138, 139–40 (1991).

36. I don't mind if you claim that Catholics should obey the Magisterium. But what is the Pope saying about the natural law that is so special that the rest of us — society at large — should accept it?

The Church has always emphasized the objective character of the natural law; the reality of God as the author of that law; and, especially, the dignity of the human person. "The guiding principle . . . of all of the Church's social doctrine", wrote Pope John Paul II, "is a correct view of the human person and of his unique value inasmuch as 'man . . . is the only creature on earth which God willed for itself.' God has imprinted his own image and likeness on man (cf. *Gn.* 1:26), conferring upon him an incomparable dignity. . . . From the Christian vision of the human person there necessarily follows a correct picture of society."[19] What is special—and essential for society to recognize—in the recent reaching of the Magisterium is the idea that relation to others is of the essence of every person.[20] This "identity" of the human person "as a spiritual and bodily being in relationship with God, with his neighbor and with the material world,"[21] builds on the traditional understanding of personhood. To find the law that governs the human person, the Magisterium looks beyond philosophical abstractions to the person of "Christ the new Adam . . . [who] fully reveals man to himself and brings to light his most high calling".[22]

---

[19] *C.A.*, nos. 11 and 13. On the human community in general, see *C.C.C.*, nos. 1877–1948.

[20] See *C.C.C.*, nos. 1878–96.

[21] *V.S.*, no. 13.

[22] Second Vatican Council, *Pastoral Constitution on the Church in the Modern World* (*Gaudium et Spes*), no. 22. See *V.S.*, no. 2.

In constitutional law, the term *person* includes corporations as well as human beings.[23] In *Roe* v. *Wade*, however, the Supreme Court held that *unborn* human beings are nonpersons and therefore have no constitutional rights.[24] That ruling rejects the implicit mandate of justice that all human beings are entitled to be regarded as persons. This mandate is especially obvious in a legal system where personhood is explicitly defined as the condition for the possession of rights. Incidentally, the nonpersonhood of the unborn child is the premise of any decision that would allow abortion in some cases or that would make abortion a matter for the states to decide.[25] If your life is subject to termination at the will of another whenever the legislature so decides, you are, in constitutional terms, a nonperson with no constitutional right to live.[26]

In philosophical terms, the classic definition is that of Boethius (c. 475–525): a person is "an individual substance of a rational nature"—that is, an individual with intellect and will.[27] Saint Thomas accepts this definition[28] and applies it to God as well as to human beings.

> "Person" signifies what is most perfect in all nature—that is, a subsistent individual of a rational nature. Hence, since everything that is perfect must be attributed to God, forasmuch as His essence contains every perfection, this name

---

[23] *Santa Clara County* v. *Southern Pacific Railroad Co.*, 118 U.S. 394 (1886).

[24] 410 U.S. 113 (1973).

[25] See *Webster* v. *Reproductive Health Services*, 492 U.S. 490, 567–68, n. 13 (1989) (opinion of Stevens); *Planned Parenthood* v. *Casey* (112 S. Ct. 2791, 2839 (1992)) (opinion of Stevens).

[26] See Charles E. Rice, *No Exception: A Pro-Life Imperative* (1991), chap. 2.

[27] Boethius, *De Duab. Nat.*, III (PL 64 1343).

[28] *S.T.*, I, Q. 29, art. 1.

"person" is fittingly applied to God; not, however, as it is applied to creatures, but in a more excellent way.[29] . . . "Person" in general signifies the individual substance of a rational [nature]. The individual in itself is undivided, but is distinct from others. Therefore "person" in any nature signifies what is distinct in that nature: thus in human nature it signifies this flesh, these bones, and this soul, which are the individuating principles of a man, and which, though not belonging to "person" in general, nevertheless do belong to the meaning of a human person. Now distinction in God is only by relation of origin . . . while relation in God is not as an accident in a subject, but is the divine essence itself. . . . In God, the individual—i.e., distinct and incommunicable substance—includes the idea of relation.[30]

The Persons in God are therefore not three isolated individuals. Rather, "relation" to the other divine Persons "is the divine essence itself".[31] This concept of a divine person as essentially involving relation to others goes beyond the classic definition of a person in general as "an individual substance of a rational nature". Saint Thomas did not apply this idea of person-as-relation to human as well as to divine persons. However, the Second Vatican Council began that application: "The Lord Jesus, when praying to the Father 'that they may all be one . . . even as we are one' (*Jn.* 17:21–22), has opened up new horizons closed to human reason by implying that there is a certain parallel between the union existing among the divine persons and the union of the sons of God in truth and love. It follows, then, that if man is the only creature on earth that

---

[29] Ibid., art. 3.
[30] Ibid., art. 4.
[31] Ibid.

God has wanted for its own sake, man can fully discover his true self only in a sincere giving of himself."[32]

More recently, John Paul II and others have further developed this idea that relation to others is of the essence of the human person just as it is of the essence of the divine Persons in the Trinity. Before he became Pope John Paul II, Cardinal Karol Wojtyla said that "the definition of Boethius determines above all the 'metaphysical site,' or in other words the dimension of being in which the personal subjectivity of man is realized, creating, so to speak, the right conditions for building upon this 'site' on the ground of experience."[33] As Pope, John Paul has inspired the construction on this "metaphysical site" of a relational understanding of personhood that is crucial in this age of individualism and alienation.

Cardinal Joseph Ratzinger writes:

> *The philosophical God is essentially self-centered*, thought simply contemplating itself. The God of Faith is basically defined by the category of relationship. . . . Thereby a completely new picture of the world, or completely new world-order is established; the highest possibility of Being no longer seems to be the detachment of him who exists in himself and needs only himself. On the contrary, the highest mode of Being includes the element of relationship. It is hardly necessary to say what a revolution it must mean for the direction of man's existence when the supreme Being no longer appears as absolute, enclosed autarchy but turns out to be at the same time involvement, creative power, which creates and bears and loves other things. . . . *The philosophical God is pure thought*: he is based on the notion that thought and thought

---

[32] Second Vatican Council, *Pastoral Constitution on the Church in the Modern World* (*Gaudium et Spes*), no. 24.

[33] Cardinal Karol Wojtyla, *Subjectivity and the Irreducible in Man*, in *The Human Being in Action* (Anna-Teresa Tymieniecka, ed., 1978), 107.

alone is divine. The God of Faith, as thought, is also love. His image is based on the conviction that to love is divine.[34]

God is a being in three persons. In this context, theologians argued, person must be understood as *relation*. According to Augustine and late patristic theology, the three persons that exist in God are in their nature relations. They are, therefore, not substances that stand next to each other, but they are real existing relations, and nothing besides. I believe this idea of the late patristic period is very important. In God, person means relation. Relation, being related, is not something superadded to the person, but it *is* the person itself. In its nature, the person exists only *as* relation. Put more concretely, the first person does not generate in the sense that the act of generating a Son is added to the already complete person, but the person *is* the deed of generating, of giving itself, of streaming itself forth. The person is identical with this act of self-donation. One could thus define the first person as a self-donation in fruitful knowledge and love. . . .

Let us summarize: in God there are three persons—which implies . . . that persons are relations, pure relatedness. Although there is in the first place only a statement about the Trinity, it is at the same time the fundamental statement about what is at stake in the concept of person. It opens the concept of person into the human spirit and provides its foundation and origin.[35]

Relation to others is no less intrinsic to the personhood of man than it is to that of God. "The issue of individualism and selfishness", wrote Professor David Schindler, "is the issue of relation. . . . Relation (to God, to all others in God) is some-

---

[34] Cardinal Joseph Ratzinger, *Introduction to Christianity* (1990), 102–3.

[35] Cardinal Joseph Ratzinger, "Retrieving the Tradition: Concerning the Notion of Person in Theology", 17 *Communio* 439, 444, 447 (Fall 1990).

thing I first am (*esse*) rather than something I first do or achieve (*agere*)."[36] Father Robert Connor summarized the significance of this new understanding of the human person as intrinsically relation to others:

> With the introduction of the notion of person in the *Pastoral Constitution of the Church in the Modern World*, no. 24, as "achieving self by the gift of self," the notion of person as "gift," and hence as relation, has universally and constantly been offered as the core concept in all the papal pronouncements and magisterial offerings in the last 26 years since Vatican II and particularly in the last 13 years in the pontificate of John Paul II. That this notion has impacted heavily in the East as a rallying point for Solidarity and in the collapse of Marxism, as well as in the West where it collides with the individualism of what we could call the "autonomous man," gives testimony to the enormous import of the notion.[37]

The erroneous "*notion of freedom*" today "exalts the isolated individual in an absolute way, and gives no place to solidarity, to openness to others and service of them."[38] On the contrary, "every man is his 'brother's keeper,' because God entrusts us to one another. And it is also in view of this entrusting that God gives everyone freedom, a freedom which possesses an *inherently relational dimension*."[39] Thus, "the full meaning of freedom [is] the gift of self in *service to God and one's brethren*."[40] Our model is the "*Crucified Christ* [who] *reveals the authentic meaning of freedom; he lives it fully in the total gift of himself* and

---

[36] David Schindler, "The One, True American Religion", *30 Days*, June 1989, pp. 55, 56.

[37] Robert A. Connor, "The Person as Resonating Existential", 66 *Am. Catholic Phil.* Q. 39, 42 (1992).

[38] *E.V.*, no. 19.

[39] Ibid.

[40] *V.S.*, no. 87.

calls his disciples to share in his freedom."[41] As Pope John Paul described it, "the deepest and most authentic meaning of life [is] that of being *a gift which is fully realized in the giving of self.*"[42]

"Human perfection," as John Paul described it in *Fides et Ratio*, "consists not simply in acquiring an abstract knowledge of the truth, but in a dynamic relationship of faithful self-giving with others. It is in this faithful self-giving that a person finds a fullness of certainty and security. At the same time, however, knowledge through belief, grounded as it is on trust between persons, is linked to truth: in the act of believing, men and women entrust themselves to the truth which the other declares to them."[43]

So if you ask: What is the Magisterium saying that is so special? the answer is that, since Vatican II and especially under the leadership of John Paul II, the Church has shown the way to a new understanding of the human person—and of freedom —that is the definitive answer to the sterile individualism and alienation of the Enlightenment.

37. So the Magisterium argues for "the Christian vision of the human person". So what? How does that relate to the problems of life in the real world?

Have you ever wondered at the paradox that the twentieth century has produced more proclamations of human rights than any century and yet has produced the greatest violations of

---

[41] Ibid., no. 85.

[42] *E.V.*, no. 49.

[43] *F.R.*, no. 32.

those rights ever seen?[44] One practical service rendered by the Magisterium, including especially the teaching of John Paul II, is its exposition of the role of relativism and autonomous individualism in fostering totalitarianism. The Magisterium opposes relativism by affirming objective moral norms, not on the basis of philosophical abstraction but in light of the creation and destiny of the human person. And it opposes alienation by affirming the person, not as an isolated, alienated individual but as one for whom relation to others is of the essence of his being because he is made in the image of the persons of the Trinity.[45]

Objective Moral Norms

Through philosophical reflection we can see man as a "rational animal", with objective moral criteria arising from his nature. That explanation is valid but it does not go far enough. John Paul II has gone beyond it by grounding the reality of objective moral norms not merely in philosophical abstractions but rather in "the truth of creation" of each human person in the image and likeness of God.[46] In his address to the 1986 International Congress on Moral Theology, the Pope said:

> That there in fact exists a moral good and evil not reducible to other human goods and evils is the necessary and immediate consequence of the *truth of creation*, which is the ultimate foundation of the *very dignity* of the human person.
>
> Called, as a person, to immediate communion with God; the object, as a person, of an entirely singular Providence,

---

[44] See Question 46, below.
[45] See Question 35, above.
[46] See also *C.C.C.*, nos. 1700–15, 1750–61.

man bears a law written in his heart that he does not give to himself, but which expresses the immutable demands of his personal *being* created by God, granted a finality by God and in itself endowed with a dignity that is infinitely superior to that of things. This law is not only made up of general guidelines, whose specification is in their respective content conditioned by different and changeable historical situations. There are moral norms that have a precise content which is immutable and unconditioned. . . .

To deny the existence of norms having such a value can be done only by someone who denies the existence of a *truth* about the person, of an immutable nature in man, based ultimately on the creative Wisdom which is the measure of all reality.[47]

The Pope called for ethical reflection to be "founded and rooted ever more deeply in a true anthropology and this, ultimately, on the metaphysics of creation which is at the center of all Christian thinking."[48]

Rational ethical reflection is completed, by finding its perfection in the theological ethical reflection. The creative Wisdom that is the measure of all reality, in the Truth of which every creature is true, has a name: the Incarnate Word, the Lord Jesus dead and risen. In Him and in view of Him man is created, because the Father—in his utterly free plan—has wanted man to participate in the only-begotten Son, in the trinitarian life itself. And, therefore, only theological ethics can give an *entirely* true response to the moral questioning of man. From this derives a true and proper competence of the Magisterium of the Church in the sphere of moral norms. Her intervention in this area cannot be seen as the

---

[47] Pope John Paul II, *Address to International Congress on Moral Theology,* Apr. 10, 1986, 31 *The Pope Speaks* 175, 177.

[48] Ibid.

equivalent of one opinion among others, even if the opinion were granted a particular authority. . . . To appeal to a "faith of the Church" in order to oppose the moral Magisterium of the Church is equivalent to denying the Catholic concept of Revelation.[49]

The Ten Commandments are specifications of the obligations of the natural law.[50] "Both the Old and the New Testaments explicitly affirm that *without love of neighbor*, made concrete in keeping the commandments, *genuine love for God is not possible*."[51] "God, who alone is good, knows perfectly what is good for man, and by virtue of his very love proposes this good to man in the commandments."[52] The positive precepts of the natural law, such as to honor one's parents, may not apply in a specific situation "in view of other duties which may be more important or urgent."[53] If his parents ordered a child to steal, he would be obliged to disobey them. "The *negative precepts* of the natural law," however, such as the prohibition of adultery, "oblige each and every individual, always and in every circumstance. . . . The Church has always taught that one may never choose kinds of behavior prohibited by the moral commandments expressed in negative form in the Old and New Testaments. . . . Jesus himself reaffirms that these prohibitions allow no exceptions."[54]

The moral law, John Paul makes clear, is not an academic abstraction. In teaching that law, the Church "does not simply present 'ideals': rather she teaches *who* man *is*, created by God in Christ, and therefore, what his true good is. The moral law

---

[49] Ibid., 177–78.

[50] See *V.S.*, no. 79.

[51] *V.S.*, no. 14.

[52] Ibid., no. 35.

[53] Ibid., no. 67, see also no. 52.

[54] *V.S.*, no. 52.

is not something extrinsic to the person; it is the very human person himself in so far as he is called *in* and *by* the creative act itself to be and to fulfill himself freely in Christ."[55]

In *Veritatis Splendor*, John Paul explained why the denial of objective moral truth reduces law to a function of raw, totalitarian power.[56] As he put it, recognition of objective moral norms is essential for freedom and "genuine democracy": "[T]here can be no freedom apart from or in opposition to the truth. . . . [O]nly by obedience to universal moral norms does man find full confirmation of his personal uniqueness and the possibility of authentic moral growth. For this very reason . . . [t]hese norms . . . represent the foundation of genuine democracy, which can . . . develop only on the basis of the equality of all its members, who possess common rights and duties. *When it is a matter of the moral norms prohibiting intrinsic evil, there are no privileges or exceptions for anyone.* It makes no difference whether one is the master of the world or the 'poorest of the poor' on the face of the earth. Before the demands of morality, we are all absolutely equal."[57]

This is applied common sense. If we do not affirm objective norms that always prohibit certain conduct, how can we define any moral limits to what the state can do? "Indeed, 'If there is no ultimate truth to guide and direct political activity, then ideas and convictions can easily be manipulated for reasons of power. As history demonstrates, a democracy without values easily turns into open or thinly disguised totalitarianism.' "[58]

---

[55] Pope John Paul II, *Address to International Congress on Moral Theology*, Apr. 10, 1986, 31 *The Pope Speaks* 178.

[56] See *V.S.*, no. 99.

[57] *V.S.*, no. 96.

[58] Ibid. no. 101

Alienation or Relation?

As discussed in the previous Question and in Question 25, the concept of person as relation was applied by Saint Thomas to the Persons of the Trinity. Its recent application by the Magisterium to human persons[59] can have a decisive impact on economic and social relations as well as on issues of the family, procreation, and bioethics. "The age in which we live", said Pope John Paul in his 1994 *Letter to Families*, "is still threatened to a great extent by 'alienation.' This is the result of 'Enlightenment' premises according to which a man is 'more' human if he is 'only' human. It is not difficult to notice how alienation from everything belonging . . . to the full richness of man threatens our times."[60] The Enlightenment sees man not as social by nature but as merely sociable, with his relations to others arising not from his nature and the demands of the common good but solely from his freely given consent. This is the origin of the "pro-choice" mentality. The expectant mother is an autonomous individual owing no duty to her child except as she chooses to consent. Marriage implies no inherent stability of relationship. Rather, it is up to each spouse to decide whether it will be permanent or temporary, monogamous or adulterous. The goal is self-fulfillment of the isolated individual unencumbered by any inherent duties or relations to others. However, if man, of his very nature, is in relationship with others, then the autonomous individual of the Enlightenment, who has no responsibility or openness to others except by his own unrestricted choice, is not only unattractive. He is inhuman.

---

[59] See *C.C.C.*, nos. 1877–96, 1939–48.

[60] *L.F.*, no. 15.

[The trinitarian understanding of personhood as inherently involving relation to others is] a model for the Christian understanding of reality. The teaching on the Trinity signifies a breakthrough from an understanding of reality that was stamped by the primacy of a substance that existed in and for itself to an understanding of reality that is marked by the primacy of person and relation. According to Christian thought, the ultimate reality is conceivable not in terms of a self-subsistent substance but of a person who is fulfilled only in a selfless relationality of giving and receiving. It could also be said that the meaning of being, from the Christian point of view, is love. . . . From this comes the fundamental model of a Christian spirituality of selfless service. The Persons of the Trinity are in fact characterized by their selflessness. Each is in his way pure self-donation, pure self-emptying.[61]

We, like the Persons of the Trinity, are not isolated individuals. Rather, we are persons only in relation to others. In his 1991 social encyclical, *Centesimus Annus*, Pope John Paul II said:

When man does not recognize in himself and in others the value and grandeur of the human person, he effectively deprives himself of the possibility of benefiting from his humanity and of entering into that relationship of solidarity and communion with others for which God created him. Indeed, it is through the free gift of self that man truly finds himself. . . . Man cannot give himself to a purely human plan for reality, to an abstract ideal or to a false utopia. As a person, he can give himself to another person or to other persons, and ultimately to God, who is the author of his being and who alone can fully accept his gift. A man is alienated if he refuses to transcend himself and to live the experi-

---

[61] Walter Kasper, *Transcending All Understanding: The Meaning of Christian Faith Today* (Boniface Ramsey, O.P., transl., 1989), 98–99.

ence of self-giving and of the formation of an authentic human community oriented toward his final destiny, which is God. A society is alienated if its forms of social organization, production and consumption make it more difficult to offer this gift of self and to establish this solidarity between people. . . . A person who is concerned solely or primarily with possessing and enjoying, who is no longer able to control his instincts and passions, or to subordinate them by obedience to the truth, cannot be free; obedience to the truth about God and man is the first condition of freedom, making it possible for a person to order his needs and desires and to choose the means of satisfying them according to a correct scale of values, so that the ownership of things may become an occasion of growth for him.[62]

"If the promotion of the self is understood in terms of absolute autonomy," said John Paul II, "people inevitably reach the point of rejecting one another. Everyone else is considered an enemy from whom one has to defend oneself. Thus society becomes a mass of individuals placed side by side, but without any mutual bonds. Each one wishes to assert himself independently of the other and in fact intends to make his own interests prevail. Still, . . . some kind of compromise must be found if one wants a society in which the maximum possible freedom is guaranteed to each individual. In this way, any reference to common values and to a truth absolutely binding on everyone is lost and social life ventures onto the shifting sands of complete relativism. At that point, *everything is negotiable, everything is open to bargaining*: even the first of the fundamental rights, the right to life."[63]

The analysis by the Magisterium of the human person as

---

[62] *C.A.*, no. 41.

[63] *E.V.*, nos. 19–20.

relation is the foundation for a conclusive answer to the failed individualism of the Enlightenment. That analysis, based on metaphysics as well as revelation, tells us that "the notion of person, besides including substance, must be formally inclusive of relation. The notion of person would take its meaning and fulfillment from love. Person as such could only take place in the plural, in the presence of another."[64] The classic definition saw a person as an individual substance of rational nature. Any relation that person might have with others was added to, and not intrinsically part of, his nature as a person. Now, however, as Cardinal Ratzinger put it, "the undivided sway of thinking in terms of substance is ended; relation is discovered as an equally valid primordial mode of reality."[65] Saint Paul said that "we are members of one another."[66] We are not isolated individuals whose only responsibility is to "look after number one". In the words of Bishop Dr. Walter Kasper, the "existence" of the human person is "possible only in co-existence with other persons. The human person is possible only in the plural; it can exist only in reciprocal acknowledgement, and it finds its fulfillment only in the communion of love. Persons thus exist only in mutual giving and receiving."[67]

Instead of the accurate, but dry and incomplete, abstractions of "substance", "rational animal", and so forth, the discussion of the person must now center on the exciting reality of *this* human being—*this* person—created in the image and likeness of God for a destiny of eternal happiness with God in heaven.

---

[64] Robert Connor, "Relation, the Thomistic *esse*, and American Culture: Toward a Metaphysic of Sanctity", 17 *Communio* 455 (Fall 1990).

[65] Ratzinger, *Introduction to Christianity* (1969, 1990), 132.

[66] Eph 4:25.

[67] Walter Kasper, *The God of Jesus Christ* (1984), 306.

And Christ showed the human person that he "can fully discover his true self only in a sincere giving of himself".[68]

To view the human person as intrinsically including relation to others is to assimilate but carry to a higher plane the affirmation of Aristotle and Aquinas that man is a social, rather than merely a sociable, animal. Libertarian and social-contract theorists tell us that we are in relation to others only to the extent that we freely consent to such relation; even the mother has the "choice" to deny her relation to the child in her womb. The emphasis on personhood as inherently involving relation to others provides a coherent and humane alternative to this sterile individualism. The "I'm aboard, pull up the gangplank" school of jurisprudence not only does not work. It is contrary to the nature of man.

---

[68] Second Vatican Council, *Pastoral Constitution on the Church in the Modern World* (*Gaudium et Spes*), no. 24.

XI

SOME APPLICATIONS
OF THE NATURAL LAW
BY THE MAGISTERIUM

38. Get down to specifics. According to what principles would the Magisterium organize society and the economy?

To begin, we have to distinguish "evangelization, Catholic social teaching, and policy statements".[1] Evangelization is bearing witness to Christ and the Gospel.[2] Catholic social teaching is based on "scripture, tradition, and reason" and "is really a subdivision of evangelization, broadly understood".[3] That teaching explains principles as guides to the formation of a sound political, economic, and social order.[4] The social teachings, however, do not endorse any particular system or solution. Specific policy statements, such as an endorsement by the American bishops of a certain civil rights bill, apply the social teachings to particular problems; those policy statements are prudential judgments and bishops, as bishops, "have no greater insight into policy matters than anyone else".[5]

Our concern in this Question is with the social teaching rather than with particularized policy statements. Although a general discussion of the social teaching of the Church is beyond the scope of this book, we can note here a few ways in

---

[1] J. Brian Benestad, "Catholic Social Teaching, Political Philosophy and Pope John Paul II's *Laborem Exercens*", *Proceedings of the Fifth Convention of the Fellowship of Catholic Scholars* (1982), 53, 58.

[2] See the call for a "new evangelization" in *V.S.*, no. 106; see also William E. May, ed. *The Church's Mission of Evangelization* (1996).

[3] J. Brian Benestad, "Catholic Social Teaching", 58, 59.

[4] On the human community generally, see *C.C.C.*, nos. 1877–1948; on the social teaching of the Church in the context of the Seventh Commandment, see nos. 2419–63.

[5] Benestad, "Catholic Social Teaching", 59.

which that teaching brings the Christian view of the person to bear on the effort to attain a just social order.[6]

The encyclicals and other pronouncements of Pope John Paul II clearly explain the foundation and principles of that social teaching. The publication in 1993 of *Veritatis Splendor* was "the first time . . . that the Magisterium . . . has set forth in detail the fundamental elements of [Christian moral] teaching and presented the principles for the pastoral discernment necessary in practical and cultural situations."[7] That encyclical declared that "obedience to universal and unchanging moral norms" is essential for a just and free civil order.[8] The moral norm, however, is not an abstraction, but a person, Jesus Christ.[9] In *Evangelium Vitae*, in 1995, John Paul summoned us to a "cultural transformation",[10] reconnecting morality with faith and freedom with truth so as to overcome the "culture of death" with a "culture of life."[11] In these and other documents,[12] we

---

[6] The virtue of justice "directs man in his relations with other men". *S.T.*, II, II, Q. 58, art. 5. The "act of justice" is: "Rendering to each one his right". Ibid., art. 1. The traditional terminology classifies justice as general or particular. See Vernon Bourke, "Justice as Equitable Reciprocity: Aquinas Updated", 27 *Am. J. of Jur.* 17, 19, 27 (1982). General, or legal, justice (often called "social justice") relates to the legal, social, and other arrangements that involve immediately the common good; it governs the duties of the individual toward the community. *S.T.*, II, II, Q. 58, art. 7. On the particular justice side, commutative justice governs the relations between or among private persons, while distributive justice relates to the duties of the community toward individuals. *S.T.*, II, II, Q. 61, art. 1.

[7] *V.S.*, nos. 114–15.

[8] Ibid., no. 85.

[9] Ibid., nos. 19, 85.

[10] Ibid., no. 96.

[11] Ibid., no. 28.

[12] See Congregation for the Doctrine of the Faith, *Instruction on Christian Freedom and Liberation*, no. 73; *V.S.*, nos. 96–99; *E.V.*, nos. 2, 71

see that the basic foundation of social life is the dignity of the human person which he possesses because he is created in the image of God with an immortal destiny which transcends the state. Because man is created in the image of God, relation to others is intrinsic to his personhood as it is to the three Persons of the Trinity. From this it follows that the civil order must follow the principle of solidarity among persons rather than the isolated individualism of the Enlightenment. Because man has an eternal destiny he cannot find his fulfillment in the state or in any temporal order. From this arises the principle of subsidiarity which denies total competence and supremacy to the state. The Magisterium offers no particular models of political organization. But it does insist that the civil order must be founded on objective moral norms, that freedom cannot be divorced from truth and that morality cannot be divorced from faith. In short, a society and civil order that would be truly free must accept the natural law and its Author as its norm.

In the 1986 *Instruction on Christian Freedom and Liberation*, the Congregation for the Doctrine of the Faith, with the approval of Pope John Paul II, said that "the great commandment of love" is "the supreme principle of Christian social morality".[13]

> The supreme commandment of love leads to the full recognition of the dignity of each individual created in God's image. From this dignity flow natural rights and duties. In the light of the image of God, freedom, which is the essential prerogative of the human person, is manifested in all its depth. Persons are the active and responsible subjects of social life. Intimately linked to the *foundation*, which is man's dignity,

---

[13] Congregation for the Doctrine of the Faith, *Instruction on Christian Freedom and Liberation* (1986), no. 171; see also *Centesimus Annus*, no. 15.

are the *principle of solidarity*[14] and the *principle of subsidiarity*.[15] By virtue of the first, man with his brothers is obliged to contribute to the common good of society at all its levels. Hence, the Church's doctrine is opposed to all the forms of social or political individualism. By virtue of the second, neither the state nor any society must ever substitute for the initiative and responsibility of individuals and of intermediate communities at the level on which they can function, nor must they take away the room necessary for their freedom. Hence, the Church's social doctrine is opposed to all the forms of collectivism.[16]

On May 1, 1991, Pope John Paul II issued the encyclical *Centesimus Annus* (*The 100th Year*) to commemorate the centenary of Pope Leo XIII's social encyclical, *Rerum Novarum*. John Paul built on intervening encyclicals, including Pope Paul VI's *Populorum Progressio* (1967) and his own *Laborem Exercens* (1981) and *Sollicitudo Rei Socialis* (1987). *Centesimus Annus* refers only obliquely to the natural law.[17] But it is a gold mine of analysis of what it means to be a person in light of John Paul's emphasis on relation to others as an intrinsic aspect of personhood.

As noted in Question 37 above, *Centesimus Annus* carried forward the emerging concept of person as relation: "Indeed, it is through the free gift of self that man truly finds him-

---

[14] See *C.C.C.*, nos. 1939–42.

[15] Ibid., no. 1894.

[16] Congregation for the Doctrine of the Faith, *Instruction on Christian Freedom and Liberation*, no. 73.

[17] See *C.A.*, nos. 13, 30; 36 *The Pope Speaks* 273, 281–82, 291–92 (1991); see also Russell Hittinger, "The Problem of the State in *Centesimus Annus*", 15 *Ford. Int'l. Law J.* 953 (1991–92); James V. Schall, S.J., "On Being Dissatisfied with Compromises: Natural Law and Human Rights", 38 *Loyola L. Rev.* 289, 301–9 (1992).

self. . . . Man cannot give himself to a purely human plan for reality, to an abstract ideal or to a false utopia. As a person, he can give himself to another person or to other persons, and ultimately to God. . . . A society is alienated if its forms of social organization, production and consumption make it more difficult to offer this gift of self and to establish this solidarity between people."[18]

In *Centesimus Annus*, the Pope condemned socialism, the "fundamental error" of which is that it "considers the individual person simply as an element, a molecule within the social organism, so that the good of the individual is completely subordinated to the functioning of the socioeconomic mechanism. Socialism likewise maintains that the good of the individual can be realized without reference to his free choice. . . . In contrast, from the Christian vision of the human person . . . the social nature of man is not completely fulfilled in the state, but is realized in various intermediary groups, beginning with the family and including economic, social, political and cultural groups which stem from human nature itself and have their own autonomy."[19] This last allusion is to the principle of subsidiarity, which every Pope since Pius XI has explicitly affirmed:

> Just as it is wrong to withdraw from the individual and commit to the community at large what private enterprise and industry can accomplish, so too, it is an injustice, a grave evil, and a disturbance of right order for a larger and higher organization to arrogate to itself functions which can be performed efficiently by smaller and lower bodies. This is a fundamental principle of social philosophy, unshaken and unchangeable, and it retains its full truth today. . . . The

---

[18] *C.A.*, no. 41; see also *V.S.*, nos. 17–20, 85–88, 99–100.
[19] *C.A.*, no. 13.

true aim of all social activity should be to help individual members of the social body, but never to destroy or absorb them.[20]

Pope John Paul II said the "first cause" of socialism's mistaken concept of the person and society is "atheism". Only "by responding to the call of God" does man become "aware of his transcendent dignity".[21] Nor can that dignity be maintained in a society that denies God: "The denial of God deprives the person of his foundation and consequently leads to a reorganization of the social order without reference to the person's dignity and responsibility."[22] The Pope noted that the collapse of the Communist regimes in central and eastern Europe was due to "the violation of the rights of workers, . . . the inefficiency of the economic system [and] atheism".[23] "The true cause of the new developments", John Paul said, "was the spiritual void brought about by atheism. . . . Marxism had promised to uproot the need for God from the human heart, but the results have shown that it is not possible to succeed in this without throwing the heart into turmoil."[24] This theme was elaborated in *Evangelium Vitae*, where the Pope said: "[*W*]*hen the sense of God is lost, there is also a tendency to lose the sense of man*, of his dignity and his life."[25]

John Paul rejected the class struggle, in which "what is pursued is not the general good of society, but a partisan interest which replaces the common good and sets out to destroy whatever stands in its way."[26] The class struggle transfers to

---

[20] Pope Pius XI, *Quadragesimo Anno* (1931), no. 79; see also *L.E.*, no. 16.

[21] *C.A.*, no. 13.

[22] Ibid.

[23] Ibid., nos. 23, 24.

[24] Ibid., no. 24; see also *V.S.*, no. 98; *E.V.*, nos 21, 96.

[25] *E.V.*, no. 21.

[26] *C.A.*, no. 14.

"internal conflict between social groups the doctrine of 'total war'", which militarism and imperialism use in international relations. Both "class struggle in the Marxist sense and militarism have the same root, namely, atheism and contempt for the human person, which place the principle of force above that of reason and law."[27]

Although *Centesimus Annus* came down hard on socialism, it offered small comfort to Western materialism. The Pope criticized the response offered to Marxism by "the affluent society or the consumer society. It seeks to defeat Marxism on the level of pure materialism by showing how a free-market society can achieve a greater satisfaction of material human needs than communism, while equally excluding spiritual values. . . . Insofar as it denies an autonomous existence and value to morality, law, culture and religion, it agrees with Marxism in the sense that it totally reduces man to the sphere of economics and the satisfaction of material needs."[28] Indeed, John Paul said that the atheism that is the "first cause" of socialism's errors is "closely connected with the rationalism of the Enlightenment, which views human and social reality in a mechanistic way. Thus there is a denial of the supreme insight concerning man's true greatness, his transcendence in respect to earthly realities, the contradiction in his heart between the desire for the fullness of what is good and his own inability to attain it, and above all, the need for salvation which results from this situation."[29]

A central feature of Enlightenment philosophy is the denial of a knowable objective truth. John Paul has repeatedly em-

---

[27] Ibid.
[28] Ibid., no. 19.
[29] Ibid., no. 13.

phasized that this error underlies totalitarianism of whatever type.

> Totalitarianism arises out of a denial of truth in the objective sense. If there is no transcendent truth, in obedience to which man achieves his full identity, then there is no sure principle for guaranteeing just relations between people. Their self-interest as a class, group or nation would inevitably set them in opposition to one another. If one does not acknowledge transcendent truth, then the force of power takes over and each person tends to make full use of the means at his disposal in order to impose his own interests or his own opinion, with no regard for the rights of others. People are then respected only to the extent that they can be exploited for selfish ends. Thus, the root of modern totalitarianism is to be found in the denial of the transcendent dignity of the human person who, as the visible image of the invisible God, is therefore by his very nature the subject of rights which no one may violate—no individual, group, class, nation or state. Not even the majority of a social body may violate these rights by going against the minority, by isolating, oppressing or exploiting it or by attempting to annihilate it.[30]

The Pope wrote favorably of "the democratic system". However:

> Nowadays there is a tendency to claim that agnosticism and skeptical relativism are the philosophy and the basic attitude which correspond to democratic forms of political life. Those who are convinced that they know the truth and firmly adhere to it are considered unreliable from a democratic point of view, since they do not accept that truth is determined by the majority or that it is subject to variation according to

---

[30] Ibid., no. 44; quoted in *V.S.*, no. 99; see also *E.V.*, nos. 20, 96.

different political trends. It must be observed in this regard that if there is no ultimate truth to guide and direct political activity, then ideas and convictions can easily be manipulated for reasons of power. As history demonstrates, a democracy without values easily turns into open or thinly disguised totalitarianism. Since it is not an ideology, the Christian faith does not presume to imprison changing sociopolitical realities in a rigid schema, and it recognizes that human life is realized in history in conditions that are diverse and imperfect. Furthermore, in constantly reaffirming the transcendent dignity of the person, the Church's method is always that of respect for freedom.[31]

In his discussion of the need "to rebuild morally and economically the countries which have abandoned communism",[32] the Pope emphasized:

Development must not be understood solely in economic terms, but in a way that is fully human. . . . The apex of development is the exercise of the right and duty to seek God, to know him and to live in accordance with that knowledge. In the totalitarian and authoritarian regimes, the principle that force predominates over reason was carried to the extreme. Man was compelled to submit to a conception of reality imposed on him by coercion and not reached by virtue of his own reason and exercise of his own freedom. This principle must be overturned and total recognition must be given to the rights of the human conscience, which is bound only to the truth, both natural and revealed. The recognition of these rights represents the primary foundation of every authentically free political order.[33]

---

[31] *C.A.*, no. 46; quoted in *V.S.*, no. 101; see also *V.S.*, nos. 16, 96–97 and *E.V.*, nos. 57, 70, 96.

[32] *C.A.*, no. 27.

[33] Ibid., no. 29.

Centesimus Annus repeatedly stresses the need for a proper understanding of the person and the need for solidarity among nations as well as among people. The Pope criticized the post-World War II process of "decolonization" in that, in some of the former colonies, "decisive sectors of the economy still remain *de facto* in the hands of large foreign companies which are unwilling to commit themselves to the long-term development of the host country."[34]

Pope John Paul declared that human nature "is made for freedom", and he stressed the need for the "social order" to bring "personal interest" into harmony with "the interests of society as a whole". Furthermore, he cautioned against the illusion of trying to create "a perfect social organization which makes evil impossible". This passage deserves full quotation as a summary of the Church's insistence on the rightful freedom of the human person and her rejection of any secular religion of politics:

> Not only is it wrong from the ethical point of view to disregard human nature, which is made for freedom, but in practice it is impossible to do so. Where society is so organized as to reduce arbitrarily or even suppress the sphere in which freedom is legitimately exercised, the result is that the life of society becomes progressively disorganized and goes into decline. Man tends toward good, but he is also capable of evil. . . .
>
> The social order will be all the more stable, the more it takes this fact into account and does not place in opposition personal interest and the interests of society as a whole, but rather seeks ways to bring them into fruitful harmony. In fact, where self-interest is violently suppressed, it is replaced by a burdensome system of bureaucratic control which dries

---

[34] Ibid., no. 20

up the wellsprings of initiative and creativity. When people think they possess the secret of a perfect social organization which makes evil impossible, they also think that they can use any means, including violence and deceit, in order to bring that organization into being. Politics then becomes a "secular religion" which operates under the illusion of creating paradise in this world. But no political society—which possesses its own autonomy and laws—can ever be confused with the kingdom of God.[35]

39. If the Pope rejects both socialism and consumerism, what's his answer? What about private property? Where does he come down on that?

Saint Thomas states:

Man has a natural dominion over external things, because, by his reason and will, he is able to use them for his own profit, as they were made on his account: for the imperfect is always for the sake of the perfect. . . . It is by this argument that [Aristotle] proves . . . that the possession of external things is natural to man. Moreover, this natural dominion of man over other creatures, which is competent to man in respect of his reason wherein God's image resides, is shown forth in man's creation (*Gen.* i.26) by the words: 'Let us make man to Our image and likeness: and let him have dominion over the fishes of the sea,' etc. . . . God has sovereign dominion over all things: and He, according to His providence, directed certain things to the sustenance of man's body. For this reason man has a natural dominion over things, as regards the power to make use of them.[36]

---

[35] Ibid., no. 25.
[36] *S.T.*, II, II, Q. 66, art. 1.

Man not only has a right to use property, he has a right to possess it as his own. This right is not absolute, however. The realism of Saint Thomas shines through his answer:

> Two things are competent to man in respect of exterior things. One is the power to procure and dispense them, and in this regard it is lawful for man to possess property. Moreover this is necessary to human life for three reasons. *First*, because every man is more careful to procure what is for himself alone than that which is common to many or to all: since each one would shirk the labor and leave to another that which concerns the community. . . . *Secondly*, because human affairs are conducted in more orderly fashion if each man is charged with taking care of some particular thing himself, whereas there would be confusion if everyone had to look after any one thing indiscriminately. *Thirdly*, because a more peaceful state is ensured to man if each one is contented with his own. . . . Quarrels arise more frequently where there is no division of the things possessed.
>
> The second thing that is competent to man with regard to external things is their use. In this respect man ought to possess external things, not as his own, but as common, so that . . . he is ready to communicate to others in their need. . . .
>
> Community of goods is ascribed to the natural law, not that the natural law dictates that all things should be possessed in common and that nothing should be possessed as one's own: but because the division of possessions is not according to the natural law, but rather arose from human agreement which belongs to positive law. . . . Hence the ownership of possessions is not contrary to the natural law, but an addition thereto devised by human reason. . . .
>
> [A] rich man does not act unlawfully if he anticipates someone in taking possession of something which at first was common property, and gives others a share: but he sins if he excludes others indiscriminately from using it. . . .

When Ambrose says: "Let no man call his own that which is common," he is speaking of ownership as regards use, wherefore he adds: "He who spends too much is a robber."[37]

In *Centesimus Annus*, Pope John Paul II emphasized the consistent teaching of the Church on "the necessity and therefore the legitimacy of private ownership as well as the limits which are imposed on it. . . . God gave the earth to the whole human race for the sustenance of all its members, without excluding or favoring anyone. . . . It is through work that man, using his intelligence and exercising his freedom, succeeds in dominating the earth and making it a fitting home. In this way he makes part of the earth his own, precisely the part he has acquired through work: this is the origin of individual property. Obviously he also has the responsibility not to hinder others from having their own part of God's gift; indeed he must cooperate with others so that together all can dominate the earth."[38]

These principles apply to the earth itself as well as to other goods. "In the beginning God entrusted the earth and its resources to the common stewardship of mankind to take care of them, master them by labor, and enjoy their fruits."[39] A government has the duty to promote the common good of its particular society and people. However, the exercise of that duty, pursuant to the principle of solidarity," cannot be divorced from the common good of the entire human family."[40] Persons have a right to migrate which is based on their dignity as persons and on the universal destination of land as of other goods. No community has a moral right absolutely to foreclose immigration. Its right to restrict immigration will depend on

---

[37] Ibid., art. 2.

[38] *C.A.*, nos. 30, 31.

[39] *C.C.C.*, no. 2402.

[40] Pope John XXIII, *Pacem in Terris*, (1963) no. 98.

a balancing of its own common good against the needs of potential immigrants. In *Pacem in Terris*, Pope John XXIII said that, "among men's personal rights we must include his right to enter a country in which he hopes to be able to provide more fittingly for himself and his dependents. It is therefore the duty of State officials to accept such immigrants and—so far as the good of their own community, rightly understood, permits—to further the aims of those who may wish to become members of a new society."[41] In his message for World Migration Day, July 25th, 1995, Pope John Paul said: "Today the phenomenon of illegal migrants has assumed considerable proportions. His irregular legal status cannot allow the migrant to lose his dignity, since he is endowed with inalienable rights, which can neither be violated nor ignored. . . . Illegal immigration should be prevented, but it is also essential to combat vigorously the criminal activities which exploit illegal immigrants." It is necessary to avoid the use of administrative regulations, meant to restrict the criterion of family membership, which result in unjustifiably forcing into an illegal situation people whose right to live with their family cannot be denied by any law."[42]

The Pope noted "another form of ownership which is becoming no less important than land: the possession of know-how, technology and skill. . . . Whereas at one time the decisive factor of production was the land and later capital, . . . today the decisive factor is increasingly man himself, that is, his knowledge, especially his scientific knowledge, his capacity for interrelated and compact organization as well as his ability to perceive the needs of others and to satisfy them."[43]

---

[41] *Pacem in Terris*, no. 106.
[42] 41 *The Pope Speaks* 8, 10 (1996).
[43] *C.A.*, no. 32.

He deplored the situation of people in the "Third World" whose "dignity is not acknowledged in any real way, and sometimes there are even attempts to eliminate them from history through coercive forms of demographic control which are contrary to human dignity." He criticized the "inhuman exploitation" through which, "for the poor, to the lack of material goods has been added a lack of knowledge and training which prevents them from escaping their state of humiliating subjection."[44]

In *Evangelium Vitae*, John Paul called for a "cultural change" which "demands from everyone the courage to *adopt a new* lifestyle . . . on the basis of a correct set of values: *the primacy of being over having, of the person over things.* This renewed life-style involves a passing *from indifference to concern for others, from rejection to acceptance of them.*"[45] And the *Catechism* affirms that "The ownership of any property makes its holder a steward of Providence, with the task of making it fruitful and communicating its benefits to others, first of all his family."[46]

In summary, in the words of John Paul II, "the right to private property . . . which is fundamental for the autonomy and development of the person, has always been defended by the Church up to our own day. At the same time the Church teaches that the possession of material goods is not an absolute right and that its limits are inscribed in its very nature as a human right."[47] The distinction between property rights and human rights is false. The right to own and dispose of property, while not absolute, is one of the most fundamental human rights. Without economic freedom, rightly understood,

---

[44] Ibid., no. 33.

[45] *E.V.*, no. 98.

[46] *C.C.C.*, no. 2404; see nos. 2401–06.

[47] *C.A.*, no. 30; see *V.S.*, no. 100.

there can be no genuine personal and political freedom. But economic freedom is not absolute.

40. So if the Magisterium affirms property rights and opposes socialism, does it therefore endorse capitalism?

That depends. The Church condemns both Marxism and liberal capitalism. They are both forms of materialism and of economism, which regards man as only an economic entity.[48] Here, as elsewhere, let the Magisterium speak for itself.

In *Centesimus Annus*, Pope John Paul II acknowledged that "the free market is the most effective instrument for utilizing resources and responding to needs."[49]

> [We endorse] not the socialist system, which in fact turns out to be state capitalism, but rather a society of free work, of enterprise and of participation. Such a society is not directed against the market, but demands that the market be appropriately controlled by the forces of society and by the state so as to guarantee that the basic needs of the whole of society are satisfied. The Church acknowledges the legitimate role of profit as an indication that a business is functioning well. . . . In fact the purpose of a business firm is not simply to make a profit, but is to be found in its very existence as a community of persons who in various ways are endeavoring to satisfy their basic needs and who form a particular group at the service of the whole of society. Profit is a regulator of the life of a business, but it is not the only one; other human and moral factors must also be considered, which in

---

[48] See Pope John Paul II, *Laborem Exercens* (1981), nos. 13, 14.

[49] *C.A.*, no. 34.

the long term are at least equally important for the life of a business.[50]

The Pope expressed particular concern about the plight of "weaker" nations:

> We have seen that it is unacceptable to say that the defeat of so-called "real socialism" leaves capitalism as the only model of economic organization. It is necessary to break down the barriers and monopolies which leave so many countries on the margins of development and to provide all individuals and nations with the basic conditions which will enable them to share in development. . . . Stronger nations must offer weaker ones opportunities for taking their place in international life, and the latter must learn how to use these opportunities by making the necessary efforts and sacrifices and by ensuring political and economic stability, the certainty of better prospects for the future, the improvement of workers' skills and the training of competent business leaders who are conscious of their responsibilities.
>
> At present, the positive efforts which have been made along these lines are being affected by the still largely unsolved problem of the foreign debt of the poorer countries. The principle that debts must be paid is certainly just. However, it is not right to demand or expect payment when the effect would be the imposition of political choices leading to hunger and despair for entire peoples. It cannot be expected that the debts which have been contracted should be paid at the price of unbearable sacrifices. In such cases it is necessary to find—as in fact is partly happening—ways to lighten, defer, or even cancel the debt compatible with the fundamental right of peoples to subsistence and progress.[51]

---

[50] Ibid., no. 35.
[51] Ibid.; see also *E.V.*, no. 18.

A persistent theme in the social teaching of the Church is that "economic freedom is only one element of human freedom. When it becomes autonomous, when man is seen more as a producer or consumer of goods than as a subject who produces and consumes in order to live, then economic freedom loses its necessary relationship to the human person and ends up by alienating and oppressing him."[52]

John Paul asked, "Can it perhaps be said that after the failure of communism capitalism is the victorious social system and that capitalism should be the goal of the countries now making efforts to rebuild their economy and society? Is this the model that ought to be proposed to the countries of the Third World, which are searching for the path to true economic and civil progress?"[53]

> The answer is obviously complex. If by "capitalism" is meant an economic system which recognizes the fundamental and positive role of business, the market, private property and the resulting responsibility for the means of production as well as free human creativity in the economic sector, then the answer is certainly in the affirmative even though it would perhaps be more appropriate to speak of a "business economy," "market economy" or simply "free economy." But if by "capitalism" is meant a system in which freedom in the economic sector is not circumscribed within a strong juridical framework which places it at the service of human freedom in its totality and which sees it as a particular aspect of that freedom, the core of which is ethical and religious, then the reply is certainly negative.
>
> The Marxist solution has failed, but the realities of marginalization and exploitation remain in the world, especially the

---

[52] *C.A.*, no. 39.
[53] Ibid., no. 42.

Third World, as does the reality of human alienation, especially in the more advanced countries.[54]

The Pope criticized "the welfare state, dubbed the 'social assistance state'" as a violation of the principle of subsidiarity. "By intervening directly and depriving society of its responsibility, the social assistance state leads to a loss of human energies and an inordinate increase of public agencies which are dominated more by bureaucratic ways of thinking than by concern for serving their clients and which are accompanied by an enormous increase in spending. In fact, it would appear that needs are best understood and satisfied by people who are closest to them and who act as neighbors to those in need."[55]

In accord with the principle of subsidiarity, the Pope stressed the importance of the family and "other intermediate communities":

> In order to overcome today's widespread individualistic mentality, what is required is a concrete commitment to solidarity and charity, beginning in the family with the mutual support of husband and wife and the care which the different generations give to one another. In this sense the family too can be called a community of work and solidarity. It can happen, however, that when a family does decide to live up fully to its vocation, it finds itself without the necessary support from the state and without sufficient resources. It is urgent therefore to promote not only family policies, but also those social policies which have the family as their principal object, policies which assist the family by providing adequate resources and efficient means of support both for bringing up children and for looking after the elderly so as to avoid distancing the latter from the family unit and in order to strengthen relations between generations.

---

[54] Ibid.

[55] Ibid., no. 48.

Apart from the family, other intermediate communities exercise primary functions and give life to specific networks of solidarity. These develop as real communities of persons and strengthen the social fabric, preventing society from becoming an anonymous and impersonal mass as unfortunately often happens today. It is in interrelationships on many levels that a person lives and that society becomes more "personalized." The individual today is often suffocated between two poles represented by the state and the marketplace. At times it seems as though he exists only as a producer and consumer of goods or as an object of state administration. People lose sight of the fact that life in society has neither the market nor the state as its final purpose, since life itself has a unique value which the state and the market must serve.[56]

The Pope also noted the Church's "preferential option for the poor, which is never exclusive or discriminatory toward other groups. This option is not limited to material poverty, since it is well known that there are many other forms of poverty, especially in modern society—not only economic, but cultural and spiritual poverty as well."[57]

"The Church", said the Pope, "has no models to present; models that are real and truly effective can only arise within the framework of different historical situations through the efforts of all those who responsibly confront concrete problems in all their social, economic, political and cultural aspects as these interact with one another. For such a task the Church offers her social teaching as an *indispensable and ideal orientation*, a teaching which, as already mentioned, recognizes the positive value of the market and of enterprise, but which at the

---

[56] Ibid., no. 49.
[57] Ibid., no. 57.

same time points out that these need to be oriented toward the common good."[58]

> [We also find legitimate] workers' efforts to obtain full respect for their dignity and to gain broader areas of participation in the life of industrial enterprises so that, while cooperating with others and under the direction of others, they can in a certain sense "work for themselves" through the exercise of their intelligence and freedom.
>
> The integral development of the human person through work does not impede but rather promotes the greater productivity and efficiency of work itself, even though it may weaken consolidated power structures. A business cannot be considered only as a "society of capital goods"; it is also a "society of persons" in which people participate in different ways and with specific responsibilities, whether they supply the necessary capital for the company's activities or take part in such activities through their labor. To achieve these goals there is still need for a broad associated workers' movement directed toward the liberation and promotion of the whole person.[59]

In sum, the teaching of the Magisterium rejects materialism and the treatment of human beings as merely economic units. That teaching is centered instead on the dignity and primacy of the human person. "It is not wrong to want to live better", wrote Pope John Paul. "What is wrong is a style of life which is presumed to be better when it is directed toward 'having' rather than 'being' and which wants to have more not in order to be more, but in order to spend life in enjoyment as an end in itself. It is therefore necessary to create lifestyles in which the quest for truth, beauty, goodness and communion with others for the sake of common growth are the factors which deter-

---

[58] Ibid., no. 43.
[59] Ibid.

mine consumer choices, savings and investments."[60] Of particular relevance to certain aspects of life in the United States, Pope John Paul criticized "consumerism", in which "people are ensnared in a web of false and superficial gratifications rather than being helped to experience their personhood in an authentic and concrete way."[61] One of the first casualties of that consumerism is the family, which is the primary cell of society and which depends on the ethic of self-giving rather than the ethic of self-gratification.

41. *What is the family and what's so special about it?*

The individualist, Enlightenment philosophy of the family[62] is reflected in American constitutional law. In *Eisenstadt* v. *Baird*, in 1972, the Supreme Court reversed the conviction of William Baird for distributing contraceptives to unmarried persons, holding that "whatever the rights of the individual to access to contraceptives may be, the rights must be the same for the unmarried and the married alike." The "marital couple", said the Court, "is not an independent entity with a mind and heart of its own, but an association of individuals each with a separate intellectual and emotional makeup. If the right of privacy means anything, it is the right of the *individual*, married or single, to be free from unwarranted governmental intrusion into matters so fundamentally affecting a person as the decision whether to bear or beget a child."[63]

---

[60] Ibid., no. 36; see also *E.V.*, no. 98.

[61] *C.A.*, no. 41.

[62] See Allan C. Carlson, *Family Questions: Reflections on the American Social Crisis* (1990), chap. 16.

[63] 405 U.S. 438, 453 (1972).

The Court thus reduces marriage to a mere personal contract, just as an agreement by one person to cut another's lawn every week is a contract. If both parties decide to terminate the lawn-cutting arrangement, or if only one wants out, the law will not compel them to continue in it. Similarly, if either spouse wants to terminate the family relation, the law will not interfere. No-fault divorce is the logical outcome of this atomization of the family.

The family, however, is not a mere social convention, to be defined and redefined according to changing norms of political correctness. The family, in Aristotle's words, is founded on "a union of those who cannot exist without each other; namely, of male and female, that the race may continue". "The family", he wrote, "is the association established by nature for the supply of men's everyday wants."[64] Aristotle described the family as the "first" social institution, the origin of the household and then of the village and of the state. The family is a society grounded in the nature of the human person. Its promotion is an essential aspect of the common good. As Pope John XXIII put it, the family is "the natural, primary cell of human society".[65]

Saint Thomas asserts that "matrimony is natural for man, and promiscuous performance of the sexual act, outside matrimony, is contrary to man's good. For this reason it must be a sin."[66] He concludes that marriage should be indivisible, that "it is contrary to the natural instinct of the human species for

---

[64] Aristotle, *Politics*, book I (Benjamin Jowett, transl.), in *Basic Works of Aristotle* (Richard McKeon, ed., 1941), 1127.

[65] Pope John XXIII, *Pacem in Terris*, no. 16.

[66] Saint Thomas Aquinas, *Summa contra Gentiles* (Vernon J. Bourke, transl., 1975), book III, chap. 122, p. 146; see also *S.T.*, Suppl., Q., 41, art. 1. On the sacrament of matrimony, see *C.C.C.*, nos. 1601–66; on conjugal love and fidelity, see nos. 2360–72.

a wife to be separated from her husband. And thus, the union of male and female in the human species must be not only lasting, but also unbroken."[67]

The Magisterium places marriage and the family (including children) in the context of the nature of the human person, who, in the words of Vatican II, "can fully discover his true self only in a sincere giving of himself".[68] Thus, Pope John Paul II stated in his 1981 apostolic exhortation, *Familiaris Consortio*, that "sexuality . . . is realized in a truly human way only if it is an integral part of the love by which a man and a woman commit themselves totally to one another until death. The total physical self-giving would be a lie if it were not the sign and fruit of a total personal self-giving, in which the whole person, including the temporal dimension, is present: if the person were to withhold something or reserve the possibility of deciding otherwise in the future, by this very fact he or she would not be giving totally."[69]

John Paul II wrote in *Centesimus Annus*:

> The first and fundamental structure for "human ecology" is the family, in which man receives his first formative ideas about truth and goodness, and learns what it means to love and to be loved, and thus what it actually means to be a person. Here we mean the family founded on marriage, in which the mutual gift of self by husband and wife creates an environment in which children can be born and develop their potentialities, become aware of their dignity and pre-

---

[67] Aquinas, *Summa contra Gentiles* (Vernon J. Bourke, transl., 1975), book III, chap 123, p. 148.

[68] Second Vatican Council, *Pastoral Constitution on the Church in the Modern World* (*Gaudium et Spes*), no. 24.

[69] Pope John Paul II, *Familiaris Consortio* (*The Community of the Family*) (1981) (hereafter cited as *F.C.*), no. 11; 27 *The Pope Speaks* 1 (1982). See *C.C.C.*, nos. 2360–72.

pare to face their unique and individual destiny. But it often happens that people are discouraged from creating the proper conditions for human reproduction and are led to consider themselves and their lives as a series of sensations to be experienced rather than as a work to be accomplished. The result is a lack of freedom, which causes a person to reject a commitment to enter into a stable relationship with another person and to bring children into the world or which leads people to consider children as one of the many "things" which an individual can have or not have, according to taste, and which compete with other possibilities. It is necessary to go back to seeing the family as the sanctuary of life. The family is indeed sacred: it is the place in which life—the gift of God—can be properly welcomed and protected against the many attacks to which it is exposed and can develop in accordance with what constitutes authentic human growth. In the face of the so-called culture of death, the family is the heart of the culture of life.[70]

In numerous respects, the family in the United States is an endangered species. To explore the current problems of the family, however, is beyond the scope of this book. Rather, the purpose here is to present affirmatively the teaching of the Magisterium on the family. That teaching is centered on the reality of the human person, who is not an isolated, autonomous entity but rather one whose very essence includes his relationship to others. In *Familiaris Consortio*, Pope John Paul II discussed the family in this context of personhood and the plan of God: "According to the plan of God, marriage is the foundation of the wider community of the family, since the very institution of marriage and conjugal love are ordained to

---

[70] *C.A.*, no. 39. On the family in the context of the Fourth Commandment, see *C.C.C.*, nos. 2196–233.

the procreation and education of children, in whom they find their crowning."[71] The Pope listed "four general tasks for the family":

1. Forming a community of persons;

2. Serving life;

3. Participating in the development of society;

4. Sharing in the life and mission of the Church.[72]

1. *Forming a community of persons.* Pope John Paul's emphasis on relation to others as the essence of personhood is reflected in his view of the family as "a community of persons" founded on love.[73] "The family originates in a marital communion . . . a *covenant,* in which man and woman 'give themselves to each other and accept each other'. . . . [P]arenthood is the event whereby the family, already constituted by the conjugal covenant of marriage, is brought about 'in the full and specific sense'. . . . *Communion* has to do with the personal relationship between the *I* and the *thou. Community* on the other hand transcends this framework and moves toward a *society,* a *we.* The family, as a community of persons, is thus the first human society. It arises whenever there comes into being the conjugal covenant of marriage, which opens the spouses to a lasting communion of love and of life, and it is brought to completion in a full and specific way with the procreation of children. The communion of the spouses gives rise to the community of the

---

[71] *F.C.,* no. 14.
[72] Ibid., no. 17.
[73] *F.C.,* no. 14.

family. The community of the family is completely pervaded by the very essence of communion."[74]

In his 1988 encyclical *On the Dignity and Vocation of Woman*, John Paul explained that this communion of human persons is modeled on the communion of divine Persons in the Trinity:

> *God*, who allows himself to be known by human beings through Christ is the *unity of the Trinity*: unity in communion. In this way new light is also thrown on man's image and likeness to God, spoken of in the book of *Genesis*. The fact that man "created as man and woman" is the image of God means not only that each of them individually is like God as a rational and free being. It also means that man and woman, created as a "unity of the two" in their common humanity, are called to live in a communion of love and in this way to mirror in the world the communion of love that is in God, through which the three Persons love each other in the intimate mystery of the one divine life. The Father, Son and Holy Spirit, one God through the unity of the divinity, exist as persons through the inscrutable divine relationship. Only in this way can we understand the truth that God in himself is love (cf. 1 *Jn.* 4:16). . . .
>
> In the "unity of the two," man and woman are called from the beginning not only to exist "side by side" or "together," but they are also called *to exist mutually "one for the other."* . . . To be human means to be called to interpersonal communion. . . . Being a person means striving toward self-realization (the council text speaks of self-discovery), which can only be achieved "*through a sincere gift of self*." The model for this interpretation of the person is God himself as Trinity, as a communion of persons. To say that man is

---

[74] *L.F.*, no. 7, quoting *Gaudium et Spes*, no. 48 and *F.C.*, no. 69; on solidarity as experienced within and around the family, see *E.V.*, no. 93.

created in the image and likeness of God means that man is called to exist "for" others, to become a gift.[75]

This meaning of person and of marriage in the divine plan requires that marriage be indissoluble. "Being rooted in the personal and total self-giving of the couple and being required by the good of the children, the indissolubility of marriage finds its ultimate truth in the plan that God has manifested in His revelation: He wills and He communicates the indissolubility of marriage as a fruit, a sign and a requirement of the absolutely faithful love that God has for man and that the Lord Jesus has for the Church."[76]

One role of the family is "welcoming, respecting and promoting each one of its members in his or her lofty dignity as a person, that is, as a living image of God."[77] In an important, countercultural passage, the Pope insisted not only that men should respect the "dignity of women" but also that society should favor women's "work in the home":

> Above all it is important to underline the equal dignity and responsibility of women with men. This equality is realized in a unique manner in that reciprocal self-giving by each one to the other and by both to the children which is proper to marriage and the family. What human reason intuitively perceives and acknowledges is fully revealed by the word of God: The history of salvation, in fact, is a continuous and luminous testimony to the dignity of women. . . .
>
> There is no doubt that the equal dignity and responsibility of men and women fully justifies women's access to pub-

---

[75] Pope John Paul II, *Mulieris Dignitatem* (1988), no. 7, 34 *The Pope Speaks* 10, 16–17 (1989); see also *L.F.*, nos. 6, 8; *E.V.*, no. 99.

[76] *F.C.*, no. 20; see Aquinas, *Summa contra Gentiles* (Vernon J. Bourke, transl., 1975), book III, chap. 123, for Aquinas' conclusion that marriage is indissoluble, as mentioned above in this Question. See also *L.F.*, no. 11.

[77] *F.C.*, no. 22.

lic functions. On the other hand the true advancement of women requires that clear recognition be given to the value of their maternal and family role, by comparison with all other public roles and all other professions. Furthermore, these roles and professions should be harmoniously combined if we wish the evolution of society and culture to be truly and fully human.

This will come about more easily if . . . a renewed "theology of work" can shed light upon and study in depth the meaning of work in the Christian life and determine the fundamental bond between work and the family, and therefore the original and irreplaceable meaning of work in the home and in rearing children. Therefore the Church can and should help modern society by tirelessly insisting that the work of women in the home be recognized and respected by all in its irreplaceable value. . . .

While it must be recognized that women have the same right as men to perform various public functions, society must be structured in such a way that wives and mothers are *not in practice compelled* to work outside the home, and that their families can live and prosper in a dignified way even when they themselves devote their full time to their own family.

Furthermore, the mentality which honors women more for their work outside the home than for their work within the family must be overcome. This requires that men should truly esteem and love women with total respect for their personal dignity, and that society should create and develop conditions favoring work in the home.[78]

2. *Serving life.* "The Sacrament of Matrimony", said Pope John Paul in 1992, "is oriented toward fruitfulness. It is an inclination which is inborn in human nature. 'By its very na-

---

[78] Ibid., nos. 22–23.

ture,' the council says, 'the institution of marriage and married love is ordered to the procreation and education of the offspring and it is in them that it finds its crowning glory.' "[79] This statement echoed his assertion in *Familiaris Consortio* that "the fundamental task of the family is to serve life, to actualize in history the original blessing of the Creator—that of transmitting by procreation the divine image from person to person. Fecundity is the fruit and the sign of conjugal love, the living testimony of the full reciprocal self-giving of the spouses: 'While not making the other purposes of matrimony of less account, the true practice of conjugal love, and the whole meaning of the family life which results from it, have this aim: that the couple be ready with stout hearts to cooperate with the love of the Creator and the Savior, who through them will enlarge and enrich His own family day by day.' "[80] The Pope criticized the prevalent antilife mentality:

> Some ask themselves if it is a good thing to be alive or if it would be better never to have been born; they doubt therefore if it is right to bring others into life when perhaps they will curse their existence in a cruel world with unforeseeable terrors. Others consider themselves to be the only ones for whom the advantages of technology are intended and they exclude others by imposing on them contraceptives or even worse means. Still others imprisoned in a consumer mentality and whose sole concern is to bring about a continual growth of material goods, finish by ceasing to understand, and thus by refusing, the spiritual riches of a new human life. The ultimate reason for these mentalities is the absence

---

[79] Pope John Paul II, General Audience, May 16, 1992, quoting the Second Vatican Council, *Pastoral Constitution on the Church in the Modern World* (*Gaudium et Spes*), no. 43; 37 *The Pope Speaks* 307, 308 (1992).

[80] *F.C.*, no. 28.

in people's hearts of God, whose love alone is stronger than all the world's fears and can conquer them.

Thus an anti-life mentality is born, as can be seen in many current issues: one thinks, for example of a certain panic deriving from the studies of ecologists and futurologists on population growth, which sometimes exaggerate the danger of demographic increase to the quality of life. But the Church firmly believes that human life, even if weak and suffering, is always a splendid gift of God's goodness. . . .

Thus the Church condemns as a grave offense against human dignity and justice all those activities of governments or other public authorities which attempt to limit in any way the freedom of couples in deciding about children. Consequently, any violence applied by such authorities in favor of contraception or, still worse, of sterilization and procured abortion must be altogether condemned and forcefully rejected. Likewise to be denounced as gravely unjust are cases where in international relations economic help given for the advancement of peoples is made conditional on programs of contraception, sterilization, and procured abortion.[81]

Pope John Paul emphasized also the *"original and primary"* right and duty of parents to educate their children, including *"education for chastity"*.[82]

3. *Participating in the development of society.* The Church insists on recognition of the family as "the first and vital cell of society".[83] The state has no right to intrude on the proper functions of the family:

---

[81] Ibid., no. 30; see *L.F.*, no. 12.

[82] Ibid., nos. 36, 37; see Pontifical Council for the Family, *The Truth and Meaning of Human Sexuality*, 25 *Origins* 529 (1996).

[83] Ibid., no. 42; see *L.F.*, no. 13.

The family and society have complementary functions in defending and fostering the good of each and every human being. But society—more specifically the State—must recognize that "the family is a society in its own original right" and so society is under a grave obligation in its relations with the family to adhere to the principle of subsidiarity. By virtue of this principle the state cannot and must not take away from families the functions that they can just as well perform on their own or in free associations; instead it must positively favor and encourage as far as possible responsible initiative by families.[84]

In Question 45 below, we will examine specific rights of the family with respect to society and the state.

4. *Sharing in the life and mission of the Church.* The Pope described the family as a "Church in miniature" in that "in its own way the family is a living image and historical representation of the mystery of the Church. . . . Christian married couples and parents . . . not only *receive* the love of Christ and become a *saved* community, but they are called upon to *communicate* Christ's love to their brethren, thus becoming a *saving* community."[85] In line with the nature of personhood as including relation to others, *Familiaris Consortio* said that "the family's sharing in the Church's mission should follow *a community pattern*: the spouses together *as a couple*, the parents and children *as a family*, must live their service to the Church and to the world."[86]

---

[84] *F.C.*, no. 45.
[85] Ibid., no. 49.
[86] Ibid., no. 50.

Pope John Paul emphasized the "absolute need" for religious instruction in the home through "family catechesis". Especially "in places where widespread unbelief or invasive secularism makes real religious growth practically impossible, 'the Church of the home' remains the one place where children and young people can receive an authentic catechesis."[87] The Pontiff struck a poignant note when he encouraged parents to persevere "with courage and great interior serenity" during their children's adolescence and youth, "when the children, as often happens, challenge or even reject the Christian faith received in earlier years. . . . A form of missionary activity can be exercised even within the family . . . when some member . . . does not have the faith or does not practice it with consistency. In such a case the other members must give him or her a living witness of their own faith in order to encourage and support him or her along the path towards full acceptance of Christ the Savior."[88]

A fitting conclusion for this discussion of the family is the marital success formula the Pope offered in his address on Boston Common in 1979: "Follow Christ! You who are married: share your love and your burdens with each other; respect the human dignity of your spouse; accept joyfully the life that God gives through you; make your marriage stable and secure for your children's sake. Follow Christ!"[89]

---

[87] Ibid., no. 52.

[88] Ibid., no. 54.

[89] Pope John Paul II, *Address*, Oct. 1, 1979, 24 *The Pope Speaks* 292, 296 (1979).

42. Why does the Church put so much emphasis on contraception? I think it enables people to exercise responsible free choice. Why does the Church oppose it?

In *Humanae Vitae*, in 1968, Pope Paul VI said that the law of God prohibits "every actions which, either in anticipation of the conjugal act, or in its accomplishment, or in the development of its natural consequences, proposes, whether as an end or a means, to render procreation impossible".[90] This teaching "is founded upon the inseparable connection—which is willed by God and which man cannot lawfully break on his own initiative—between the two meanings of the conjugal act: the unitive meaning and the procreative meaning".[91] In *Familiaris Consortio*, John Paul stressed the "objective standards" that govern here as in other areas: "The Second Vatican Council clearly affirmed that when there is a question of harmonizing conjugal love with the responsible transmission of life, the moral aspect of any procedure does not depend solely on sincere intentions or on an evaluation of motives. It must be determined by *objective standards*. These, *based on the nature of the human person and his or her acts*, preserve the full sense of mutual self-giving and human procreation in the context of true love."[92]

In his audience of Sept. 17, 1983, the Pope added to the above reasons the fact that the contraceptor usurps the role of God by making himself (or herself) the arbiter of when life begins:

---

[90] Pope Paul VI, *Humanae Vitae* (1968), no. 14. See *C.C.C.*, no. 2366.

[91] Pope Paul VI, *Humanae Vitae* (1968), no. 12.

[92] *F.C.*, no. 32. On the virtue of chastity, to which all people are called according to their state in life, see *C.C.C.*, nos. 2337–50.

At the origin of every human person there is a creative act of God. No man comes into existence by chance; he is always the object of God's creative love. From this fundamental truth of faith and reason it follows that the procreative capacity, inscribed in human sexuality, is—in its deepest truth —a cooperation with God's creative power.

It also follows that men and women are not the arbiters, are not the masters of this same capacity, called as they are, in it and through it, to be participants in God's creative decision. When, therefore, through contraception, married couples remove from the exercise of their conjugal sexuality its potential procreative capacity, they claim a power which belongs solely to God: the power to decide, *in a final analysis*, the coming into existence of a human person. They assume the qualification not of being cooperators in God's creative power, but the ultimate depositaries of the source of human life.

In this perspective, contraception is to be judged, objectively, so profoundly unlawful as never to be, for any reason, justified. To think or to say the contrary is equal to maintaining that in human life situations may arise in which it is lawful not to recognize God as God.[93]

The teachings of John Paul II have stressed relation to others as an essential element of personhood. In this context the practice of contraception is essentially degrading to the person: "When couples, by means of recourse to contraception, separate these two meanings that God the Creator has inscribed in the being of man and woman and in the dynamism of their sexual communion, they act as 'arbiters' of the divine plan and they 'manipulate' and degrade human sexuality and with it themselves and their married partner by altering its

---

[93] Pope John Paul II, *Discourse*, Sept. 17, 1983, 28 *The Pope Speaks* 356–57 (1983).

value of 'total' self-giving. Thus the innate language that expresses the total reciprocal self-giving of husband and wife is overlaid through contraception, by an objectively contradictory language, namely, that of not giving oneself totally to the other. This leads not only to a positive refusal to be open to life but also to a falsification of the inner truth of conjugal love, which is called upon to give itself in personal totality."[94]

To practice natural family planning,[95] the man and woman must communicate with each other. Contraception, by contrast, is a deliberate frustration of communication. The contraceptors withhold something of themselves from each other. Instead of a mutual self-donation, the sexual act tends to become a noncommunicative exercise in mutual masturbation, with the other person regarded as an object. Contraception involves a refusal both to take the possible consequences of the act and to accept the other as he or she is without alteration by a chemical, a device, or surgery. In this light, contraception is the antithesis of the relational essence of personhood through which "man can fully discover his true self only in a sincere giving of himself".[96]

John Paul, before he became Pope, emphasized that "the person is the kind of good which does not admit of use and cannot be treated as an object of use and as such the means to an end. . . . The person is a good towards which the only proper and adequate attitude is love."[97] Note the contrast between this view and the "utilitarian principle" of the Enlightenment, which would allow the human person, whether in con-

---

[94] *F.C.*, no. 32.

[95] See Question 43 below.

[96] Second Vatican Council, *Pastoral Constitution on the Church in the Modern World (Gaudium et Spes)*, no. 24.

[97] Karol Wojtyla, *Love and Responsibility* (H. T. Willets, transl., 1981), 41.

traception or elsewhere, to be treated as a means to another's end.[98]

Contraception is so rooted in contemporary culture that it is easy to forget that the Anglican Lambeth Conference of 1930 was the first occasion on which a Christian denomination said that contraception could ever be objectively right under any circumstances.[99] "Lambeth", said editor James Douglas of the London *Sunday Express*, "has delivered a fatal blow to marriage, to motherhood, to fatherhood, to the family and to morality."[100] In 1931, when a committee of the Federal Council of Churches followed Lambeth by endorsing "careful and restrained" use of contraceptives, the *Washington Post* editorially replied:

> It is impossible to reconcile the doctrine of the divine institution of marriage with any modernistic plan for the mechanical regulation or suppression of human birth. The church must either reject the plain teachings of the Bible or reject schemes for the "scientific" production of human souls. Carried to its logical conclusion, the committee's report if carried into effect would sound the death-knell of marriage as a holy institution, by establishing degrading practices which would encourage indiscriminate immorality. The suggestion that the use of legalized contraceptives would be "careful and restrained" is preposterous.[101]

Contraception is the defining vice of this era. The general acceptance of the morality of the act of contraception is a major factor in the following developments:

---

[98] Ibid., 40.

[99] See *New York Times*, Aug. 15, 1930, p. 1, col. 6.

[100] *New York Times*, Aug. 17, 1930, p. 5, col. 1.

[101] *Washington Post*, Mar. 22, 1931.

Abortion. Contraception is the prevention of life, while abortion is the taking of life. But both involve the willful separation of the unitive and procreative aspects of sex. The contraceptive mentality tends to require abortion as a backup. And many so-called contraceptives are abortifacient in that they cause the destruction of the developing human being. In *Evangelium Vitae*, Pope John Paul noted that

> the pro-abortion culture is especially strong precisely where the Church's teaching on contraception is rejected. Certainly, from the moral point of view contraception and abortion are *specifically* different evils: the former contradicts the full truth of the sexual act as the proper expression of conjugal love, while the latter destroys the life of a human being. . . . But despite their differences of nature and moral gravity, contraception and abortion are often closely connected, as fruits of the same tree. It is true that in many cases contraception and even abortion are practiced under the pressure of real-life difficulties, which nonetheless can never exonerate from striving to observe God's law fully. Still, in very many other instances such practices are rooted in a hedonistic mentality unwilling to accept responsibility in matters of sexuality, and they imply a self-centered concept of freedom, which regards procreation as an obstacle to personal fulfillment. The life which could result from a sexual encounter thus becomes an enemy to be avoided at all costs, and abortion becomes the only possible decisive response to contraception. The close connection between . . . contraception and . . . abortion . . . is being demonstrated in an alarming way by the development of chemical products, intrauterine devices and vaccines which, distributed with the same ease as contraceptives, really act as abortifacients in the very early stages of the development of the life of the new human being."[102]

---

[102] *E.V.*, no. 13.

[T]here exists in contemporary culture a certain Promethean attitude which leads people to think that they can control life and death by taking the decisions about them into their own hands.[103]

Euthanasia. Once the contraceptive ethic and abortion accustomed people to the idea that burdensome lives are not worth living, the way was clear for euthanasia for the aged and the "useless". If man is the arbiter of when life begins, he will predictably make himself the arbiter of when life ends. Euthanasia is postnatal abortion, as abortion is prenatal euthanasia.

Pornography. Like contraception, which reduces sexual relations to an exercise in mutual masturbation, pornography is the separation of sex from life and the reduction of sex to an exercise in self-gratification. Pope Paul VI, in *Humanae Vitae*, warned that contraception would cause women to be viewed as sex objects, that "man, growing used to the employment of anti-conceptive practices, may finally lose respect for the woman and, no longer caring for her physical and psychological equilibrium, may come to the point of considering her as a mere instrument of selfish enjoyment, and no longer as his respected and beloved companion."[104]

In vitro fertilization. Contraception is the taking of the unitive without the procreative. In vitro fertilization is the reverse. Various refinements of this technique include the freezing of spare embryos and their later use for experimentation or as

---

[103] *E.V.*, no. 15.

[104] Pope Paul VI, *Humanae Vitae* (1968), no. 17. On pornography as an offense against chastity in the context of the Sixth Commandment, see *C.C.C.*, no. 2354.

spare parts for persons in need of new organs. The treatment of human beings as objects is obvious here.

Promiscuity. According to the natural moral law and the Commandments, sex is reserved for marriage because sex is inherently connected with procreation and the natural way to raise children is in a marriage. But if, through contraception, we claim the power to decide whether sex will have anything to do with procreation, why should we have to reserve sex for marriage?

Divorce. In the natural order, marriage should be permanent because sex is inherently related to procreation and children should be raised in a home with parents permanently married to each other. But if it is wholly our decision whether sex will have any relation to children, why should marriage be permanent? If sex and marriage are not intrinsically related to new life, marriage loses its reason for permanence. It tends to become a temporary alliance for individual gratification—what Pope Paul VI called "the juxtaposition of two solitudes".[105]

Homosexual activity. If sex has no inherent relation to procreation, and if man, rather than God, is the arbiter of whether and when it will have that relation, why not let Freddy marry George and Erica marry Susan? The contraceptive society cannot say that homosexual activity is objectively wrong without condemning itself. Objections to the legitimization of the homosexual "life-style" are reduced to the pragmatic and the esthetic. Homosexual activity, like contraception, also frustrates the interpersonal communion that is intrinsic to the conjugal act. And where that act should be open to life, homosexual

---

[105] "Conversations with Pope Paul VI", *McCall's*, Oct. 1967, pp. 93, 138.

activity is a dead end. It rejects life and focuses instead on ex-crement, which is dead.

It is increasingly obvious not only that contraception is con-trary to the nature and dignity of the person but also that it is hostile to the common good. The Church's teaching here is a providential and prophetic call to reason and sanity.

43. Isn't natural family planning the same as contracep-tion? Isn't the intent of both the same, to avoid having children?

No, on both counts. The differences between natural family planning (NFP) and contraception were spelled out in *Famil-iaris Consortio*:

> When, . . . by means of recourse to periods of infertility, the couple respect the inseparable connection between the unitive and procreative meanings of human sexuality, they are acting as "ministers" of God's plan and they "benefit from" their sexuality according to the original dynamism of "total" self-giving, without manipulation or alteration.
>
> In the light of the experience of many couples and of the data provided by the different human sciences, theological reflection is able to perceive and is called to study further the difference, both anthropological and moral, between con-traception and recourse to the rhythm of the cycle: It is a difference which is much wider and deeper than is usually thought, one which involves in the final analysis two irrecon-cilable concepts of the human person and of human sexual-ity. The choice of the natural rhythms involves accepting the cycle of the person, that is, the woman, and thereby accept-ing dialogue, reciprocal respect, shared responsibility, and self-control. To accept the cycle and to enter into dialogue

means to recognize both the spiritual and corporal character of conjugal communion and to live personal love with its requirement of fidelity. In this context the couple comes to experience how conjugal communion is enriched with those values of tenderness and affection which constitute the inner soul of human sexuality in this physical dimension also. In this way sexuality is respected and promoted in its truly and fully human dimension and is never "used" as an "object" that, by breaking the personal unity of soul and body, strikes at God's creation itself at the level of the deepest interaction of nature and person.[106]

NFP, however, is *"not an end in itself"*.[107] The Second Vatican Council declared that "marriage and married love are by nature ordered to the procreation and education of children."[108] As Paul VI stated in *Humanae Vitae*, it is only "for grave motives", "serious motives", and "just motives" that married couples may rightly choose to avoid pregnancies even by partial abstinence.[109] "The Encyclical Humanae Vitae", said Pope John Paul II, "presents 'responsible parenthood' as an expression of high ethical value. *In no way is it exclusively directed* to limiting, much less excluding, children; it means also the willingness to accept a larger family. Above all, . . . 'responsible parenthood' implies 'a deeper relationship with the objective moral order instituted by God—the order of which a right conscience is the true interpreter'."[110]

---

[106] *F.C.*, no. 32. See *C.C.C.*, nos. 2368–72; *E.V.*, nos. 88, 97.

[107] Pope John Paul II, *Address*, June 8, 1984, 29 *The Pope Speaks* 246 (1984).

[108] Second Vatican Council, *Pastoral Constitution on the Church in the Modern World, Gaudium et Spes*, no. 50; see also no. 48.

[109] Pope Paul VI, *Humanae Vitae* (1968), nos. 10, 16.

[110] Pope John Paul II, Audience, Sept. 5, 1984, *L'Osservatore Romano* (English ed.), Sept. 10, 1984, p. 10.

If NFP is used without serious reason, it becomes, in design rather than in technique, an alternate form of contraception. An antichild mentality is wrong whether it is implemented by natural means or by pills and devices. In any event, education on contraception should emphasize the personal and social advantages of large families. At the Capitol Mall in Washington, D.C., on October 7, 1979, John Paul reminded us of this point:

> Decisions about the number of children and the sacrifices to be made for them must not be taken only with a view to adding to comfort and preserving a peaceful existence. Reflecting upon this matter before God, with the graces drawn from the sacrament, and guided by the teaching of the Church, parents will remind themselves that it is certainly less serious to deny their children certain comforts or material advantages than to deprive them of the presence of brothers and sisters, who could help them to grow in humanity and to realize the beauty of life at all its ages and in all its variety.[111]

In a 1990 address to participants in a seminar on NFP, Pope John Paul II examined NFP in the context of "the total vision of the human person". In this analysis we see the emerging concept of a person-as-relation applied to the specific issue of NFP in terms that illuminate that concept as the key to understanding other moral issues as well. It merits a lengthy presentation here in the Pope's own words:

> Church teaching about such a delicate and urgent issue in the life of spouses and society is often misunderstood and opposed *because it is presented in an inadequate and unilateral fashion.* It stops at the negative judgment concerning contraception, which is always an intrinsically dishonest act; yet it

---

[111] Pope John Paul II, *Address*, Oct. 7, 1979, in *The Pope in America* (Wanderer Press, 1979), 79–80.

rarely makes any effort to understand this norm in the life of "the total vision of the human person and vocation, which is not only natural and earthly, but also supernatural and eternal."[112] In truth, only *within the framework of responsibility for love and for life* can the underlying reasons for prohibiting "actions which have the aim of and are used as a means for making procreation impossible"[113] be understood. Only within the context of values such as these can spouses find the inspiration which allows them to overcome, with the help of God's grace, the difficulties which they inevitably face when, under unfavorable social conditions and in an environment marked by readily available hedonism, they seek to follow a path which conforms to the Lord's will. It is only by deepening the Christian concept of this "responsibility for love and for life" that one can grasp the "difference, both anthropological and moral, between contraception and recourse to the rhythm of the cycle."[114] *"Responsibility for love and for life!"* That expression reminds us of the greatness of the vocation of spouses, called to be free and conscious collaborators of the God who is love, who creates through love and calls to love. The term "responsibility" is, therefore, ethically decisive because in it is combined the dignity of the "gift" which is received and, on the other hand, the value of the "freedom" to which it is entrusted so that it might bear fruit. The greater the gift, the greater the responsibility of the subject who freely accepts it. And what gift is greater on the natural plane than the vocation of a man and woman to express faithful and indissoluble love which is open to the transmission of life?

In conjugal love and in transmitting life, the human being *cannot forget his or her dignity as a person*; it raises the natural

---

[112] Pope Paul VI, *Humanae Vitae* (1968), no. 7.

[113] Ibid., no. 14.

[114] *F.C.*, no. 32

order to a certain level, one which is no longer merely biological. That is why the Church teaches that *responsibility
for love is inseparable from responsibility for procreation.* The
biological phenomenon of human reproduction, wherein the
human person finds his or her beginnings, also has as its end
the emergence of a new person, unique and unrepeatable,
made in the image and likeness of God. The dignity of the
procreative act in which the interpersonal love of the spouses
finds its culmination in the new person, in a son or daughter, emerges from that fact. That is why the Church teaches
that openness to life in conjugal relations protects the very
authenticity of the love relationship, saving it from the risk
of descending to the level of mere utilitarian enjoyment. . . .

In applying this scientific knowledge to regulating fertility, *technology in no way substitutes for the involvement of the
persons* and neither does it intervene by manipulating the nature of the relationship, as is the case with contraception in
which the unitive meaning of the conjugal act is deliberately
separated from its procreative meaning. On the contrary, in
practising natural methods *science must always be joined with
self-control*, since, in using them, virtue—that perfection belonging specifically to the person—is necessarily a factor.

Thus we can say that periodic continence, practised to
regulate procreation in a natural way, *requires profound understanding of the person and love.* In truth, that requires mutual listening and dialogue by spouses, attention and sensitivity for the other spouse and constant self-control; all of
these are qualities which express real love for the person
of the spouse for what he or she is, and not for what one
may wish the other to be. The practice of natural methods
requires personal growth by the spouses in a joint effort to
strengthen their love.

This intrinsic connection between science and moral virtue
constitutes the specific and morally qualifying element for
recourse to natural methods. It is a part of the complete in-

tegral training of teachers and of couples, and, in it, it should be clear that what is of concern here is more than just simple "instruction" divorced from the moral values proper to teaching people about love. In short, it allows people to see that it is not possible to practice natural methods as a "licit" variation of the decision to be closed to life, which would be substantially the same as that which inspires the decision to use contraceptives: only if there is a basic openness to fatherhood and motherhood, understood as collaboration with the Creator, does the use of natural means become an integrating part of the responsibility for love and for life.[115]

NFP, when justified by a serious reason, involves an openness to life and an accepting intent. For sufficient reason, the husband and wife refrain from sexual activity during the fertile period, and they engage in such activity at other times. But they are open to life in that they do nothing to frustrate the nature of the sexual act, and they are open to new life if God so wills. The contracepting couple, by contrast, reject even partial abstinence. They engage in sexual activity when they so choose. But, rather than having an accepting intent open to life, they use drugs, plugs, or other devices to prevent the creation of new life. Those who rightly practice NFP recognize that God is in charge. The contraceptors, by contrast, put themselves in charge. They make themselves rather than God the arbiters of whether and when life shall begin. They seek the unitive aspects of the act, but they deliberately frustrate the procreative. They say to God: "We want the recreational, you keep the procreational." Ironically, because the essence of contraception is noncommunication, a withholding of self, they end up frustrating the unitive aspect as well as the procre-

---

[115] Pope John Paul II, *Address* (Dec. 14, 1990), *Position Paper* 215 (Nov. 1991), 323–26; see 36 *The Pope Speaks* 126 (1991).

ational. And, as noted in the previous Question, this deliberate separation of sex from procreation is not only wrong in itself but is also the source of numerous other evils.

44. *What insight does the Magisterium offer on homosexual activity and "gay rights"?*

In *Bowers* v. *Hardwick*, in 1986, the Supreme Court upheld the Georgia prohibition of consensual sodomy.[116] "Until 1961, all 50 States outlawed sodomy."[117] In his concurring opinion, Chief Justice Warren Burger reviewed the long tradition of sodomy prohibitions:

> Decisions of individuals relating to homosexual conduct have been subject to state intervention throughout the history of Western Civilization. Condemnation of those practices is firmly rooted in Judaeo-Christian moral and ethical standards. Homosexual sodomy was a capital crime under Roman law. . . . During the English Reformation when powers of the ecclesiastical courts were transferred to the King's Courts, the first English statute criminalizing sodomy was passed: 25 *Hen.* VIII, c.6. Blackstone described "the infamous crime against nature" as an offense of "deeper malignity" than rape, an heinous act "the very mention of which is a disgrace to human nature," and "a crime not fit to be named." . . . The common law of England, including its prohibition of sodomy, became the received law of Georgia and the other Colonies. . . . To hold that the act of homosexual sodomy is somehow protected as a fundamental right would be to cast aside millenia of moral teaching.[118]

---

[116] 478 U.S. 186 (1986).
[117] 478 U.S. at 193 (opinion of Court).
[118] 478 U.S. at 196–97.

Saint Thomas, quoting Saint Augustine, said that of all "the sins belonging to lust, 'that which is against nature is the worst.'"[119]

In every genus, worst of all is the corruption of the principle on which the rest depend. Now the principles of reason are those things that are according to nature, because reason presupposes things as determined by nature, before disposing of other things according as it is fitting. . . . In matters of action it is most grave and shameful to act against things as determined by nature. Therefore, since by the unnatural vices man transgresses that which has been determined by nature with regard to the use of venereal actions, it follows that in this matter this sin is gravest of all. After it comes incest, which . . . is contrary to the natural respect we owe persons related to us. With regard to the other species of lust they imply a transgression merely of that which is determined by right reason, on the presupposition, however, of natural principles.[120]

Just as the ordering of right reason proceeds from man, so the order of nature is from God Himself: Wherefore in sins contrary to nature, whereby the very order of nature is violated, an injury is done to God, the Author of nature. Hence, Augustine says (*Conf.* iii.8): "Those foul offenses that are against nature should be everywhere and at all times detested and punished, such as were those people of Sodom, which should all nations commit, they should all stand guilty of the same crime, by the law of God, which hath not so made men that they should so abuse one another. For even that very intercourse which should be between God and us is violated, when that same nature, of which He is the Author, is polluted by the perversity of lust.[121]

---

[119] *S.T.,* II, II, Q. 154, art. 12.
[120] Ibid.
[121] Ibid.

The statements of the teaching Church have consistently affirmed that homosexual acts are intrinsically wrong but that persons with homosexual tendencies are entitled to respect and should not be subjected to unjust discrimination.[122] And those statements have stressed the importance of prayer, "frequent reception of the sacraments of penance and the Eucharist", and "devotion to the Immaculate Mother of God."[123] Incidentally, since homosexual acts are intrinsically disordered, the inclination toward those acts, while not itself sinful, is disordered even if it is not acted upon.[124]

The *Catechism of the Catholic Church* states:

> 2357. Homosexuality refers to relations between men or between women who experience an exclusive or predominant sexual attraction toward persons of the same sex. It has taken a great variety of forms through the centuries and in different cultures. Its psychological genesis remains largely unexplained. Basing itself on Sacred Scripture, which presents homosexual acts as acts of grave depravity, tradition has always declared that "homosexual acts are intrinsically disordered." They are contrary to the natural law. They close the sexual act to the gift of life. They do not proceed from a genuine affective and sexual complementarity. Under no circumstances can they be approved.

---

[122] *See* Congregation for the Doctrine of the Faith, *Declaration on Sexual Ethics* (1975); Congregation for the Doctrine of the Faith, *Letter to the Bishops of the Catholic Church on the Pastoral Care of Homosexual Persons* (1986); *C.C.C.*, nos. 2357–59.

[123] Congregation for the Doctrine of the Faith, *Declaration on Sexual Ethics* (1975), no. 12.

[124] See Congregation for the Doctrine of the Faith, *Letter to the Bishops of the Catholic Church on the Pastoral Care of Homosexual Persons* (1986); C.D.F., *Responding to Legislative Proposals on Discrimination Against Homosexuals*, 22 *Origins* 174 (Aug. 6, 1992); John F. Harvey, O.S.F.S., *The Truth about Homosexuality* (1996).

2358. The number of men and women who have deep-seated homosexual tendencies is not negligible. This inclination, which is objectively disordered, constitutes for most of them a trial. They must be accepted with respect, compassion, and sensitivity. Every sign of unjust discrimination in their regard should be avoided. These persons are called to fulfill God's will in their lives and, if they are Christians, to unite to the sacrifice of the Lord's Cross the difficulties they may encounter from their condition.

2359. Homosexual persons are called to chastity. By the virtues of self-mastery that teach them inner freedom, at times by the support of disinterested friendship, by prayer and sacramental grace, they can and should gradually and resolutely approach Christian perfection.[125]

Pope John Paul approved the final text of the *Catechism* on June 25, 1992.[126] One month later, on July 23rd, the Congregation for the Doctrine of the Faith issued publicly a slightly revised text of a letter it had sent on June 25th to the Catholic bishops.[127] This letter, *Responding to Legislative Proposals on Discrimination against Homosexuals*, is a "background resource" and not a doctrinal statement. But it is a compact, yet comprehensive statement of the Church's position on the legislative as well as the moral issues involved. The text of the letter is set forth here in full because it is a summary review and application of the principles, discussed in previous Questions in this book, governing the limits of the human law in relation to the natural and divine laws.

---

[125] *C.C.C.* nos. 2357–59.

[126] 37 *The Pope Speaks* 377 (1992).

[127] See *The Wanderer*, July 30, 1992, p. 1.

Foreword

Recently, legislation has been proposed in various places which would make discrimination on the basis of sexual orientation illegal. In some cities, municipal authorities have made public housing, otherwise reserved for families, available to homosexual (and unmarried heterosexual) couples. Such initiatives, even where they seem more directed toward support of basic civil rights than condonement of homosexual activity or a homosexual lifestyle, may in fact have a negative impact on the family and society. Such things as the adoption of children, the employment of teachers, the housing needs of genuine families, landlords' legitimate concerns in screening potential tenants, for example, are often implicated.

While it would be impossible to anticipate every eventuality in respect to legislative proposals in this area, these observations will try to identify some principles and distinctions of a general nature which should be taken into consideration by the conscientious legislator, voter or church authority who is confronted with such issues.

The first section will recall relevant passages from the Congregation for the Doctrine of the Faith's [CDF's] "Letter to the Bishops of the Catholic Church on the Pastoral Care of Homosexual Persons" of 1986. The second section will deal with their application.

I. Relevant Passages from the CDF's "Letter"

1. The letter recalls that the CDF's "Declaration on Certain Questions concerning Sexual Ethics" of 1975 "took note of the distinction commonly drawn between the homosexual condition or tendency and individual homosexual actions"; the latter are "intrinsically disordered" and "in no case to be approved of" (*Letter*, no. 3).

2. Since "[i]n the discussion which followed the publication of the (aforementioned) declaration . . . , an overly be-

nign interpretation was given to the homosexual condition itself, some going so far as to call it neutral or even good," the letter goes on to clarify:

"Although the particular inclination of the homosexual person is not a sin, it is a more or less strong tendency ordered toward an intrinsic moral evil; and thus the inclination itself must be seen as an objective disorder. Therefore special concern and pastoral attention should be directed toward those who have this condition, lest they be led to believe that the living out of this orientation in homosexual activity is a morally acceptable option. It is not" (*Letter*, no. 3).

3. "As in every moral disorder, homosexual activity prevents one's own fulfillment and happiness by acting contrary to the creative wisdom of God. The church, in rejecting erroneous opinions regarding homosexuality, does not limit but rather defends personal freedom and dignity realistically and authentically understood" (*Letter*, no. 7).

4. In reference to the homosexual movement, the letter states: "One tactic used is to protest that any and all criticism of or reservations about homosexual people, their activity and lifestyle are simply diverse forms of unjust discrimination" (*Letter*, no. 9).

5. "There is an effort in some countries to manipulate the church by gaining the often well-intentioned support of her pastors with a view to changing civil statutes and laws. This is done in order to conform to these pressure groups' concept that homosexuality is at least a completely harmless, if not an entirely good, thing. Even when the practice of homosexuality may seriously threaten the lives and well-being of a large number of people, its advocates remain undeterred and refuse to consider the magnitude of the risks involved" (*Letter*, no. 9).

6. "She (the church) is also aware that the view that homosexual activity is equivalent to or as acceptable as the sexual expression of conjugal love has a direct impact on so-

ciety's understanding of the nature and rights of the family and puts them in jeopardy" (*Letter*, no. 9).

7. "It is deplorable that homosexual persons have been and are the object of violent malice in speech or in action. Such treatment deserves condemnation from the Church's pastors wherever it occurs. It reveals a kind of disregard for others which endangers the most fundamental principles of a healthy society. The intrinsic dignity of each person must always be respected in word, in action and in law.

"But the proper reaction to crimes committed against homosexual persons should not be to claim that the homosexual condition is not disordered. When such a claim is made and when homosexual activity is consequently condoned, or when civil legislation is introduced to protect behavior to which no one has any conceivable right, neither the church nor society at large should be surprised when other distorted notions and practices gain ground, and irrational and violent reactions increase" (*Letter*, no. 10).

8. "What is at all costs to be avoided is the unfounded and demeaning assumption that the sexual behavior of homosexual persons is always and totally compulsive and therefore inculpable. What is essential is that the fundamental liberty which characterizes the human person and gives him his dignity be recognized as belonging to the homosexual person as well" (*Letter*, no. 11).

9. "In assessing proposed legislation, the bishops should keep as their uppermost concern the responsibility to defend and promote family life" (*Letter*, no. 17).

II. Applications

10. "Sexual orientation" does not constitute a quality comparable to race, ethnic background, etc., in respect to nondiscrimination. Unlike these, homosexual orientation is an objective disorder (cf. *Letter*, no. 3) and evokes moral concern.

11. There are areas in which it is not unjust discrimination to take sexual orientation into account, for example, in the placement of children for adoption or foster care, in employment of teachers or athletic coaches, and in military recruitment.

12. Homosexual persons, as human persons, have the same rights as all persons, including the right of not being treated in a manner which offends their personal dignity (cf. *Letter*, no. 10). Among other rights, all persons have the right to work, to housing, etc. Nevertheless, these rights are not absolute. They can be legitimately limited for objectively disordered external conduct. This is sometimes not only licit but obligatory. This would obtain moreover not only in the case of culpable behavior but even in the case of actions of the physically or mentally ill. Thus it is accepted that the state may restrict the exercise of rights, for example, in the case of contagious or mentally ill persons, in order to protect the common good.

13. Including "homosexual orientation" among the considerations on the basis of which it is illegal to discriminate can easily lead to regarding homosexuality as a positive source of human rights, for example, in respect to so-called affirmative action or preferential treatment in hiring practices. This is all the more deleterious since there is no right to homosexuality (cf. *Letter*, no. 10), which therefore should not form the basis for judicial claims. The passage from the recognition of homosexuality as a factor on which basis it is illegal to discriminate can easily lead, if not automatically, to the legislative protection and promotion of homosexuality. A person's homosexuality would be invoked in opposition to alleged discrimination, and thus the exercise of rights would be defended precisely via the affirmation of the homosexual condition instead of in terms of a violation of basic human rights.

14. The "sexual orientation" of a person is not compara-

ble to race, sex, age, etc. also for another reason than that given above which warrants attention. An individual's sexual orientation is generally not known to others unless he publicly identifies himself as having this orientation or unless some overt behavior manifests it. As a rule, the majority of homosexually oriented persons who seek to lead chaste lives do not publicize their sexual orientation. Hence the problem of discrimination in terms of employment, housing, etc., does not usually arise.

Homosexual persons who assert their homosexuality tend to be precisely those who judge homosexual behavior or lifestyle to be either "completely harmless, if not an entirely good, thing" (cf. *Letter*, no. 3),[128] and hence worthy of public approval. It is from this quarter the one is more likely to find those who seek to "manipulate the church by gaining the often well-intentioned support of her pastors with a view to changing civil statutes and laws" (cf. *Letter*, no. 5),[129] those who use the tactic of protesting that "any and all criticism of or reservations about homosexual people . . . are simply diverse forms of unjust discrimination" (cf. *Letter*, no. 9)

In addition, there is a danger that legislation which would make homosexuality a basis for entitlements could actually encourage a person with a homosexual orientation to declare his homosexuality or even to seek a partner in order to exploit the provisions of the law.

15. Since in the assessment of proposed legislation "uppermost concern" should be given to "the responsibility to defend and promote family life" (cf. *Letter*, no. 17), strict attention should be paid to the single provisions of proposed measures. How would they affect adoption or foster care? Would they protect homosexual acts, public or private? Do they confer equivalent family status on homosexual unions,

---

[128] The quote is from *Letter*, no. 9.
[129] Ibid.

for example, in respect to public housing or by entitling the homosexual partner to the privileges of employment, which could include such things as "family" participation in the health benefits given to employees (cf. *Letter*, no. 9)?

16. Finally, where a matter of the common good is concerned, it is inappropriate for church authorities to endorse or remain neutral toward adverse legislation even if it grants exceptions to church organizations and institutions. The church has the responsibility to promote family life and the public morality of the entire civil society on the basis of fundamental moral values, not simply to protect herself from the application of harmful laws (cf. *Letter*, no. 17).[130]

This statement is applied common sense. It would make no more sense to force a day-care center to hire an acknowledged or practicing homosexual than it would to make a bank hire an acknowledged or practicing thief.

The political "gay rights" movement, moreover, does not seek merely to prevent legal sanctions against those who may have homosexual inclinations but do not act on them. It seeks rather to legitimize homosexual activity as normal and even as a preferred constitutional right. Pope John Paul II restated not a merely sectarian doctrine but a reality of nature when he noted:

The good "of the human community is strictly linked to the health of the family institution. When, in its legislation, the civil power fails to recognize the specific value which the duly constituted family brings to the good of society; when it behaves like an indifferent spectator before the ethical values of sexual life and of the life of matrimony, then, far from promoting the good and the permanence of human values, it favors by such behavior the dissolution of morals."

---

[130] 22 *Origins* 174 (Aug. 6, 1992).

It would not, therefore, contribute to personal and social good to think up laws whose aim would be to place on an equal footing with the natural family founded on matrimony and to recognize as legitimate *de facto unions* which do not involve any *taking on of responsibility* and any *guarantee of stability*, which are essential elements of the union between man and woman as it was intended by God the Creator and confirmed by Christ the Redeemer. It is one thing to guarantee the rights of persons and quite another to encourage a misunderstanding by presenting a disorder as a situation that is right and good in itself.[131]

In 1994, the Pope denounced the European Parliament's approval of homosexual marriage and the adoption of children by homosexual couples. The Parliament, he said, "does not merely defend people with homosexual *tendencies* by rejecting unjust discrimination in their regard. . . . The Church agrees with that. . . . What is not morally acceptable is the legal approval of homosexual *activity*. . . . [T]he attempt has been made [by the Parliament] to tell the inhabitants of this continent that moral evil, deviation, a kind of slavery, is the way to liberation, thus distorting the true meaning of the family."[132]

Laws and judicial decisions in the United States increasingly legitimize homosexual activity under the cloak of nondiscrimination, or they accord to homosexual (or heterosexual) "domestic partnerships" a legal status comparable to that of the traditional family.[133] The legal recognition of some form of

---

[131] Pope John Paul II, *Address to the National Convention of the Union of Italian Catholic Jurists*, Dec. 16, 1989, quoting Pope John Paul II, *Insegnamenti* (1986), vol. IX–I, p. 1140; 35 *The Pope Speaks* 212, 213 (1990); see the related discussion in *L.F.*, no. 17.

[132] 39 *The Pope Speaks* 249, 250 (1994).

[133] See Vada Berger, "Domestic Partnership Initiatives", 40 *DePaul L. Rev.* 417 (1990).

homosexual "marriage" is likely.[134] These developments should prompt us to ask whether we have become what G. K. Chesterton described as a "people that have lost the power of astonishment at their own actions".[135]

45. Okay. So the Pope thinks the state should promote the family. But how?

Two specifics come to mind. One is revision of the federal tax structure in the United States, which "has become increasingly biased against families with children. The main reason for this is the steady decline in the value of the personal exemption applying to children, which is the tax allowance for the cost of raising children."[136] The main objective of tax reform should be promotion of the functional equivalent of the "family wage", so that, in the words of John Paul II, "a workman's wages should be sufficient to enable him to support himself, his wife and his children."[137]

The second proposal that comes to mind is restoration of legal restrictions on divorce.[138] "Legal integrity, social health, and political liberty all require of the nation's lawmakers a

---

[134] See the discussion of the "traditional, liberal and postmodern" models of marriage in David Orgon Coolidge, *Same-Sex Marriage?*, 38 *So. Tex. L. Rev.* 1, 95 (1997).

[135] G. K. Chesterton, *A Chesterton Anthology* (P. J. Kavanagh, ed., 1985), 359.

[136] Robert Rector, "Reducing the Tax Burden on the Embattled American Family", *Backgrounder* (Heritage Foundation), Aug. 12, 1991, p. 2.

[137] *C.A.*, no. 8; see Allan C. Carlson, "Hard Times for Breadwinners: The Fall of the Family Wage since World War II", *The Family in America* (Rockford Institute), May 1991.

[138] On divorce as a social evil, see *C.C.C.*, nos. 2382–86.

critical reassessment of 'no fault' divorce. Though now well entrenched in every state, 'no fault' has recently aroused opposition that may signal a promising shift."[139] As Pope John Paul stated, "Conjugal communion is characterized not only by its unity but also by its indissolubility."[140] For the common good, the state ought to forbid divorce or restrict it as far as it practically can. A civil divorce is not an intrinsic evil in the sense that abortion, as the execution of the innocent, is such an evil and can never be rightly tolerated by the law.[141] A civil divorce does not affect the reality of the marriage; indeed, a civil divorce may sometimes be justified for the protection of the spouse or children. An incremental strategy would therefore be appropriate to restrict divorce as a means of restoring respect for the family.

In *Evangelium Vitae*, John Paul said: *"a family policy must be the basis and the driving force of all social policies.* For this reason there need to be set in place social and political initiatives capable of guaranteeing conditions of true freedom of choice in matters of parenthood. It is also necessary to rethink labour, urban, residential and social service policies so as to harmonize working schedules with time available for the family, so that it becomes effectively possible to take care of children and the elderly."[142] It would be a mistake, however, to devote this answer to a catalogue of specific legislative proposals.[143] Instead, it will be helpful to set forth the comprehensive statement of

---

[139] Bryce J. Christensen, "Taking Stock: Assessing Twenty Years of 'No Fault' Divorce", *The Family in America* (Rockford Institute), Sept. 1991, p. 8

[140] *F.C.*, no. 20.

[141] See, generally, Charles E. Rice, *No Exception: A Pro-Life Imperative* (1990).

[142] *E.V.*, no. 90.

[143] On relations between the family and society, see *C.C.C.*, nos. 2207–13; see also *L.F.*, no. 17.

family rights issued by the Holy See, with the approval of Pope John Paul II, on October 22, 1983. This document, the *Charter of the Rights of the Family*, stated in its preamble that:

> The rights of the person, even though they are expressed as rights of the individual, have a fundamental social dimension which finds an innate and vital expression in the family.

> The family is based on marriage, that intimate union of life in complementarity between a man and a woman which is constituted in the freely contracted and publicly expressed indissoluble bond of matrimony, and is open to the transmission of life.

> Marriage is the natural institution to which the mission of transmitting life is exclusively entrusted.

> The family, a natural society, exists prior to the state or any other community, and possesses inherent rights which are inalienable. . . .

> Society, and in a particular manner the state and international organizations, must protect the family through measures of a political, economic, social and juridical character, which aim at consolidating the unity and stability of the family so that it can exercise its specific function.[144]

The *Charter* itself is a summary of the obligations in justice of the state and society toward the family. We present it here in full as a useful guide to the principles and objectives that ought to guide legislative efforts with respect to the family:

---

[144] 29 *The Pope Speaks* 78, 80 (1984).

Article 1

All persons have the right to a free choice of their state of life and, thus, to marry and establish a family or to remain single.

a. Every man and every woman, having reached the age of marriage and having the necessary capacity, has the right to marry and establish a family without any discrimination whatsoever; legal restrictions to the exercise of this right, whether they be of a permanent or temporary nature, can be introduced only when they are required by grave and objective demands of the institution of marriage itself and its social and public significance; they must respect in all cases the dignity and the fundamental rights of the person.

b. Those who wish to marry and establish a family have the right to expect from society the moral, educational, social and economic conditions which will enable them to exercise their right to marry in all maturity and responsibility.

c. The institutional value of marriage should be upheld by the public authorities; the situation of non-married couples must not be placed on the same level as marriage duly contracted.

Article 2

Marriage cannot be contracted except by the free and full consent of the spouses duly expressed.

a. With due respect for the traditional role of the families in certain cultures in guiding the decision of their children, all pressure which would impede the choice of a specific person as spouse is to be avoided.

b. The future spouses have the right to their religious liberty. Therefore, to impose as a prior condition for marriage a denial of faith or a profession of faith which is contrary to conscience, constitutes a violation of this right.

c. The spouses, in the natural complementarity which exists between man and woman, enjoy the same dignity and equal rights regarding the marriage.

Article 3

The spouses have the inalienable right to found a family and to decide on the spacing of births and the number of children to be born, taking into full consideration their duties toward themselves, their children already born, the family and society, in a just hierarchy of values and in accordance with the objective moral order which excludes recourse to contraception, sterilization and abortion.

a. The activities of public authorities and private organizations which attempt in any way to limit the freedom of couples in deciding about their children constitute a grave offense against human dignity and justice.

b. In international relations, economic aid for the advancement of peoples must not be conditioned on acceptance of programs of contraception, sterilization or abortion.

c. The family has a right to assistance by society in the bearing and rearing of children. Those married couples who have a large family have a right to adequate aid and should not be subjected to discrimination.

Article 4

Human life must be respected and protected absolutely from the moment of conception.

a. Abortion is a direct violation of the fundamental right to life of the human being.

b. Respect of the dignity of the human being excludes all experimental manipulation or exploitation of the human embryo.

c. All interventions on the genetic heritage of the human person that are not aimed at correcting anomalies constitute a violation of the right to bodily integrity and contradict the good of the family.

d. Children, both before and after birth, have the right to special protection and assistance, as do their mothers during pregnancy and for a reasonable period of time after child-birth.

e. All children, whether born in or out of wedlock, enjoy the same right to social protection, with a view to their integral personal development.

f. Orphans or children who are deprived of the assistance of their parents or guardians must receive particular protection on the part of society. The state, with regard to foster-care or adoption, must provide legislation which assists suitable families to welcome into their home children who are in need of permanent or temporary care. This legislation must, at the same time, respect the natural rights of the parents.

g. Children who are handicapped have the right to find in the home and the school an environment suitable to their human development.

Article 5

Since they have conferred life on their children, parents have the original, primary and inalienable right to educate them; hence they must be acknowledged as the first and foremost educators of their children.

a. Parents have the right to educate their children in conformity with their moral and religious convictions, taking into account the cultural traditions of the family which favor the good and the dignity of the child; they should also receive from society the necessary aid and assistance to perform their educational role properly.

b. Parents have the right to choose freely schools or other means necessary to educate their children in keeping with their convictions. Public authorities must ensure that public subsidies are so allocated that parents are truly free to exercise this right without incurring unjust burdens. Parents should not have to sustain, directly or indirectly, extra charges which would deny or unjustly limit the exercise of this freedom.

c. Parents have the right to ensure that their children are not compelled to attend classes which are not in agreement with their own moral and religious convictions. In particular, sex education is a basic right of the parents and must always be carried out under their close supervision, whether at home or in educational centers chosen and controlled by them.

d. The rights of parents are violated when a compulsory system of education is imposed by the state from which all religious formation is excluded.

e. The primary rights of parents to educate their children must be upheld in all forms of collaboration between parents, teachers and school authorities, and particularly in forms of participation designed to give citizens a voice in the functioning of schools and in the formulation and implementation of educational policies.

f. The family has the right to expect that the means of social communication will be positive instruments for the building up of society, and will reinforce the fundamental values of the family. At the same time the family has the right to be adequately protected, especially with regard to its youngest members, from the negative effects and misuse of mass media.

Article 6

The family has the right to exist and to progress as a family.

a. Public authorities must respect and foster the dignity, lawful independence, privacy, integrity and stability of every family.

b. Divorce attacks the very institution of marriage and of the family.

c. The extended family system, where it exists, should be held in esteem and helped to carry out better its traditional role of solidarity and mutual assistance, while at the same time respecting the rights of the nuclear family and the personal dignity of each member.

Article 7

Every family has the right to live freely its own domestic religious life under the guidance of the parents, as well as the right to profess publicly and to propagate the faith, to take part in public worship and in freely chosen programs of religious instruction, without suffering discrimination.

Article 8

The family has the right to exercise its social and political function in the construction of society.

a. Families have the right to form associations with other families and institutions, in order to fulfill the family's role suitably and effectively, as well as to protect the rights, foster the good and represent the interests of the family.

b. On the economic, social, juridical and cultural levels, the rightful role of families and family associations must be recognized in the planning and development of programs which touch on family life.

Article 9

Families have the right to be able to rely on an adequate family policy on the part of public authorities in the juridical, economic, social and fiscal domains, without any discrimination whatsoever.

a. Families have the right to economic conditions which assure them a standard of living appropriate to their dignity and full development. They should not be impeded from acquiring and maintaining private possessions which would favor stable family life; the laws concerning inheritance or transmission of property must respect the needs and rights of family members.

b. Families have the right to measures in the social domain which take into account their needs, especially in the event of the premature death of one or both parents, of the abandonment of one of the spouses, of accident, or sickness or invalidity, in the case of unemployment, or whenever the family has to bear extra burdens on behalf of its members for reasons of old age, physical or mental handicaps or the education of children.

c. The elderly have the right to find within their own family or, when this is not possible, in suitable institutions, an environment which will enable them to live their later years of life in serenity while pursuing those activities which are compatible with their age and which enable them to participate in social life.

d. The rights and necessities of the family, and especially the value of family unity, must be taken into consideration in penal legislation and policy, in such a way that a detainee remains in contact with his or her family and that the family is adequately sustained during the period of detention.

Article 10

Families have a right to a social and economic order in which the organization of work permits the members to live together, and does not hinder the unity, well-being, health and the stability of the family, while offering also the possibility of wholesome recreation.

a. Remuneration for work must be sufficient for establishing and maintaining a family with dignity, either through a suitable salary, called a "family wage," through other social measures such as family allowances or the remuneration of the work in the home of one of the parents; it should be such that mothers will not be obliged to work outside the home to the detriment of family life and especially of the education of the children.

b. The work of the mother in the home must be recognized and respected because of its value for the family and for society.

Article 11

The family has the right to decent housing, fitting for family life and commensurate to the number of the members; in a physical environment that provides the basic services for the life of the family and the community.

Article 12

The families of migrants have the right to the same protection as that accorded other families.

a. The families of immigrants have the right to respect for their own culture and to receive support and assistance toward their integration into the community to which they contribute.

b. Emigrant workers have the right to see their family united as soon as possible.

c. Refugees have the right to the assistance of public authorities and international organizations in facilitating the reunion of their families.[145]

---

[145] Ibid., 78, 81–86 (emphasis added).

Unfortunately, this charter of family rights is countercultural today. The prevailing culture and legal system, at least in the United States, is founded on antilife premises hostile to the very existence of the family.

46. What does the Magisterium see as the origin of the antilife mentality?

In a remarkable address to the College of Cardinals on April 4, 1991, Cardinal Joseph Ratzinger, prefect of the Congregation for the Doctrine of the Faith, outlined the origins of "the war on life today".[146] It is such a compelling statement that we can do no better than to let Cardinal Ratzinger speak for himself:

The Biblical Foundation

The essential point of departure is . . . the biblical view of man. . . . First, man is created in the image and likeness of God. . . . Second, all human beings are one because they come from a single father, Adam, and a single mother, Eve, 'the mother of all the living.' Gen. 3:20. . . . Both aspects, the divine dignity of the human race and the oneness of its origin and destiny, are definitively sealed in the figure of the second Adam, Christ: the Son of God died for all, to unite everyone in the definitive salvation of divine filiation.

Rights Proclaimed and Yet Denied

On the one hand, the modern age boasts of having discovered the idea of human rights inherent in every human being and antecedent to any positive law, and of having pro-

---

[146] See excerpts in Questions 5 and 26 above.

claimed these rights in solemn declarations. On the other hand, these rights, thus acknowledged in theory, have never been so profoundly and radically denied on the practical level. The roots of this contradiction are to be sought at the height of the modern age: in the Enlightenment theories of human knowledge and the vision of human freedom connected with them, and in the theories of the social contract and their idea of society.

The Enlightenment

The fundamental dogma of the Enlightenment is that man must overcome the prejudices inherited from tradition; he must have the boldness to free himself from every authority in order to think on his own, using nothing but his own reason. From this point on, the search for truth is no longer conceived of as a community effort in which human beings joined in space and time help each other to discover better what is difficult to discover on one's own. Reason, free from any bond, from any relation with what is other, is turned back on itself. It winds up being thought of as a closed, independent tribunal. Truth is no longer an objective datum, apparent to each and everyone, even through others. It gradually becomes something merely external, which each one grasps from his own point of view, without ever knowing to what extent his viewpoint corresponds to the object in itself or with what others perceive.

The same truth about the good becomes unattainable. The idea of the good in itself is put outside of man's grasp. The only reference point for each person is what he can conceive on his own as good. Consequently, freedom is no longer seen positively as a striving for the good which reason uncovers with help from the community and tradition, but is rather defined as an emancipation from all conditions which prevent each one from following his own reason. . . .

Why do even Christians, even persons of great moral formation, think that the norms regarding human life could and should be part of the compromises necessary to political life? Why do they fail to see the insuperable limits of any legislation worthy of the name—the point at which "right" becomes injustice and crime? . . . One reason is reflected in the opinion of those who hold that there must be a separation between personal ethical convictions and the political sphere in which laws are formulated. Here, the only value to be respected would be the complete freedom of choice of each individual, depending on his own private opinions. In a world in which every moral conviction lacks a common reference to the truth, such a conviction has the value of a mere opinion. It would be an expression of intolerance to seek to impose that conviction on others through legislation, thus limiting their freedom. Social life, which cannot be established on any common, objective referent, should be thought of as the result of a compromise of interests, with a view to guaranteeing the maximum freedom possible for each one. In reality, however, wherever the decisive criterion for recognizing rights becomes that of the majority, wherever the right to express one's own freedom can prevail over the right of a voiceless minority, there is the might that has become the criterion of right. . . .

A False Idea of Conscience

A second reason which explains the extent of a mentality opposed to life, I think, is the very concept of morality that today is widespread. Often, a merely formal idea of conscience is joined to an individualistic view of freedom, understood as the absolute right to self-determination on the basis of one's own convictions. This view is no longer rooted in the classical conception of the moral conscience, in which (as Vatican II said) a law resounds which man does not give himself, but which he must obey. In this conception, which belongs to the entire Christian tradition, conscience is the capacity to be open to the call of truth that is objective, universal, and the same for all who can and must seek it. It is not isolation, but communion; *cum scire* in the truth concerning the good, which accompanies human beings in the intimacy of their spiritual nature. It is in this relationship with common and objective truth that conscience finds its dignity, a dignity which must always be guaranteed by a continuing formation. For the Christian this naturally entails a *sentire cum Ecclesia*, and so, an intrinsic reference to the authentic Magisterium of the Church.

On the other hand, in the new conception, clearly Kantian in origin, conscience is detached from its constitutive relationship with a content of moral truth and is reduced to a mere formal condition of morality. Its suggestion, "do good and avoid evil," would have no necessary and universal reference to the truth concerning the good, but would be linked only with the goodness of the subjective intention. Concrete actions, instead, would depend for their moral qualification on the self-understanding of the individual, which is always culturally and circumstantially determined. In this way, conscience becomes nothing but subjectivity elevated to being the ultimate criterion of action. The fundamental Christian idea that nothing can be opposed to conscience no longer has the original and inalienable meaning that truth can only be imposed in virtue of itself, i.e., in personal interiority. Instead, we have the divinization of subjectivity, the infallible oracle of which is conscience, never to be doubted by anyone or anything. . . .

The Distortion of Sexuality

On a second level, reflecting a more personalist approach, we find an anthropological dimension. . . . Western culture

344 / Fifty Questions on the Natural Law

increasingly affirms a new dualism, where some of its characteristic traits converge: individualism, materialism, utilitarianism, and the hedonist ideology of self-fulfillment for oneself. In fact, the body is no longer perceived naturally by the subject as the concrete form of all of his relations with God, other persons, and the world, i.e., as that datum which in the midst of a universe being built, a conversation in course, a history rich in meaning, one can participate in positively only by accepting its rules and its language. Rather, the body appears to be a tool to be utilized for one's well-being, worked out and implemented by technical reason which figures out how to draw the greatest profit from it.

In this way even sexuality becomes depersonalized and exploited. Sexuality appears merely as an occasion for pleasure and no longer as an act of selfgiving or as the expression of a love in which another is accepted completely as he or she is, and which opens itself to the richness of life it bears, i.e., a baby who will be the fruit of that love. The two meanings of the sexual act, unitive and procreative, become separated. Union is impoverished, while fruitfulness is reduced to the sphere of a rational calculation: "A child? Certainly. But when and how I want one."

It becomes clear that such a dualism between technology and the body viewed as an object permits man to flee from the mystery of being. In reality, birth and death, the appearance and the passing of another, the arrival and the dissolution of the ego, all direct the subject immediately to the question of his own meaning and his own existence. And perhaps to escape this anguishing question, he seeks to guarantee for himself the most complete dominion possible over these two key moments in life; he seeks to put them under his own control. It is an illusion to think that man is in complete possession of himself, that he enjoys absolute freedom, that he can be manufactured according to a plan which leaves nothing uncertain, nothing to chance, nothing in mystery.

Machismo and Feminism

A world which makes such an absolute option for efficiency, a world which so approves of a utilitarian logic, a world which for the most part thinks of freedom as an absolute right of the individual and conscience as a totally solitary, subjectivist court of appeal, necessarily tends to impoverish all human relations to the point of considering them finally as relations of power, and not of allowing the weakest human beings to have the place which is their due. From this point of view, utilitarian ideology heads in the direction of *machismo*, and *feminism* becomes the legitimate reaction against the exploitation of woman.

However, so-called *feminism* is frequently based on the same utilitarian presuppositions as *machismo* and, far from liberating women, contributes rather to [their] enslavement.

When, in line with the dualism just described, woman denies her own body, considering it simply as an object to be used for acquiring happiness through self-achievement, she also denies her own femininity, a properly feminine gift of self and her acceptance of another person, of which motherhood is the most typical sign and the most concrete realization. . . . An authentic feminism, working for the advancement of woman in her integral truth and for the liberation of all women, would also work for the advancement of the whole human person and for the liberation of all human beings. This feminism would, in fact, struggle for the recognition of the human person in the dignity which is due to him or her from the sole fact of existence, of being willed and created by God, and not for his or her usefulness, power, beauty, intelligence, wealth, or health. It would strive to advance an anthropology which values the essence of the person as made for the gift of self and the acceptance of the other, of which the body, male or female, is the sign and instrument.

Contraception

It is precisely by developing an anthropology which presents man in his personal and relational wholeness that we can respond to the widespread argument that the best way to fight against abortion would be to promote contraception. . . . It must be noted, in fact, that contraception and abortion both have their roots in that depersonalized and utilitarian view of sexuality and procreation which we have just described and which in turn is based on a truncated notion of man and his freedom.

It is not a matter of assuming a stewardship that is responsible and worthy of one's own fertility as the result of a generous plan that is always open to the possible acceptance of new, unforeseen life.

It is rather a matter of ensuring complete control over procreation, which rejects even the idea of an unplanned child. Understood in these terms, contraception necessarily leads to abortion as a "backup solution." One cannot strengthen the contraceptive mentality without strengthening at the same time the ideology which supports it, and therefore, without implicitly encouraging abortion. On the contrary, if one develops the idea that man only discovers himself fully in the generous gift of himself and in the unconditional acceptance of the other, simply because the latter exists, then abortion will increasingly appear as an absurd crime.

An individualistic type of anthropology, as we have seen, leads one to consider objective truth as inaccessible, freedom as arbitrary, conscience as a tribunal closed in on itself. Such an anthropology leads woman not only to hatred toward men, but also to hatred toward herself and toward her own femininity, and above all, toward her own motherhood.

Man without God

More generally, a similar anthropology leads human beings to hatred toward themselves. Man despises himself; he is no longer in accord with God who found His human creation to be "something very good." On the contrary, man today sees himself as the destroyer of the world, an unhappy product of evolution. In reality, man who no longer has access to the infinite, to God, is a contradictory being, a failed product. Thus, we see the logic of sin: By wanting to be like God, man seeks absolute independence. To be self-sufficient, he must become independent, he must be emancipated even from love, which is always a free grace, not something that can be produced or made. However, by making himself independent of love, man is separated from the true richness of his being and becomes empty. Opposition to his own being is inevitable. "It is not good to be a human being"— the logic of death belongs to the logic of sin. The road to abortion, to euthanasia and the exploitation of the weakest lies open.

To sum up everything, then, we can say that the ultimate root of hatred for human life, of all attacks on human life, is the loss of God. Where God disappears, the absolute dignity of human life disappears as well. In light of the revelation concerning the creation of man in the image and likeness of God, the intangible sacredness of the human person has appeared. Only this divine dimension guarantees the full dignity of the human person. Therefore, a purely vitalist argument, as we often see used (e.g., in the sense intended by A. Schweitzer), can be a first step, but remains insufficient and never reaches the intended goal. In the struggle for life, talking about God is indispensable. Only in this way does the metaphysical foundation of human dignity become apparent; only in this way does the value of the weak, of the disabled, of the nonproductive, of the incurably ill become apparent; only in this way can we relearn and rediscover, too, the value of suffering: the greatest lesson on human dignity always remains the cross of Christ; our salvation has its origin not in what the Son of God did, but in His suffering, and whoever does not know how to suffer does not know how to live.[147]

Pope John Paul has confirmed this analysis in his urging of a "civilization of love" to replace the current "civilization of use": "Positivism . . . results in agnosticism in theory and in utilitarianism in practice and in ethics. . . . Utilitarianism is a civilization of production and of use, a civilization of things and not of persons, a civilization in which persons are used in the same way as things are used. In . . . a civilization of use, woman can become an object for man, children a hindrance for parents, the family an institution obstructing the freedom of its members. . . . If an individual is exclusively concerned with use, he can reach the point of killing love by killing the fruit of love. For the culture of use, the 'blessed fruit of your womb' (Lk. 1:42) becomes in a certain sense an 'accursed fruit.' "[148]

The Pope described "the heart of the tragedy being experienced by modern man [as] *the eclipse of the sense of God and of man*, typical of a social and cultural climate dominated by secularism. . . . . The eclipse of the sense of God and of man inevitably leads to a *practical materialism*, which breeds individualism, utilitarianism and hedonism. . . . In the materialistic perspective described so far, *interpersonal relations are seriously impoverished*. The first to be harmed are women, children, the sick or suffering, and the elderly. The criterion of personal

---

[147] Cardinal Joseph Ratzinger, *Address* to Consistory of College of Cardinals, Apr. 4, 1991, "The Problem of Threats to Human Life", *L'Osservatore Romano* (English ed.), Apr. 8, 1991, p. 2; 36 *The Pope Speaks* 332–43 (1991) [headings added].

[148] *L.F.*, nos. 13, 21.

dignity—which demands respect, generosity and service—is replaced by the criterion of efficiency, functionality and usefulness: others are considered not for what they 'are,' but for what they 'have, do and produce.' This is the supremacy of the strong over the weak.

"*It is at the heart of the moral conscience* that the eclipse of the sense of God and of man, with all its various and deadly consequences for life, is taking place. . . . The moral conscience, both individual and social, is today subjected, also as a result of the penetrating influence of the media, to an *extremely serious and mortal danger*: that of *confusion between good and evil*, precisely in relation to the fundamental right to life."[149]

In sum, "we are facing an enormous and dramatic clash between good and evil, death and life, the 'culture of death' and the 'culture of life.' We find ourselves not only faced with but necessarily in the midst of this conflict. We are all involved and we all share in it, with the inescapable responsibility of *choosing to be unconditionally pro-life.*[150]

"In the struggle for life, talking about God is indispensable."[151] The prevailing culture today rests on a "depersonalized and utilitarian view of sexuality and procreation", which leads from contraception to abortion to euthanasia because that view is based on "a truncated notion of man and his freedom".[152]

---

[149] *E.V.*, nos. 21, 23, 24.

[150] *E.V.*, no. 28.

[151] Cardinal Joseph Ratzinger, *Address* to Consistory of College of Cardinals, Apr. 4, 1991, "The Problem of Threats to Human Life", *L'Osservatore Romano* (English ed.), Apr. 8, 1991, p. 2; 36 *The Pope Speaks* 332–43 (1991).

[152] Ibid.

47. Hasn't the Church changed her position on abortion? Didn't Aquinas deny that life begins at conception? Anyway, is abortion always wrong?

The Catholic Church has always taught that all direct, intended abortion at every stage of pregnancy is seriously wrong.[153] The penalties imposed by canon law, however, have developed in accord with the growth of knowledge of prenatal development. Thus a decree of Pius IX in 1869 rejected the outmoded distinction between animated and unanimated fetuses and ruled that a "person who procures a successful abortion" incurs an automatic excommunication regardless of that distinction.[154] As for Saint Thomas, he, of course, knew nothing of the ovum and process of fertilization and gestation. His lack of modern scientific knowledge led him to conclude that human life began, and ensoulment took place, not at conception, but some time later, probably forty days later for males and eighty for females. Aquinas based his position on the science of his day, which we now know to be wrong.[155] He concluded that abortion was not homicide until ensoulment, although he regarded abortion at every stage as a grave sin. "In his *Commentary on*

---

[153] On abortion generally, see *C.C.C.*, nos. 2270–75.

[154] See Germain Grisez, *Abortion: The Myths, the Realities and the Arguments* (1970), 177; *Code of Canon Law* (1983), Canon 1398.

[155] See discussion and citations in Grisez, *Abortion*, 154–55; John T. Noonan, Jr., ed., *The Morality of Abortion: Legal and Historical Perspectives* (1970), 1, 22–26; Rudolph J. Gerber, "When Is the Human Soul Infused?" 22 *Laval théologique et philosophique* 234, 236 (1966); *S.T.*, I, Q. 76, art. 3; *S.T.*, I, Q. 118, art. 2; *S.T.*, II, II, Q. 64, art. 8; *S.T.*, III, Q. 68, art. 11; Stephen J. Heaney, "Aquinas and the Humanity of the Conceptus", 15 *Human Life Rev.* 63 (1989).

Sentences of Peter Lombard, Thomas Aquinas taught that all abortions are a 'grave sin' . . . , 'among evil deeds' . . . and 'against nature.' "[156]

The Second Vatican Council affirmed that "life must be protected with the utmost care from the moment of conception: abortion and infanticide are abominable crimes."[157] The *Declaration on Procured Abortion*, issued with the approval of Pope Paul VI in 1974, stated that "whatever the civil law may decree in this matter, it must be taken as absolutely certain that a man may never obey an intrinsically unjust law, such as a law approving abortion in principle. He may not take part in any movement to sway public opinion in favor of such a law, nor may he vote for that law. He cannot take part in applying such a law. Doctors and nurses, for example, must not be forced into the position of cooperating proximately in abortion and thus of having to choose between the law of God and the pursuit of their profession."[158]

The condemnation of abortion has been reaffirmed on several occasions by Pope John Paul II, who stated at the Capitol Mall in Washington, D.C., on October 7, 1979:

> Let me repeat what I told the people during my recent pilgrimage to my homeland: "If a person's right to life is violated at the moment in which he is first conceived in his mother's womb, an indirect blow is struck also at the whole of the moral order, which serves to ensure the inviolable goods of man. Among those goods, life occupies the first place. The Church defends the right to life, not only in re-

---

[156] Msgr. William B. Smith, "Questions Answered", *Homiletic and Pastoral Review*, Oct. 1992, pp. 73, 74, quoting Thomas Aquinas, *Comm. in Sent.*, book IV, dist. 31.

[157] Second Vatican Council, *Pastoral Constitution on the Church in the Modern World (Gaudium et Spes)*, no. 51.

[158] 19 *The Pope Speaks* 250, 260 (1975).

gard to the majesty of the Creator, who is the First Giver of this life, but also in respect of the essential good of the human person. Human life is precious because it is the gift of a God whose love is infinite; and when God gives life, it is forever. . . ."

And so, we will stand up every time that human life is threatened. When the sacredness of life before birth is attacked, we will stand up and proclaim that no one ever has the authority to destroy unborn life. When a child is described as a burden or is looked upon only as a means to satisfy an emotional need, we will stand up and insist that every child is a unique and unrepeatable gift of God, with the right to a loving and united family.[159]

The duty of the civil law to protect the right to life was emphasized also in the *Instruction on Bioethics*, issued in 1987, with papal approval, by the Congregation for the Doctrine of the Faith. Although the *Instruction*, with respect to the civil law, immediately focused on the "possible recognition by positive law and the political authorities of techniques of artificial transmission of life and the experimentation connected with it [which] would widen the breach already opened by the legalization of abortion",[160] the principles it enunciated apply to legalized abortion itself.

The *Instruction* declared that "the fruit of human generation, from the first moment of its existence, that is to say from the moment the zygote has formed, demands the unconditional respect that is morally due to the human being in his bodily and spiritual totality. The human being is to be respected and treated as a person from the moment of conception; and

---

[159] *The Pope in America* (1979), 79–80.

[160] Congregation for the Doctrine of the Faith, *Instruction on Bioethics* (1987), III; see 32 *The Pope Speaks* 137 (1987).

therefore from the same moment his rights as a person must be recognized, among which in the first place is the inviolable right of every innocent human being to life."[161]

This emphasis on the rights of the unborn "from the moment of conception" assumes special importance in light of early abortifacient technology.[162] The dominant abortion of the near future will be accomplished by pill, implant, or other device rather than by surgery. Abortion is becoming a truly private matter, and the only way to restrict such early abortions will be by licensing and other regulations. However, political support for restraints on such "private" abortions will be unattainable apart from the restoration of the public conviction that human life is sacred because it is the gift of God.[163]

The *Instruction on Bioethics* rejected the gradualist notion that the law can legitimately tolerate violations of the right to life. It recognized that the "civil law . . . must sometimes tolerate, for the sake of public order, things which it cannot forbid without a greater evil resulting." "However," the *Instruction* continued, "the inalienable rights of the person must be recognized and respected by civil society and the political authority. These human rights depend neither on single individuals nor on parents; nor do they represent a concession made by society and the state; they pertain to human nature and are inherent in the person by virtue of the creative act from which the person took his or her origin."[164] Among the "fundamental rights" that "must be recognized and respected" by the civil law, the

---

[161] Ibid., I, 1.

[162] See *E.V.*, no. 13.

[163] See Rice, *No Exception*, chap. 5.

[164] Congregation for the Doctrine of the Faith, *Instruction on Bioethics* (1987), III.

Instruction enumerated first "every human being's right to life and physical integrity from the moment of conception until death".[165]

The *Instruction* noted:

> In various states, certain laws have authorized the direct suppression of innocents: the moment a positive law deprives a category of human beings of the protection which civil legislation must accord them, the state is denying the equality of all before the law. When the state does not place its power at the service of the rights of each citizen, and in particular of the more vulnerable, the very foundations of a state based on law are undermined. . . . As a consequence of the respect and protection which must be ensured for the unborn child from the moment of his conception, *the law must provide appropriate penal sanctions for every deliberate violation of the child's rights.* The law cannot tolerate—indeed it must expressly forbid—that human beings, even at the embryonic stage, should be treated as objects of experimentation, be mutilated or destroyed with the excuse that they are superfluous or incapable of developing normally.[166]

The Church admits no exception to her prohibition of all direct, intended abortions. However, the Church recognizes that some operations, such as those involving a cancerous womb or an extrauterine pregnancy, may be justified to avoid an imminent danger to the mother's life even though they result in the unintended death of the unborn child. If a pregnant woman has a cancerous uterus that imminently threatens to cause her death and the operation cannot be postponed until the baby it contains is able to survive outside the womb, then the uterus may be removed even though the removal results

---

[165] Ibid.
[166] Ibid.

in the death of the unborn child. Similarly, when the embryo lodges in the fallopian tube and grows there, the damaged portion of the tube, containing the developing human being, may be removed where it is clearly and imminently necessary to save the mother's life.

Such operations are moral even under Catholic teaching.[167] Morally, they are considered indirect abortions and are justified by the principle of the double effect because the death of the child is an unintended effect of an operation independently justified by the necessity of saving the mother's life.[168]

---

[167] National Conference of Catholic Bishops, *Ethical and Religious Directives for Catholic Health Facilities* (1971), paras. 10–17

[168] "To be licitly applied, the principle of the double effect imposes four limiting norms:

"1. The action (removal of the diseased womb) is good; it consists in excising an infected part of the human body.

"2. The good effect (saving the mother's life) is not obtained by means of the evil effect (death of the fetus). It would be just the opposite, e.g., if the fetus were killed in order to save the reputation of an unwed mother.

"3. There is sufficient reason for permitting the unsought evil effect that unavoidably follows. Here the Church's guidance is essential in judging that there is sufficient reason.

"4. The evil effect is not intended in itself, but is merely allowed as a necessary consequence of the good effect.

"Summarily, then, the womb belongs to the mother just as completely after a pregnancy as before. If she were not pregnant, she would clearly be justified to save her life by removing a diseased organ that was threatening her life. The presence of the fetus does not deprive her of this fundamental right." John A. Hardon, S.J., *The Catholic Catechism* (1975), 337.

Saint Thomas justifies killing in self-defense on the basis of the double effect because "the act of self-defense may have two effects, one is the saving of one's life, the other is the slaying of the aggressor. Therefore this act, since

They do not involve the intentional killing of the unborn child for the purpose of achieving another good—for example, the preservation of the mother's life. Morally, therefore, such operations may be justified. Legally, they are not considered to be abortions at all. No prosecution has ever been attempted in this country based on the removal of such a condition, even where the mother's life was not immediately threatened. There would be no need, therefore, to provide a specific exception for such cases in legislation prohibiting abortion.

Apart from cases such as the extrauterine pregnancy and the cancerous uterus, there appears to be no medical or psychiatric justification for terminating a pregnancy, whether such justification is alleged on the ground of a heart disease or other condition of the mother or on the ground that she will commit suicide if she is not allowed to kill her unborn child.[169] Even if there were medical indications for such abortion, it should not be allowed. If two people are on a one-man raft in the middle of the ocean, the law does not permit one to throw the other overboard even to save his own life.[170] Otherwise, might would make right. In maternity cases, the duty of the doctor is to use his best efforts to save both his patients, the mother

---

one's intention is to save one's own life, is not unlawful. . . . And yet, though proceeding from a good intention, an act may be rendered unlawful, if it be out of proportion to the end", *S.T.*, II, II, Q. 64, art. 7.

[169] David C. Wilson, "The Abortion Problem in the General Hospital", in Harold Rosen, *Abortion in America* (1967); see discussion in Kenneth D. Whitehead, *Respectable Killing: The New Abortion Imperative* (1972), 93; Frederick L. Good, *Marriage, Morals & Medical Ethics* (1951), 148–49; and see the discussion of testimony at a Rhode Island legislative hearing, *The Wanderer*, Apr. 23, 1981, p. 3, col. 1.

[170] See *Regina* v. *Dudley and Stephens*, 14 Q.B.D. 273, 15 Cox C.C. 273 (1884); *U.S.* v. *Holmes*, Fed. Cas. No. 15,383 (1842).

and her child. He should not be given a license to kill either of them intentionally.

If an exception should not be made where the life of the mother is concerned, it follows that it should not be made for any lesser reason. To allow abortion to prevent injury to the mother's mental or physical health (where her life is not in danger) is to allow killing for what ultimately amounts to convenience. And to kill the unborn child because he may be defective is to do exactly what the Nazis did to the Jews whose lives they regarded as not worth living.

Politically, the most appealing cases in which to allow abortion are those involving rape and incest. Of the two, rape is the broader category. Every act of intercourse by a girl below the age of legal consent is rape, whether forcible or statutory or both. The fact that the intercourse is incestuous does not change its character as a rape. An act of intercourse, incestuous or otherwise, performed by an adult woman against her will or where she is incapable of consent is also rape. Proabortion literature misleadingly refers to "rape *or* incest" as if they were totally separate categories. But the only case of pregnancy resulting from incestuous intercourse that would not fall within the broader category of rape would be that resulting from a voluntary act of intercourse by an adult woman capable of consent.

To perform abortion for rape or incest is to kill the child because of the identity of his father; this no society can rightly allow. The unborn child is an innocent nonaggressor who should not be killed because of the offense of his father. With respect to rape, the woman has the right to resist her attacker and thus she has the right to resist his sperm. Measures can be taken, consistent with the law and Catholic teaching, promptly after rape, which are not intended to abort and which may prevent conception. However, once the innocent third party, the child, is conceived, he should not be killed. The state and society, in all cases of troubled pregnancy, have the duty to solve the problems constructively with personal and financial support through delivery and beyond. It is not enough merely to forbid the abortion without providing all necessary help. A license to kill, however, is never a constructive solution to a troubled pregnancy.[171]

In *Evangelium Vitae*, after stating that the death penalty should not be used "except in cases of absolute necessity,"[172] John Paul said, "If such great care must be taken to respect every life, even that of criminals and unjust aggressors, the commandment 'You shall not kill' has absolute value when it refers to the *innocent person*. And all the more so in the case of weak and defenseless human beings, who find their ultimate defence against the arrogance and caprice of others only in the absolute binding force of God's commandment."[173]

The Pope condemned the deliberate killing of the innocent:

> Therefore, by the authority which Christ conferred upon Peter and his Successors, and in communion with the Bishops of the Catholic Church, *I confirm that the direct and voluntary killing of an innocent human being is always gravely immoral.* This doctrine, based upon that unwritten law which man, in the light of reason, finds in his own heart (cf. *Rom* 2:14–15), is reaffirmed by Sacred Scripture, transmitted by the Tradition of the Church and taught by the ordinary and universal Magisterium.
>
> The deliberate decision to deprive an innocent human being of his life is always morally evil and can never be licit either as an end in itself or as a means to a good end. . . .

---

[171] See Rice, *No Exception*, 74–76.

[172] *E.V.*, no. 56,

[173] *E.V.*, no. 57.

"Nothing and no one can in any way permit the killing of an innocent human being, whether a fetus or an embryo, an infant or an adult, an old person, or one suffering from an incurable disease, or a person who is dying. Furthermore, no one is permitted to ask for this act of killing, either for himself or herself or for another person entrusted to his or her care, nor can he or she consent to it, either explicitly or implicitly. Nor can any authority legitimately recommend or permit such an action."[174]

Evangelium Vitae defined "procured abortion" as "*the deliberate and direct killing, by whatever means it is carried out, of a human being in the initial phase of his or her existence, extending from conception to birth.* The moral gravity of procured abortion is apparent in all its truth if we recognize that we are dealing with murder. . . . The one eliminated is a human being at the very beginning of life. No one more absolutely *innocent* could be imagined."[175]

"Human life is sacred because from its beginning it involves 'the creative action of God', and it remains forever in a special relationship with the Creator, who is its sole end. God alone is the Lord of life from its beginning until its end: no one can, in any circumstance, claim for himself the right to destroy directly an innocent human being."[176]

"Some people", continued John Paul,

> try to justify abortion by claiming that the result of conception, at least up to a certain number of days, cannot yet be considered a personal human life. But in fact, "from the time that the ovum is fertilized, a life is begun which is neither that of the father nor the mother; it is rather the life of a

---

[174] *E.V.*, no. 57 (quoting *Declaration on Euthanasia* (1980)).

[175] *E.V.*, no. 58.

[176] *E.V.*, no. 53 (quoting *Instruction on Bioethics* (1987)).

new human being with his own growth. It would never be made human if it were not human already.... [M]odern genetic science ... has demonstrated that from the first instant there is established the programme of what this living being will be: a person, this individual person with his characteristic aspects already well determined. Right from fertilization the adventure of a human life begins, and each of its capacities requires time—a rather lengthy time—to find its place and to be in a position to act." Even if the presence of a spiritual soul cannot be ascertained by empirical data, the results themselves of scientific research on the human embryo provide "a valuable indication for discerning by the use of reason a personal presence at the moment of the first appearance of a human life: how could a human individual not be a human person?" ... *"The human being is to be respected and treated as a person from the moment of conception*; and therefore from that same moment his rights as a person must be recognized, among which in the first place is the inviolable right of every innocent human being to life."[177]

John Paul went on to declare: "Therefore, by the authority which Christ conferred upon Peter and his Successors, in communion with the Bishops—who on various occasions have condemned abortion and who ... albeit dispersed throughout the world, have shown unanimous agreement concerning this doctrine—*I declare that direct abortion, that is, abortion willed as an end or as a means, always constitutes a grave moral disorder*, since it is the deliberate killing of an innocent human being. This doctrine is based upon the natural law and upon the written Word of God, is transmitted by the Church's Tradition and taught by the ordinary and universal Magisterium."[178] As John

---

[177] *E.V.*, no. 60 (quoting *Declaration on Procured Abortion* (1974) and *Instruction on Bioethics* (1987)).

[178] *E.V.*, no. 62.

Paul said, "a law which violates an innocent person's natural right to life is unjust and, as such, is not valid as a law."[179]

"[C]ivil law", according to *Evangelium Vitae*,

> must ensure that all members of society enjoy respect for certain fundamental rights which innately belong to the person. . . . First and fundamental among these is the inviolable right to life of every innocent human being. While public authority can sometimes choose not to put a stop to something which—were it prohibited—would cause more serious harm, it can never presume to legitimize as a right of individuals . . . an offence against other persons caused by the disregard of so fundamental a right as the right to life. The legal toleration of abortion or of euthanasia can in no way claim to be based on respect for the conscience of others, precisely because society has the right and the duty to protect itself against the abuses which can occur in the name of conscience and under the pretext of freedom. . . . "[A]ny government which refused to recognize human rights or acted in violation of them, would not only fail in its duty; its decrees would be wholly lacking in binding force." The doctrine on the necessary *conformity of civil law with the moral law* is in continuity with the whole tradition of the Church. . . . This is the clear teaching of Saint Thomas Aquinas. . . . Disregard for the right to life, precisely because it leads to the killing of the person whom society exists to serve, is what most directly conflicts with the possibility of achieving the common good. Consequently, a civil law authorizing abortion or euthanasia ceases by that very fact to be a true, morally binding civil law. Abortion and euthanasia are thus crimes which no human law can claim to legitimize. There is no obligation in conscience to obey such laws; instead there is a *grave and clear obligation to oppose them by conscientious objection*.[180]

---

[179] *E.V.*, no. 90.

[180] *E.V.*, no. 71–73, quoting *Pacem in Terris*.

One final note on the corrupting effect of permissive abortion laws: In his letter of June 21, 1991, to the bishops of the world, Pope John Paul II stated:

> When legislative bodies enact laws that authorize putting innocent people to death and states allow their resources and structures to be used for these crimes, individual consciences, often poorly formed, are all the more easily led into error. In order to break this vicious circle, it seems more urgent than ever that we should forcefully reaffirm our common teaching, based on sacred Scripture and Tradition, with regard to the inviolability of innocent human life.[181]

48. How does the Magisterium apply the natural law to euthanasia? Can the natural law tell us when to "pull the plug" in a particular case?

Before reviewing the statements of the Magisterium,[182] it will be helpful to note some aspects of the euthanasia issue today. *Euthanasia* is derived from a Greek term meaning happy death or good death. Euthanasia can be voluntary, with the consent of the victim, or involuntary. It can be active, as when the victim is shot or poisoned. Or it can be passive, as when treatment is refused by the victim or withheld from him.

Suicide is no longer treated as a crime in Great Britain and the United States, although assisting another person to commit suicide is a crime in most American states. Active euthanasia is still treated as homicide and is therefore illegal as well

---

[181] 37 *The Pope Speaks* 15–16 (1992).
[182] On euthanasia generally, see *C.C.C.*, nos. 2276–83.

as immoral. As the intentional killing of the innocent, active euthanasia can never be morally justified even for motives of mercy. "Therefore it is in no way lawful to slay the innocent."[183]

With respect to passive euthanasia, the civil law, until recently, generally coincided with the Catholic teaching that one is morally obliged to use all ordinary means of treatment but that extraordinary means are optional. Recent years have seen an expansion of the right of patients—and of those who act for them if they are incompetent—to refuse medical treatments which might have been regarded as ordinary, and therefore required, in earlier years. The more important change, however, has been with respect to the provision of food and water to incompetent patients. Until recently, food and water, even artificially provided rather than taken by mouth, was not regarded as a merely optional form of treatment. Today, however, a competent adult has the constitutional right to starve himself to death, where he is refusing naturally or artificially provided food and water. Recent decisions have established the right of an incompetent patient to have artificially provided food and water withdrawn or withheld when his family and physicians decide that he would have wanted it that way or that it is in his "best interest".[184]

The current issues do not involve the genuinely debatable cases of withdrawing or withholding medical treatments from imminently dying patients or where such treatments are use-

---

[183] *S.T.*, II, II, Q. 64, art. 6.

[184] See *Matter of Conroy*, 486 A.2d 1209 (N.J. 1985); *Cruzan* v. *Director, Missouri Dept. of Health*, 110 S. Ct. 2841, 111 L. Ed. 2d 224 (1990); see, generally, Rita Marker, "The 'Right to Die' Movement and the Artificial Provision of Nutrition and Hydration", *International Review of Natural Family Planning and Human Life Issues* 193, 194 (1988); Rice, *No Exception*, 17–40.

less to sustain life or are unduly burdensome. Rather, in the present controversy, several things must be kept in mind:

1. These are not dying patients. Nancy Cruzan's life expectancy was thirty years.[185]

2. These patients are not in significant discomfort.[186]

3. The issue is not the withholding of medical treatments such as antibiotics or surgical procedures. Rather it is the withholding of food and water with the precise intent to cause the death of the patient.

4. Human biological life is itself a good. It is not a good merely if it is useful for other purposes such as pleasure or achievement.

The euthanasia movement employs a functional definition of personhood: a human being is entitled to treatment as a person only to the extent that he can perform in some useful way. Related to this definition is the concept of law as will: entitlement to personhood does not follow from one's nature as a human being. Instead, the legislature or courts can decree which innocent human beings may be treated as nonpersons so as to be intentionally killed.

In *Washington v. Glucksberg*[187] and *Vacco v. Quill*[188] the Supreme Court upheld state laws forbidding assisted suicide. In assisted suicide, the physician, by prescribing or administering a lethal drug or treatment, intentionally and actively helps

---

[185] *Cruzan* v. *Director, Missouri Dept. of Health*, 110 S. Ct. 2841, 111 L. Ed. 2d at 234, n. 1 (1990).

[186] See ibid.; *Brophy* v. *New England Sinai Hospital*, 497 N.E.2d 626 (Mass. 1986); *Guardianship of Jane Doe*, 583 N.E.2nd 1263 (Mass. 1992).

[187] 521 U.S. 702 (1997)

[188] 521 U.S. 793 (1997).

the patient kill himself. The distinction, however, between active intervention and passive withholding of treatment or food and water is not likely to impose an effective barrier to active killing; the intent and effect of both the active and the passive measures are the same—to kill. In *Vacco*, the Court said that "a State may prohibit assisting suicide while permitting patients to refuse . . . lifesaving treatment [and] it may permit palliative care . . . which may have the . . . unintended 'double effect' of hastening the patient's death."[189] "[W]hen a doctor provides . . . palliative care . . . the physician's purpose and intent is, or may be, only to ease his patient's pain."[190] "Palliative care" includes what the proponents of assisted suicide referred to as "terminal sedation, . . . a process [those proponents] characterize as induc[ing] barbiturate coma and then starv[ing] the person to death."[191]

While the physician's intent in such cases may be to relieve pain, it may instead be to kill. It is very difficult for the law to distinguish cases in which pain-relieving palliatives and sedation are used for proper medical reasons from cases where they are used with intent to kill. The Supreme Court allows the states to decline even to try to make that distinction. We can expect officials and courts to defer to medical judgment in such cases, barring exceptional circumstances. This will enable physicians to sedate their willing patients to death as long as they are circumspect about it. The experience in Holland, where active assisted suicide is tolerated, indicates that such practices will not be limited to willing patients and will be extended to others who, in the physician's judgment, would be better off dead, including incompetents who will have the

---

[189] 521 U.S. at 807, n. 11.

[190] 521 U.S. at 802.

[191] 521 U.S. at 807, n. 11.

desire to die attributed to them. "The 1990 Remmelink Report by Dutch researcher P. J. van der Maas found involuntary euthanasia in 30.76 percent of the cases studied. *The New England Journal of Medicine* published a 1995 study by him in which 22.5 percent of euthanized patients had not given doctors their consent."[192]

It is also difficult for the law to determine whether the intent is to kill when the technique is not sedation but the withdrawal of nutrition and hydration. Competent patients are allowed by the law to starve and dehydrate themselves to death. As to incompetents, the *Cruzan* case allowed withdrawal of food and water from an incompetent "vegetative" patient who was not dying, was not in significant discomfort and had a life expectancy of 30 years.[193] The intent in removing the tube was clearly to end Nancy Cruzan's life for the purpose of relieving her, in accord with her desire, of a burdensome or useless life.

Withdrawal of food and water will not endure as a usual technique for intentional killing of patients. Since the law acquiesces in intentional killing by starvation and dehydration, it makes no sense for it to forbid such killing by a painless injection. It will become increasingly possible to reduce the pain of starvation and dehydration. However, at best, it is a difficult way to die and it takes several days. That it will be replaced by a painless injection or death pill is a foregone conclusion.

If you can subject an incompetent, even one who is awake and conscious, to the discomfort of starvation and dehydration with the intent to cause his death, why can you not put him out of his misery with a painless injection? And why should this merciful release be available only to those already incompetent before the question arises? Should not an AIDS patient have

---

[192] *Washington Times*, Nov. 4, 1997, p. A2.
[193] *Cruzan v. Director, Mo. Dept. of Health*, 497 U.S. 261 (1990).

a right to a painless injection, if he wants it, to spare him the misery of a slow, agonizing death? And if he declines the injection despite his condition, could that not indicate his incapacity to make a rational decision and thus authorize his "caregivers" to give him that merciful release for his own good? Leo Alexander, M.D., author of the seminal analysis of the Nazi euthanasia program,[194] commented in 1984 on the American situation: "It is much like Germany in the 20's and 30's—the barriers against killing are being removed."[195]

The Magisterium has addressed the euthanasia issue several times over the past few decades. Pope Pius XII elaborated the distinction between ordinary means of medical treatment, which are morally obligatory, and the more burdensome or disproportionate extraordinary means, which are optional.[196]

Evangelium Vitae stated the governing principles:

> Here we are faced with one of the more alarming symptoms of the "culture of death," which is advancing above all in prosperous societies, marked by an attitude of excessive preoccupation with efficiency and which sees the growing number of elderly and disabled people as intolerable and too burdensome. These people are very often isolated by their families and by society, which are organized almost exclusively on the basis of criteria of productive efficiency, according to which a hopelessly impaired life no longer has any value.

---

[194] Leo Alexander, M.D., "Medical Science under Dictatorship", 241 *New England J. of Med.* 39, 44–46 (1949).

[195] See Joseph R. Stanton, M.D., "The New Untermenschen", *Human Life Review*, Fall 1985, pp. 77, 82.

[196] Pope Pius XII, *Address*, Nov. 24, 1957, 4 *The Pope Speaks* 393 (1958). See also Congregation for the Doctrine of the Faith, *Declaration on Euthanasia* (1980), 25 *The Pope Speaks* 289 (1980).

For a correct moral judgment on euthanasia, in the first place a clear definition is required. *Euthanasia in the strict sense* is understood to be an action or omission which of itself and by intention causes death, with the purpose of eliminating all suffering. "Euthanasia's terms of reference, therefore, are to be found in the intention of the will and in the methods used."

Euthanasia must be distinguished from the decision to forego so-called "aggressive medical treatment," in other words, medical procedures which no longer correspond to the real situation of the patient, either because they are by now disproportionate to any expected results or because they impose an excessive burden on the patient and his family. In such situations, when death is clearly imminent and inevitable, one can in conscience "refuse forms of treatment that would only secure a precarious and burdensome prolongation of life, so long as the normal care due to the sick person in similar cases is not interrupted. . . ." It needs to be determined whether the means of treatment available are objectively proportionate to the prospects for improvement. To forego extraordinary or disproportionate means is not the equivalent of suicide or euthanasia; it rather expresses acceptance of the human condition in the face of death. . . .

Pius XII affirmed that it is licit to relieve pain by narcotics, even when the result is decreased consciousness and a shortening of life, "if no other means exist, and if, in the given circumstances, this does not prevent the carrying out of other religious and moral duties." In such a case, death is not willed or sought, even though for reasonable motives one runs the risk of it: there is simply a desire to ease pain effectively by using the analgesics which medicine provides. All the same, "it is not right to deprive the dying person of consciousness without a serious reason": as they approach death people ought to be able to satisfy their moral and family duties, and above all they ought to be able to prepare in a fully conscious way for their definitive meeting with God.

Taking into account these distinctions, in harmony with the Magisterium of my Predecessors and in communion with the Bishops of the Catholic Church, *I confirm that euthanasia is a grave violation of the law of God*, since it is the deliberate and morally unacceptable killing of a human person. This doctrine is based upon the natural law and upon the written word of God, is transmitted by the Church's Tradition and taught by the ordinary and universal Magisterium.

Depending on the circumstances, this practice involves the malice proper to suicide or murder.

Suicide is always as morally objectionable as murder. . . .

To concur with the intention of another person to commit suicide and to help in carrying it out through so-called "assisted suicide" means to cooperate in, and at times to be the actual perpetrator of, an injustice which can never be excused, even if it is requested. In a remarkably relevant passage Saint Augustine writes that "it is never licit to kill another: even if he should wish it, indeed if he request it because, hanging between life and death, he begs for help in freeing the soul struggling against the bonds of the body and longing to be released; nor is it licit even when a sick person is no longer able to live. . . ."

The choice of euthanasia becomes more serious when it takes the form of a *murder* committed by others on a person who has in no way requested it and who has never consented to it. The height of arbitrariness and injustice is reached when certain people, such as physicians or legislators, arrogate to themselves the power to decide who ought to live and who ought to die.[197]

The 1992 statement of the United States Catholic Bishops' Committee for Pro-Life Activities dealt with the problem of

---

[197] *E.V.*, nos. 64–66 (quoting *Declaration on Euthanasia* (1980); Pope Pius XII, *Address*, Feb. 24, 1957; and *Lumen Gentium*, no. 25.

"withholding or withdrawing of medically assisted nutrition and hydration". The bishops said:

> In answering this question one should avoid two extremes.
>
> First, it is wrong to say that this could not be a matter of killing simply because it involves an omission rather than a positive action. In fact a deliberate omission may be an effective and certain way to kill, especially to kill someone weakened by illness. . . . Thus "euthanasia includes not only active mercy killing but also the omission of treatment when the purpose of the omission is to kill the patient."
>
> Second, we should not assume that all or most decisions to withhold or withdraw medically assisted nutrition and hydration are attempts to cause death. To be sure, any patient will die if all nutrition and hydration are withheld. But sometimes other causes are at work—for example, the patient may be imminently dying, from an already existing terminal condition. At other times, although the shortening of the patient's life is one foreseeable result of an omission, the real purpose of the omission was to relieve the patient of a particular procedure that was of limited usefulness to the patient or unreasonably burdensome for the patient and the patient's family or caregivers. This kind of decision should not be equated with a decision to kill or with suicide.
>
> The harsh reality is that some who propose withdrawal of nutrition and hydration from certain patients do directly intend to bring about a patient's death and would even prefer a change in the law to allow for what they see as more "quick and painless" means to cause death. In other words, nutrition and hydration (whether orally administered or medically assisted) are sometimes withdrawn not because a patient is dying, but precisely because a patient is not dying (or not dying quickly) and someone believes it would be better if he or she did, generally because the patient is perceived as having an unacceptably low "quality of life" or as imposing burdens on others.

When deciding whether to withhold or withdraw medically assisted nutrition and hydration, or other forms of life support, we . . . must be sure that it is not our intent to cause the patient's death—either for its own sake or as a means to achieving some other goal such as the relief of suffering. . . .

As Christians who trust in the promise of eternal life we recognize that death does not have the final word. Accordingly we need not always prevent death until the last possible moment; but we should never intentionally cause death or abandon the dying person as though he or she were unworthy of care and respect. . . .

When a patient is not competent to make his or her own decisions, a proxy decision-maker who shares the patient's moral convictions, such as a family member or guardian, may be designated to represent the patient's interests and interpret his or her wishes. Here, too, moral limits remain relevant—that is, morally the proxy may not deliberately cause a patient's death or refuse what is clearly ordinary means, even if he or she believes the patient would have made such a decision.[198]

In the different context of world hunger, Pope John Paul II affirmed "the basic right to nutrition that properly belongs to each human person" and urged the participants in the International Conference on Nutrition "to strive to ensure that no person will be refused his or her daily bread and necessary health care".[199] These mandates of justice are relevant to the proposed removal of nutrition and hydration, whether naturally or artificially supplied. An appropriate response to such proposals would be to invoke the first two corporal works of

---

[198] 24 *Origins* 705 (1992).

[199] Pope John Paul II, *Address* to the International Conference on Nutrition, Dec. 5, 1992; 38 *The Pope Speaks*, 142, 144–45 (1993).

mercy: "Feed the hungry. Give drink to the thirsty."[200] These apply even to the functionally useless. "Amen I say to you, as long as you did it for one of these, the least of my brethren, you did it for me."[201]

49. *Why is the Church opposed to science and technology? If we are "pro-life" and want children, why can't we use in vitro fertilization, surrogate motherhood, and other techniques, if necessary, to enable us to have them? And what's wrong with experimenting on aborted babies or using their tissues for transplants to save lives?*

This Question is appropriate to end our inquiry into the application of the natural law by the Magisterium. Married couples who want, but cannot have, children merit sympathy and encouragement. When technology offers them a chance to conceive a child, for example by in vitro fertilization and transfer of the resulting embryo into the mother's own womb, it seems like a direct answer to a prayer. The Catholic Church is virtually alone in her refusal to countenance such techniques. To many, that opposition confirms the suspicion that the natural law, in the hands of the Church, is a negative and legalistic instrument of clerical oppression. In truth, however, the Church's position here, as with contraception, offers the only principled alternative to the utilitarianism that ultimately would reduce man—and woman—to the status of a depersonalized object of science. The position of the Magisterium was spelled out in

---

[200] See Leo J. Trese, *The Faith Explained* (1959), 193 (1991 ed., 164).
[201] Mt 25:40.

the 1987 *Instruction on Bioethics*, a remarkably countercultural document.[202]

The Church claims no "particular competence in the area of the experimental sciences".[203] However, "science and technology require, for their own intrinsic meaning, an unconditional respect for the fundamental criteria of the moral law: that is to say, they must be at the service of the human person, of his inalienable rights and his true and integral good according to the design and will of God. . . . Science without conscience can only lead to man's ruin."[204]

The human body cannot be considered as a mere complex of tissues, organs and functions, nor can it be evaluated in the same way as the body of animals; rather it is a constitutive part of the person who manifests and expresses and lays down the purposes, rights and duties which are based upon the bodily and spiritual nature of the human person. Therefore this law cannot be thought of as simply a set of norms on the biological level; rather it must be defined as the rational order whereby man is called by the Creator to direct and regulate his life and actions and in particular to make use of his own body. . . . Artificial interventions on procreation and on the origin of human life . . . are not to be rejected on the ground that they are artificial. . . . [Rather, they require] moral evaluation in reference to the dignity of the human person.[205]

---

[202] Congregation for the Doctrine of the Faith, *Instruction on Bioethics* (1987) (the formal title is *Instruction on Respect for Human Life in Origin and the Dignity of Procreation*); see 32 *The Pope Speaks* 137 (1987).

[203] Congregation for the Doctrine of the Faith, *Instruction on Bioethics* (1987), Introduction, no. 1. See also *C.C.C.*, nos. 2295–301, 2373–79.

[204] Congregation for the Doctrine of the Faith, *Instruction on Bioethics* (1987), Introduction, no. 2.

[205] Ibid., Introduction, no. 3.

The *Instruction* affirmed the sacredness of human life from "the moment of conception" so that "no one can, in any circumstances, claim for himself the right to destroy directly an innocent human being."[206] The first part of the *Instruction* discussed the respect due to human embryos. It affirmed that "*the human being must be respected — as a person — from the very first instant of his existence. . . .* 'From the time that the ovum is fertilized, a new life is begun which is neither that of the father nor of the mother; it is rather the life of a new human being with his own growth. It would never be made human if it were not human already.'"[207]

The *Instruction* approved prenatal diagnosis and medical interventions for the purpose of "safeguarding or healing" the unborn child, but it condemned prenatal diagnosis "when it is done with the thought of possibly inducing an abortion depending upon the results".[208]

Experimentation on the unborn child for his own therapeutic benefit can be legitimate. However:

> Research, even when limited to the simple observation of the embryo, would become illicit were it to involve risk to the embryo's physical integrity or life. . . . *If the embryos are living, whether viable or not, they must be respected just like any other human person; experimentation on embryos which is not directly therapeutic is illicit.* No objective, even though noble in itself, such as a foreseeable advantage to science, to other human beings or to society, can in any way justify experimentation on living human embryos or fetuses, whether viable or not, either inside or outside the mother's

---

[206] Ibid., Introduction, no. 5.

[207] Ibid., I, 1, quoting from Congregation for the Doctrine of the Faith, *Declaration on Procured Abortion* (1974).

[208] Congregation for the Doctrine of the Faith, *Instruction on Bioethics* (1987), I, 2.

womb. The informed consent ordinarily required for clinical experimentation on adults cannot be granted by the parents, who may not freely dispose of the physical integrity or life of the unborn child. Moreover, experimentation on embryos and fetuses always involves risk, and indeed in most cases it involves the certain expectation of harm to their physical integrity or even their death. . . . *The corpses of human embryos and fetuses, whether they have been deliberately aborted or not, must be respected just as the remains of other human beings.* In particular, they cannot be subjected to mutilation or autopsies if their death has not yet been verified and without the consent of the parents or of the mother. Furthermore, the moral requirements must be safeguarded, that there be no complicity in deliberate abortion and that the risk of scandal be avoided. Also, in the case of dead fetuses, as for the corpses of adult persons, all commercial trafficking must be considered illicit and should be prohibited.[209]

The *Instruction* condemned the use for experimentation of embryos obtained by in vitro fertilization: "Those embryos which are not transferred into the body of the mother and are called 'spare' are exposed to an absurd fate, with no possibility of their being offered safe means of survival which can be licitly pursued."[210]

The *Instruction* rejected all forms of artificial fertilization, whether in vitro fertilization or artificial insemination and whether homologous, using the sperm of the husband, or heterologous, using the sperm of a third party. One objection to these procedures is that they often involve the intentional destruction of embryos, who are human beings. And "the abortion-mentality which has made this procedure possible . . . leads, whether one wants it or not, to man's domi-

---

[209] Ibid., I, 4.
[210] Ibid., I, 5.

nation over the life and death of his fellow human beings and can lead to a system of radical eugenics."[211] Apart from their involvement with the destruction of embryos, the techniques of artificial fertilization are condemned on their own grounds:

> *The fidelity of the spouses in the unity of marriage involves reciprocal respect of their right to become a father and a mother only through each other.* The child has the right to be conceived, carried in the womb, brought into the world and brought up within marriage: it is through the secure and recognized relationship to his own parents that the child can discover his own identity and achieve his own proper human development. . . . By reason of the vocation and social responsibilities of the person, the good of the children and of the parents contributes to the good of civil society; the vitality and stability of society require that children come into the world within a family and that the family be firmly based on marriage. The tradition of the Church and anthropological reflection recognize in marriage and in its indissoluble unity the only setting worthy of truly responsible procreation.[212]

Heterologous artificial fertilization, in which the sperm of a man other than her husband is used to fertilize the woman's ovum, involves an obvious intrusion of a third party into the conjugal relationship. *"Fertilization of a married woman with the sperm of a donor different from her husband and fertilization with the husband's sperm of an ovum not coming from his wife are morally illicit. Furthermore, the artificial fertilization of a woman who is unmarried or a widow, whoever the donor may be, cannot be morally justified."*[213]

Surrogate motherhood is of two types. In one, the woman "carries in pregnancy an embryo to whose procreation she has

---

[211] Ibid., II.

[212] Ibid., II, A, 1.

[213] Ibid., II, A, 2.

contributed the donation of her own ovum, fertilized through insemination with the sperm of a man other than her husband. She carries the pregnancy with a pledge to surrender the child once it is born to the party who commissioned or made the agreement for the pregnancy."[214] In the other type, which is a sort of rental of the womb, the woman "is genetically a stranger to the embryo [implanted in her uterus] because it has been obtained through the union of the gametes of 'donors.' She carries the pregnancy with a pledge to surrender the baby once it is born to the party who commissioned or made the agreement for the pregnancy."[215] The *Instruction* condemned surrogate motherhood of both types as "*contrary to the unity of marriage and to the dignity of the procreation of the human person*".[216]

With respect to homologous artificial fertilization, where the sperm is provided by the mother's own husband, the *Instruction* emphasized:

> [There is an] "inseparable connection, willed by God and unable to be broken by man on his own initiative, between the two meanings of the conjugal act: the unitive meaning and the procreative meaning." . . . Contraception deliberately deprives the conjugal act of its openness to procreation and in this way brings about a voluntary dissociation of the ends of marriage. Homologous artificial fertilization, in seeking a procreation which is not the fruit of a specific act of conjugal union, objectively effects an analogous separation between the goods and the meanings of marriage. Thus, *fertilization is licitly sought when it is the result of a con-*

---

[214] Ibid., II, A, 3; see *In re Baby M.*, 525 A.2d 1128 (1987), affirmed in part, reversed in part, 109 N.J. 396, 537 A.2d 1227 (1988).

[215] Congregation for the Doctrine of the Faith, *Instruction on Bioethics* (1987), II, A, 3.

[216] Ibid.

jugal act which is per se suitable for the generation of children to which marriage is ordered by its nature and by which the spouses become one flesh. But from the moral point of view procreation is deprived of its proper perfection when it is not desired as the fruit of the conjugal act, that is to say of the specific act of the spouses' union.[217]

The cloning of human beings, of course, is an obvious violation of the principles affirmed in the *Instruction*, which said that "attempts or hypotheses for obtaining a human being without any connection with sexuality through 'twin fission,' cloning or parthenogenesis are to be considered contrary to the moral law, since they are in opposition to the dignity both of human procreation and of the conjugal union."[218]

The countercultural nature of the Church's teaching in this area is clear from the *Instruction*'s explanation as to why conception must occur only through the conjugal act in marriage:

The moral value of the intimate link between the goods of marriage and between the meanings of the conjugal act is based upon the unity of the human being, a unity involving body and spiritual soul. Spouses mutually express their personal love in the "language of the body," which clearly involves both "spousal meanings" and parental ones. The conjugal act by which the couple mutually express their self-gift at the same time expresses openness to the gift of life. It is an act that is inseparably corporal and spiritual. It is in their bodies and through their bodies that the spouses consummate their marriage and are able to become father and mother. In order to respect the language of their bodies and their natural generosity, the conjugal union must take place with respect for its openness to procreation; and the procre-

---

[217] Ibid., II, B, 4, quoting Pope Paul VI, *Humanae Vitae* (1968).

[218] Congregation for the Doctrine of the Faith, *Instruction on Bioethics* (1987), I, 6.

ation of a person must be the fruit and the result of married love. The origin of the human being thus follows from a procreation that is "linked to the union, not only biological but also spiritual, of the parents, made one by the bond of marriage." Fertilization achieved outside the bodies of the couple remains by this very fact deprived of the meanings and the values which are expressed in the language of the body and in the union of human persons.

Only respect for the link between the meanings of the conjugal act and respect for the unity of the human being make possible procreation in conformity with the dignity of the person. In his unique and unrepeatable origin, the child must be respected and recognized as equal in personal dignity to those who gave him life. The human person must be accepted in his parents' act of union and love; the generation of a child must therefore be the fruit of that mutual giving which is realized in the conjugal act wherein the spouses cooperate as servants and not as masters in the work of the Creator who is Love.

In reality, the origin of a human person is the result of an act of giving. The one conceived must be the fruit of his parents' love. He cannot be desired or conceived as the product of an intervention of medical or biological techniques; that would be equivalent to reducing him to an object of scientific technology. No one may subject the coming of a child into the world to conditions of technical efficiency which are to be evaluated according to standards of control and dominion.

The moral relevance of the link between the meanings of the conjugal act and between the goods of marriage, as well as the unity of the human being and the dignity of his origin, demand that the procreation of a human person be brought about as the fruit of the conjugal act specific to the love between spouses.[219]

---

[219] Ibid.

The technique of in vitro fertilization and embryo transfer, even when the sperm of the husband is used, is intrinsically wrong because "*the generation of the human person is objectively deprived of it proper perfection: namely, that of being the result and fruit of a conjugal act* in which the spouses can become 'co-operators with God for giving life to a new person.' "[220] "A medical intervention", however, can be licit "when it seeks to assist the conjugal act either in order to facilitate its performance or in order to achieve its objective once it has been normally performed".[221] An example would seem to be the low tubal ovum transfer: Where a blockage in the fallopian tube prevents access of the sperm to the ovum, the ovum can be surgically placed below the blockage, thus enabling contact with the sperm in normal conjugal relations.[222]

In an important segment the *Instruction* expressed sympathy and concern for those who desire, but cannot have, children:

> On the part of the spouses, the desire for a child is natural: It expresses the vocation to fatherhood and motherhood inscribed in conjugal love. This desire can be even stronger if the couple is affected by sterility which appears incurable. Nevertheless, marriage does not confer upon the spouses the right to have a child, but only the right to perform those natural acts which are *per se* ordered to procreation.
>
> *A true and proper right to a child would be contrary to the child's dignity and nature. The child is not an object to which one has a right, nor can he be considered as an object of ownership: Rather, a child is a gift, "the supreme gift" and the most gratuitous gift of marriage, and is a living testimony of the mutual*

---

[220] Ibid., II, B, 5.

[221] Ibid., II, B, 7.

[222] See Donald De Marco, "New Reproductive Technologies and Church Teaching", *International Review of Natural Family Planning and Human Life Issues* (1988), 279.

giving of his parents. For this reason, the child has the right, as already mentioned, to be the fruit of the specific act of the conjugal love of his parents; and he also has the right to be respected as a person from the moment of his conception. . . . Sterile couples must not forget that "even when procreation is not possible, conjugal life does not for this reason lose its value. Physical sterility in fact can be for spouses the occasion for other important services in the life of the human person, for example, adoption, various forms of educational work and assistance to other families and to poor or handicapped children."

Many researchers are engaged in the fight against sterility. While fully safeguarding the dignity of human procreation, some have achieved results which previously seemed unattainable. Scientists therefore are to be encouraged to continue their research with the aim of preventing the causes of sterility and of being able to remedy them so that sterile couples will be able to procreate in full respect for their own personal dignity and that of the child to be born.[223]

The *Instruction* stressed the duty of the civil law to protect the unborn child's right to life and to impose "appropriate penal sanctions for every deliberate violation of the child's rights".[224] The *Instruction* also specified other duties of the civil law, especially with respect to the family:

The political authority is bound to guarantee to the institution of the family, upon which society is based, the juridical protection to which it has a right. From the very fact that it is at the service of people, the political authority must also be at the service of the family. Civil law cannot grant

---

[223] Congregation for the Doctrine of the Faith, *Instruction on Bioethics* (1987), II, B, 8; quoting from Second Vatican Council, *Pastoral Constitution on the Church in the Modern World* (*Gaudium et Spes*), no. 50, and Pope John Paul II, *Familiaris Consortio* (1981), no. 14, See also *C.C.C.*, no. 2373–79.

[224] Congregation for the Doctrine of the Faith, *Instruction on Bioethics*, III.

approval to techniques of artificial procreation which, for the benefit of third parties (doctors, biologists, economic or governmental powers), take away what is a right inherent in the relationship between spouses; and, therefore, civil law cannot legalize the donation of gametes between persons who are not legitimately united in marriage.

Legislation must also prohibit, by virtue of the support which is due to the family, embryo banks, post-mortem insemination and "surrogate motherhood."

It is part of the duty of the public authority to ensure that the civil law is regulated according to the fundamental norms of the moral law in matters concerning human rights, human life and the institution of the family. Politicians must commit themselves, through their interventions upon public opinion, to securing in society the widest possible consensus on such essential points and to consolidating this consensus wherever it risks being weakened or is in danger of collapse. [225]

In its conclusion, the *Instruction* expressed the hope that "all will understand the incompatibility between recognition of the dignity of the human person and contempt for life and love, between faith in the living God and the claim to decide arbitrarily the origin and fate of a human being". [226] The principles of the *Instruction* were more briefly reaffirmed in *Evangelium Vitae*, which declared that "human embryos or fetuses . . . as human beings . . . have a right to the same respect owed to a child once born, just as to every person." [227]

---

[225] Ibid.
[226] Ibid., Conclusion.
[227] *E.V.*, no. 63; see also *L.F.*, no. 19.

XII

THE FUTURE OF
THE NATURAL LAW

50. Isn't the natural law a terminal case, a dying relic of the past? Isn't it unrealistic to expect people to take it seriously today?

No, on both counts.

The Enlightenment has failed in its effort to build a good society without God. The Constitution of the United States recognized the power of the state and federal governments to affirm the existence of God and to encourage belief in God while maintaining neutrality among religious sects. Beginning in 1961, however, the Supreme Court imposed on government the impossible task of suspending judgment on the existence of God.[1] Government is now required to maintain neutrality not merely among theistic creeds but between theism and nontheism. Justice William Brennan, in his concurring opinion in the 1963 school prayer case, captured the meaning of that ruling when he argued that the words "under God" could be kept in the pledge of allegiance:

> This general principle might also serve to insulate the various *patriotic exercises* and activities used in the public schools and elsewhere which, whatever may have been their origins, *no longer have a religious purpose or meaning*. The reference to divinity in the revised pledge of allegiance, for example, *may merely recognize the historical fact that our Nation was believed to have been founded "under God."*[2]

---

[1] *Torcaso* v. *Watkins*, 367 U.S. 488 (1961); *Engle* v. *Vitale*, 370 U.S. 421 (1962); *Abington School District* v. *Schempp*, 374 U.S. 203 (1963); see also *Lee* v. *Weisman*, 112 S.Ct. 2649, 120 L. Ed. 2d 467 (1992).

[2] *Abington School District* v. *Schempp*, 374 U.S. at 303–4 (emphasis added).

It is now unconstitutional, according to the Supreme Court, for the President officially to affirm that the Declaration of Independence is in fact true when it proclaims the existence of "Nature's God", the "Creator", the "Supreme Judge of the World", and "Divine Providence". These words may be recited only as a historical commemoration without any affirmation that in fact they are true.[3] Government thus can neither affirm nor deny the existence of God. But when government suspends judgment on the existence of God, it gives implicit preference to agnosticism. That is why agnostic secular humanism is now our national religion.

The Declaration of Independence recognized the "Laws of Nature and of Nature's God" and affirmed that "all Men . . . are endowed by their Creator with certain unalienable Rights". There are, in other words, God-given limits that no government can rightly exceed. The Supreme Court's false neutrality, however, implicitly rejects the natural moral law as a limit on government action. The preference for agnostic secularism requires, for example, that the right to life of the unborn child, and that of his retarded brother and grandmother, must be evaluated in secular, utilitarian terms; in such an evaluation they are guaranteed losers. By refusing to affirm that life is a gift of God, the government of the United States implies that it is a gift of the state. And the state acts accordingly.

The Supreme Court, in this matter, reflects as well as promotes a secular consensus. The law of God, if it is acknowledged at all, is widely regarded as irrelevant to "practical"

---

[3] Ibid. See discussion in *Sherman v. School District 21 of Wheeling Township*, 980 F. 2d 437 (7th Cir., 992); see also Justice Brennan's reference to the Pledge of Allegiance as a form of "ceremonial deism" that has "lost through rote repetition any significant religious content", *Lynch v. Donnelly*, 465 U.S. 668, 716 (1984) (dissenting opinion).

problems of government as well as to private life. The Supreme Court mirrors what we have become in this respect. Pope John Paul II aptly described legalized abortion as a consequence of "theoretical and practical materialism which, by rejecting God, ends up rejecting even man in his essential, transcendent dimension; it is a result of consumerist hedonism which puts immediate interests as the goal of human activity."[4]

Ideas have consequences. When secularism and relativism are combined with the prevailing contraceptive ethic, it becomes easy to cite reasons for pessimism. In the public schools, we give the students sex instruction and condoms, yet we refuse to let them pray or even see the Ten Commandments on their classroom wall.[5] In 1950, 4.0 percent of all births in the United States were out of wedlock; in 1960 the figure was 5.3 percent; in 1993 it was 31 percent, and the figure for births to unwed black mothers was 68.7 percent.[6] The immediate victims of the culture of "free love", as John Paul put it, are "the children . . . condemned in fact to be orphans of living parents".[7] Every member of the Supreme Court accepts the principle of *Roe* v. *Wade* that innocent human beings can be defined as nonpersons and subjected to execution at the discretion of others; even the "pro-life" justices on the Court accept the constitutional non-personhood of the unborn child—they argue that the state legislatures should be allowed to decide whether and under what conditions that child may be legally executed.[8] The death toll

---

[4] *Address to Italian Pro-Life Movement*, Jan 25, 1986, 31 *The Pope Speaks* 128, 129 (1986); see Charles E. Rice, *50 Questions on Abortion, Euthanasia and Related Issues* (1986), 5–6.

[5] See *Stone v. Graham*, 449 U.S. 39 (1980).

[6] *New York Times*, July 26, 1992, sec. 1, p. 1; *Information Please Almanac* (1997), 841; *Statistical Abstract of the United States* (1996), 79.

[7] *L.F.*, no. 14.

[8] See Charles E. Rice, *No Exception: A Pro-Life Imperative* (1990), chap. 2.

from legalized abortion in the United States approaches forty million and more. And the end of the legalized killing is not in sight. "I predict", said Cardinal John O'Connor in 1989, "that the 'right to die'—which really means that hospitals and doctors and other health care 'providers' will be *required* to kill—will dwarf the abortion phenomenon in magnitude, in numbers, in horror."[9]

Utilitarian positivism can set no effective limits to the depersonalization and execution of inconvenient human beings, to the disintegration of the family, and to the other manifestations of Enlightenment jurisprudence. The only effective alternative is a return to respect for the law of God, including the natural law. Bishop Dr. Walter Kasper writes:

> We Christians cannot counter the threat to humanity merely by an appeal to a minimal consensus founded in natural law. . . . [Vatican II] affirms that the dignity of the human person is recognized with the help of human reason according to the experience of centuries, *but in all its fullness* is only shown forth through divine revelation. . . . It is precisely the Christian faith that defends and perpetuates the legacy of Western humanism, and sanctions it by an ultimate theological foundation, just as it did in the cultural disintegration at the end of the ancient world. For the one, all-encompassing and all-transcending reality of God makes all human beings brothers and sisters, it is the pledge of the absolute dignity of each individual human being, and the ultimate foundation of the solidarity of all women and men. . . . Indeed, it is clear today that only religious presuppositions can ensure the survival of the modern idea and promotion of human rights, for our secularized modern civilization is unable to do so. . . . The God of the Christian faith is not,

---

[9] Cardinal John O'Connor, "A Cardinal's Chilling Warning", *New Covenant*, May 1989, pp. 23, 24.

like the God of the Enlightenment, a vague and empty transcendence, an open but empty horizon. . . . In Jesus Christ, the new Adam, God not only made manifest himself . . . , but also revealed human beings to themselves, and revealed that the meaning of human existence is that of existing for others. Human rights thus need to be interpreted in the light of the Christian commandment to love our neighbor as ourselves.[10]

Secular jurisprudence does not work. Every society, like every man, has to have a god, an ultimate authority. If it is not the real God, it will be a god of man's own making. This may be the individual himself, the consensus, the courts—whatever. Ultimately, in the absence of an acknowledged higher interpreter, the state will assume that moral authority. Natural law offers the only coherent alternative with which to limit the power of the state and to promote the common good. But the natural law makes no ultimate sense apart from God because the only enduring basis for the dignity of the human person is the fact that he is an immortal creature made in the image and likeness of God. Only in this light can the person be said to have rights absolutely beyond the power of the state to abridge. Moreover, the natural law makes no practical sense without an accepted, visible interpreter of its meaning. Christ, who is God, is the author of the natural law and the only appropriate interpreter in his Vicar, the Pope. Without acceptance of the Magisterium, natural law becomes grist for endless debating mills, with its meaning determined by the shifting consensus. Inevitably, that consensus will be defined by those in power, in the media, finance, and the state.

---

[10] Walter Kasper, "The Theological Foundations of Human Rights", 50 *Jurist* 148, 160–64 (1990).

The teachings of Saint Thomas are not merely the thoughts of a long-dead philosopher. Through the Magisterium, Aquinas offers a living jurisprudence. It is time for those who accept natural law jurisprudence, as explained by Saint Thomas and integrated into the teaching of the Magisterium to make their case. And it is an attractive case. For example, the Magisterium's insistence that personhood intrinsically involves relation to others is not only the answer to the failed individualism of the Enlightenment but also a prescription for a humane, civilized order. In his 1991 address to the Congress of the International Thomas Aquinas Society, John Paul II described the "teaching" of Saint Thomas as "still valid today for the renewal of a civilization where ethics will find its place and be able to direct life in all its dimensions".[11] The Pope noted "how true is that which Thomas calls the 'anguish of the learned' when they do not find an adequate solution to man's ultimate questions. Anguish today results from the fact that our civilization does not offer man the right way. So many people today find themselves lost in blind alleys. The Christian thinker is called therefore to begin an open and sincere dialogue in light of transcendent truths, leading to that truth which takes away this human sense of being lost, inasmuch as it is truth anchored in Christ, the light of the world and the redeemer of the human person."[12]

The sterility of most academic debate on the natural law arises from tacit acceptance of the Enlightenment ground rules, which limit discussion to the merely philosophical and exclude the affirmation as reality of the divine law and the truth, who is Christ. It is time to break that mold. The teachings of Saint Thomas and the Magisterium must be presented not as

---

[11] 37 *The Pope Speaks* 52, 55 (1992).
[12] Ibid., 54.

hypotheses but as truth, which they are.[13] Cardinal Edouard Gagnon recounted a conversation about teaching the truth that he had with Pope John Paul II:

> The Holy Father . . . told me, "error makes its way because truth is not taught. We must teach the truth whenever we see something which is against the truth. We must teach truth, repeat it, not attacking the ones who teach errors because that would never end—they are so numerous. We have to teach the truth." He told me truth has a grace attached to it. Anytime we speak the truth, we conform to what Christ teaches and what is being taught us by the Church. Every time we stand up for the truth, there is an internal grace of God that accompanies that truth. The truth may not immediately enter in the mind and heart of those to whom we talk, but the grace of God is there and at the time they need it, God will open their heart and they will accept it. He said, error does not have grace accompanying it. It might have all the external means, but it does not have the grace of God accompanying it. This encouraged me very much.[14]

The objective here must be free acceptance by the American people of the truth of the principles of the natural and divine laws as presented by Saint Thomas and the Magisterium. "This may appear to be a radical fantasy, but sooner or later the moral bankruptcy of the godless state will be so evident that it will be 'respectable' to advocate a radical solution. It must be the Catholic solution."[15] "Written testimonies alone, however, will not suffice. Much more important are living tes-

---

[13] Ibid. See also Pope John Paul II, *The Mission of the Redeemer* (*Redemptoris Missio*), no. 3; 36 *The Pope Speaks* 138, 139–40 (1991).

[14] *Lay Witness* (Mar. 1990), 6–7 (Catholics United for the Faith, 50 Washington Ave., New Rochelle, N.Y. 10801).

[15] Charles E. Rice, *Beyond Abortion: The Theory and Practice of the Secular State* (1979), 135.

timonies. As Pope Paul VI observed, 'Contemporary man listens more willingly to witnesses than to teachers, and if he listens to teachers it is because they are witnesses.'"[16]

The essential need is for a restoration of faith. "Make a note of the difference there is", said Saint John Vianney, the Curé of Ars, "between believing in the existence of God and believing in him."[17] More than six decades ago, Bertrand Russell said that a grave danger faced the United States—that it would be Catholic in 150 years. Archbishop Fulton J. Sheen responded that if the United States "is to be Catholic, it will have to do two more things than it is doing now: It will have to begin to think, and it will have to begin to pray."[18] The more important element is prayer.[19] And because the critical issues involve attacks on motherhood and life, it is appropriate to ask the intercession of Mary, the mother of Life, especially through the Rosary.[20] As Pope Paul VI said, "The Rosary should be con-

---

[16] *L.F.*, no. 23, quoting *Address to the Council of the Laity*, (1974); see also, *V.S.*, no. 107.

[17] Saint John Vianney, "Sermon on the First Commandment", in *Thoughts of the Curé D'Ars* (1984), 50.

[18] Fulton J. Sheen, *Moods and Truths* (1932), 191.

[19] On prayer generally, see *C.C.C.*, nos. 2558–758; on the Our Father, see nos. 2759–865.

[20] Methodist Reverend J. Neville Ward described the Rosary as an "inexhaustible source of help in the spiritual life". *Five for Sorrow, Ten for Joy* (1973), 105; see also Francis J. Ripley, "Mary—Test of True Ecumenism", *Position Paper* 169 (Jan. 1988), 2; Kenneth A. Briggs, "Marian Devotions: An Ecumenical Upsurge", *New York Times*, June 7, 1979, p. A8, col. 1. For a discussion of Martin Luther's devotion to Mary, see Paul H. Hallett, "Lutheran Mariology", *National Catholic Register*, May 23, 1982, p. 5, col. 1. "It is devotion to Mary", wrote Methodist pastor Donald Charles Lacy, "that helps unite us as Christians. When Protestants lose their widespread hangup that Roman Catholics have worshipped and do worship her, they can perceive by the power of the Holy Spirit an authentic ecumenism that calls us 'to be

sidered as one of the best, most efficacious prayers in common that the Christian family is invited to recite. We like to think and sincerely hope that when the family gathering becomes a time of prayer, the Rosary is a frequent, favored manner of praying."[21]

Pope John Paul II concluded his 1987 encyclical, *Mother of the Redeemer*, by noting:

> The Church . . . sees Mary deeply rooted in humanity's history, in man's eternal vocation according to the providential plan which God has made for him from eternity. She sees Mary maternally present and sharing in the many complicated problems which today beset the lives of individuals, families and nations; she sees her helping the Christian people in the constant struggle between good and evil, to ensure that it "does not fall," or if it has fallen, that it "rises again."[22]

In *Veritatis Splendor*, the Pope described Mary as "mother of each and every one of us, the mother who obtains for us

---

one.' When many Roman Catholics stop apologizing for their emphasis on her in order not to offend the Protestant community, they can put her back where she rightfully belongs. . . . Ecumenically, the Blessed Mother of God provides that means for us to value again with joy and confidence chastity and purity. . . . Roman Catholics (and Orthodox for that matter) do not hold a monopoly on her! She belongs to all of us who profess her Son as Savior and Lord." "Devotion to Mary Should Go Beyond Denominations", *Our Sunday Visitor*, Aug. 16, 1987, p. 3. See Rice, *No Exception*, 118. The Catechism of the Catholic Church emphasizes the importance of prayer to Mary, especially the Hail Mary and including the Rosary. *C.C.C.*, nos. 2673–82; see also no. 1674.

[21] Pope Paul VI, *Apostolic Exhortation, Devotion to the Blessed Virgin Mary* (*Marialis Cultus*), Feb. 2, 1974; 19 *The Pope Speaks* 49, 83 (1974).

[22] Pope John Paul II, *Redemptoris Mater* (1987), no. 52; 32 *The Pope Speaks* 195, 197 (1987). On Mary as Mother of Christ and Mother of the Church, see *C.C.C.*, nos. 963–75; see also *F.R.*, no. 108.

divine mercy. . . . To us too she addresses the command she gave to the servants at Cana, in Galilee during the marriage feast: 'Do whatever he tells you' (*Jn* 2:5)."[23]

In his 1990 encyclical, *The Mission of the Redeemer*, John Paul said, "God is preparing a great springtime for Christianity, and we can already see its first signs."[24] The "terminal case" and "dying relic of the past" is not the natural law but the Enlightenment. It has failed. It has nothing to offer. It is time for the alternative: The Truth, who is a person, Christ.

---

[23] *V.S.*, no. 120.

[24] Pope John Paul II, *Redemptoris Missio*, no. 2; 36 *The Pope Speaks* 138, 180 (1991).

Index